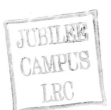

By the same author

An Introduction to Anglo-Saxon England
Roman Britain and Early England: A.D. 43–871

The World of Bede

Peter Hunter Blair

CAMBRIDGE
UNIVERSITY PRESS

Published by the Press Syndicate of the University of Cambridge
The Pitt Building, Trumpington Street, Cambridge CB2 1RP
40 West 20th Street, New York, NY 10011–4211, USA
10 Stamford Road, Oakleigh, Melbourne, 3166, Australia

First published by Martin Secker and Warburg Limited 1970
This edition first published by Cambridge University Press 1990

Printed in Great Britain by Athenæum Press Ltd, Gateshead
Reprinted 1995

British Library cataloguing in publication data

Blair, Peter Hunter, *1912–1982*
The world of Bede.
Reissue with corrections.
1. Bede, the Venerable. Saint, 673–735
I. Title   II. Lapidge, Michael, *1942–*
270.2092

Library of Congress cataloguing in publication data applied for

ISBN 0 521 39138 5 hardback
ISBN 0 521 39819 3 paperback

[FP]

Contents

PART FOUR

LEARNING, TEACHING AND WRITING

Foreword

Peter Hunter Blair's *The World of Bede* was first published in 1970. At the time of its publication there had not been a monograph on Bede worthy of the name for over fifty years (the last being *The Venerable Bede: His Life and Writings* by G. F. Browne, published in London by SPCK in 1919), and the standard monograph on Bede was still Karl Werner's (by then outdated) *Beda der ehrwürdige und seine Zeit* (Vienna, 1881). The prospective student of Bede and his Northumbrian context could do no better in 1970 than to consult the collection of essays by various distinguished scholars edited by A. Hamilton Thompson and published by the Clarendon Press in 1935 under the title *Bede, his Life, Times, and Writings*. The appearance of Hunter Blair's book changed this situation immeasurably. It gave us the results of a lifetime's thinking and reading about Bede and Northumbria by an eminent Bedan scholar, distilled into a readable and engaging book, written in a style that is immediately accessible to the non-professional scholar and which carries the weight of its learning lightly and modestly – as in all Hunter Blair's scholarly publications – but which is supplied with ample documentation for those who would pursue its arguments. The most striking feature of *The World of Bede* is that it is based almost entirely on its author's reading in the primary sources, above all Bede's own Latin writings, as well as the manuscript evidence for Northumbrian learning (accessible through E. A. Lowe's *Codices Latini Antiquiores*). For this reason, Hunter Blair's book stands up well to the passage of time: being concerned with Bede himself, and not with the industry of Bedan scholarship, Hunter Blair's arguments are as fresh and relevant as they were twenty years ago. Indeed George Brown, who has recently written the only general monograph on Bede which deserves comparison with *The World of Bede*, could describe Hunter Blair's book as 'one of the best books on Bede and his milieu' (*Bede the Venerable* (Boston, 1987), p. 142). The high reputation which Hunter Blair's book still enjoys among Anglo-Saxon scholars encouraged the Cambridge University Press to undertake a photographic reprint; I have taken the opportunity of correcting a number of misprints (for the detection of many of which I am indebted to the generous assistance of David Dumville) and adding some brief *Bibliographical Addenda* (pp. 327–9).

Michael Lapidge
Cambridge
January 1990

Preface

Writing from his bed of sickness to the Patriarch of Alexandria in the summer of 598 Gregory the Great was able to pass on the joyful news, but lately arrived in Rome, that large numbers of the English had been baptised on Christmas Day 597. He thought it necessary to tell the Patriarch that the English were a people who lived in a remote corner of the world and who had until recently worshipped sticks and stones. Almost exactly a hundred and fifty years later the great English missionary, Boniface, wrote from Germany to the abbot of Wearmouth and Jarrow asking him if he would send him some of the works of the monk Bede whose scriptural scholarship had lately made him eminent among his people as a shining beacon of the church.

I have tried to show in this book how it was that a seed sown in this chill northern soil flourished so greatly that some of those who were nurtured upon its fruits became for a short while, before the age of the Vikings, the spiritual, intellectual and artistic leaders of much of northern and western Europe. I have deliberately confined myself to what has seemed to me the most interesting aspect of Bede's times – the transition from illiterate paganism to the kind of world which enabled him to indulge to the full his delight in learning, teaching and writing. This choice has compelled the omission of much else that is relevant, and in particular I have not thought myself competent to write of his theological and spiritual teaching.

My debt to the work of others will be apparent from the references and from the Select Bibliography, but I cannot forebear to mention the name of Charles Plummer whose volume of notes to his edition of the *Ecclesiastical History* I have so often found to contain what I thought I had discovered for myself. It will be evident that much of Part IV of the book could not well have been written without many profitable hours spent with E. A. Lowe's *Codices Latini Antiquiores*. I am deeply indebted also to Professor Dorothy Whitelock who has read the whole of the book in typescript, to its great profit, and to Dr F. H. Stubbings I owe my thanks for his helpful criticisms of my translations of passages in Bede's writings. The final stages of preparing the book for the press have been greatly eased by help given me by my wife. Yet the greatest debt of all is to Bede himself. I hope that I may have succeeded in conveying to my readers at least something of what manner of man he was – the scholar who never spared himself in the search for truth, the monk who loved music and was deeply moved by the beauty of his church all brightly lit for a festal day, the teacher whose last thought was for the pupils of his school, and the endearingly humble man who chose the images of griddle, frying-pan and oven to illustrate stages in the growth of spiritual understanding.

Emmanuel College
Cambridge
24. xi. 1969

List of Abbreviations

The following abbreviations are used for works cited frequently in the footnotes. Other works cited under abbreviated titles in the footnotes can be easily identified by reference to the *Select Bibliography*.

AdVC *Adomnan's Life of Columba*, ed. and tr. A. O. and M. O. Anderson, Edinburgh and London, 1961.

AVC *Vita Sancti Cuthberti Auctore Anonymo*, ed. and tr. B. Colgrave, *Two Lives of St Cuthbert*, Cambridge, 1940.

AVCeol *Vita Ceolfridi Abbatis Auctore Anonymo*, ed. C. Plummer, *Venerabilis Baedae Opera Historica*, Oxford, 1896, I, pp. 388–404, under the title *Historia Abbatum Auctore Anonymo*. Tr. D. Whitelock, *EHD*, No. 155, pp. 697–708.

BR *Benedicti Regula*, ed. R. Hanslik, *Corpus Scriptorum Ecclesiasticorum Latinorum*, LXXV, Vindobonae, 1960.

BdTR *Bedae Liber De Temporibus Major Sive De Temporum Ratione*, ed. C. W. Jones, *Bedae Opera De Temporibus*, The Mediaeval Academy of America, Publication No. 41, Cambridge, Mass., 1943, pp. 173–291.

BVC *Vita Sancti Cuthberti Auctore Beda*, ed. and tr. B. Colgrave, *Two Lives of St Cuthbert*, Cambridge, 1940.

CCSL *Corpus Christianorum Series Latina*, Typographi Brepols, Turnholti – *in progress*.

CI *Cassiodori Senatoris Institutiones*, ed. R. A. B. Mynors, Oxford, 1937. Tr. L. W. Jones, *An Introduction to*

Divine and Human Reading by Cassiodorus Senator, New York, 1946.

CLA   *Codices Latini Antiquiores, A Palaeographical Guide to Latin Manuscripts prior to the ninth century,* E. A. Lowe, Oxford, 1934–71.

EHD   *English Historical Documents,* ed. D. C. Douglas, Vol. I, c. 500–1042, ed. D. Whitelock, London, 1979.

EHR   *English Historical Review.*

EVW   *Vita Wilfridi Episcopi Auctore Eddio Stephano,* ed. and tr. B. Colgrave, *The Life of Bishop Wilfrid by Eddius Stephanus,* Cambridge, 1927.

GE   *Gregorii I Papae Registrum Epistolarum,* ed. P. Ewald and L. M. Hartmann, *MGH Epist.* 2 vols., Berlin 1891, 1899.

HAbb   *Historia Abbatum Auctore Beda,* ed. C. Plummer, *Venerabilis Baedae Opera Historica,* Oxford, 1896, I, pp. 364–87.

HE   *Historia Ecclesiastica Gentis Anglorum Auctore Beda,* ed. C. Plummer, *Venerabilis Baedae Opera Historica,* Oxford, 1896, Vol. I, Text, Vol. II, Notes. Tr. D. Whitelock, *EHD,* No. 51, pp. 639–747, with some passages omitted.

HOM   *Bedae Venerabilis Homeliarum Evangelii Libri II,* ed. D. Hurst, *CCSL* CXXII, Pars III, *Opera Homiletica,* Turnholti, 1955.

LEU   E. A. Lowe, *English Uncial,* Oxford, 1960.

MGH   *Monumenta Germaniae Historica.*

PL   *Patrologia Latina,* ed. J. P. Migne, 221 vols. Paris, 1844–64.

Rev. Bén.   *Revue Bénédictine.*

RS   Rolls Series – *Chronicles and Memorials of Great Britain and Ireland,* London, 1858–96.

Settimane   *Settimane di Studio del Centro Italiano di studi Sull'Alto Medioevo,* Spoleto.

TASA   H. M. and J. Taylor, *Anglo-Saxon Architecture,* 2 vols., Cambridge, 1965.

PART ONE

Alter Orbis

I

Change in the West

'Bede, a servant of Christ and priest of the monastery of the blessed apostles Peter and Paul, which is in Wearmouth and Jarrow. . .' Bede so describes himself near the end of what he regarded as the last of his major works, *The Ecclesiastical History of the English Nation.* And he continues: 'I was born on an estate of the same monastery and when I was seven years old my kinsmen entrusted me for my education to the most reverend abbot Benedict and later to Ceolfrith. Since then I have passed the whole of my life within the walls of this same monastery and devoted all my time to studying the Scriptures. Amid the observance of monastic discipline and the daily charge of singing in the church, my delight has always been in learning, teaching or writing. In the 19th year of my life I became a deacon, and in the 30th year I advanced to the office of priesthood, on each occasion at the hands of the most reverend bishop John, and at the bidding of abbot Ceolfrith. From the time when I received priest's orders until reaching the age of 59 I have concerned myself with making these brief commentaries on Holy Scripture from the works of the venerable fathers, for my own needs as well as the needs of my brethren, or even with adding something more towards their understanding and interpretation.'[1] There follows a list of his works under some twenty-five titles, making a total of some sixty separate books.

It is scarcely surprising that no account of Bede's life was written in the early years after his death, since a life such as his offered little scope to writers of the currently fashionable hagiography. Beyond the moving story of his death, written by one of his fellow-monks, there is little more to be told of either lesser incident or greater episode in the near sixty years of his life. We know, that towards the end of his life he visited his former pupil Egbert who, at that time, was bishop of York and that a second visit was only prevented by ill-health.[2] His description of Cuthbert's cell on Farne has sometimes been regarded as evidence that he had visited the island and it may also be that he went to Lindisfarne,[3] but even if there were other unrecorded journeys about Northumbria there are no grounds for thinking that he had travelled more widely. William of Malmesbury was certainly right in refusing to credit those who said that he had been to Rome, and rash only in believing that Pope Sergius had invited him.[4] Some of Bede's works began to circulate in England during his own lifetime, but there is no evidence that his reputation became more widespread until after his death.

The date of his terrestrial birth had no great significance for a man who regarded life as the brief pilgrimage of an exile from eternity, and later chroniclers, driven to precision by the rigidity of annals, drew differing conclusions from the little that Bede recorded about his age. He seems to say that he finished his *Ecclesiastical History* in 731 and that he was aged 59 when he compiled the list of his works which forms its epilogue, so suggesting that he was born *c.* 672, entrusted to the care of abbot Benedict *c.* 679, ordained deacon *c.* 691 and priest *c.* 702. The place of his birth is unknown though it probably lay close to either Wearmouth or Jarrow on land which was part of their original endowments. The translator of the *History* into Old English rendered Bede's Latin *natus in territorio eiusdem monasterii* by the words *acenned on sundurlonde pæs ylcan mynstres*, but the compound *sundorland* (*sundurlond*), indicating land set apart for a special purpose, is not uncommon in northern English place-names and it is wiser to regard it in this passage as translating *territorium* rather than as referring to the place now called Sunderland.[5]

Bede never refers to any of his kinsmen by name, nor is anything known about them from any other source, but we may infer that they were Christians and, in view of their association with such a man as Benedict Biscop, probably from the ranks of the well-born. At this time it was a common practice for parents who were anxious for their children to be educated, to entrust them to the care of a monastery at an early age, but such a step did not necessarily imply lifelong devotion to monasticism, still less any desire to be rid of an unwanted child. John, from whom in later years Bede received the orders first of deacon and then of priest, was the bishop of Hexham. It was to Acca, John's successor in the see at Hexham, that Bede dedicated most of his theological works, often expressing himself towards him in terms of the deepest affection. At 19 Bede was several years below the canonical age of 25 for ordination to the diaconate. He may have shown exceptional ability as a young man, but we do not know how strictly the canonical age for ordination was enforced in England at this time.

Not all of Bede's writings can be exactly dated, but so far as we know, his two earliest works – the *De Arte Metrica* and the *De Schematibus et Tropis* – were composed in 701 or 702, both of them being designed for the use of teachers in the schoolroom.[6] His last work was a letter which he wrote towards the end of 734, the year before his death, to his former pupil Egbert who was then bishop of York and who was to become its first *de facto* archbishop in the following year.[7] The 60 or so volumes which Bede wrote over a period of some 30 years represent his labours during those parts of his day which were not occupied by teaching in the monastic school or by the fulfilment of his prime duty, the daily observance of the monastic rule and the daily praise of God in the church. Music was one of Bede's great delights. We know that he was skilled in the recitation of vernacular English poetry and songs,[8] and it seems likely that the great interest and joy which he repeatedly shows in the music of the liturgy was first kindled by the visit of Abbot John, the *archicantor* of St Peter's church in Rome who came to Wearmouth to teach the Roman chant, possibly in the very year in which Bede entered the monastery as a boy of seven.[9]

Shortly before his death when, by his calculations the English had been living in Britain for rather less than 300 years, Bede, though not without concern for the evils seemingly foretold by the simultaneous appearance of two comets, was able to contemplate a Christian country whose people were enjoying times of stability, peace and prosperity. A king had lately died in Kent after ruling his kingdom for more than 34 years, Rochester had lost a bishop who was said to have been as familiar with Greek and Latin as he was with his native tongue, and in Canterbury the archbishopric had recently changed hands after a tenure of more than 37 years. The rulers of Kent, who could trace their royal ancestry far back beyond the days of Augustine, the first archbishop, had become, like the rulers of the other petty kingdoms south of Humber, subject to the suzerainty of Æthelbald, king of Mercia, who himself reigned for 41 years. North of Humber, Bede's own Northumbria was governed by a king to whom he was glad to send the first draft of his *Ecclesiastical History* for criticism and comment, and who, after reigning for 12 years, lived for a further 27 as a monk in St Cuthbert's monastery at Lindisfarne. Enjoying stability within, the English were no longer at war with their external neighbours. The Picts, now rejoicing in membership of the universal church, were observing a treaty of peace with the English, and likewise the Scots, living contentedly within their own boundaries, were not contemplating any attack against the English. Only among the Britons did hostility remain, hostility which rested partly on understandable feelings of personal antagonism towards their conquerors, but which also had a theological basis exemplified by their continuing refusal to unite in the observances of the universal catholic church.[10]

Bede was about 13 years old when Ecgfrith, king of Northumbria, was killed in battle against the Picts at Dunnichen Moss in Forfar in the summer of 685, only four months after the dedication of the new church of St Paul at Jarrow, and for the remaining 50 years of his life the records do not tell of any major battle fought anywhere in Britain, nor do they tell of any attack against Britain's coastline. Had he been born half a century earlier Bede might well have found himself involved directly in some of the many wars arising from the attempts of ambitious rulers to extend their boundaries or to win supremacy over neighbours, and had he died a little more than half a century later he would have witnessed the first Viking attack on his own monastery. But, in his sight, the headlands and lofty cliffs had been set to defend the earth against the raging storms of the sea not against the attacks of pirates, just as the resolute hearts of God's faithful people protected the church against the boisterous waves of persecution.[11] Neither Jarrow nor Wearmouth nor Lindisfarne nor many another coastal or island monastery could have prospered as they did unless the seas had been more their protection than their enemy. Stability had been achieved and for a while a balance was maintained.

Yet for all the serenity of his surroundings, Bede would have agreed with William of Malmesbury's description of his birthplace as lying in the most distant corner of the world, on the furthest shore of an island which some called another world (*alter orbis*) because there were not many geographers who had discovered its existence.[12] Long before Bede's birth, Gregory the Great, writing to Eulogius, bishop of Alexandria, described the English as a people who lived in a corner of the world and who, until lately, had put their trust in the worship of sticks and stones.[13] Bede himself had a deep sense of his remoteness from the centre of things, though it was a sense that would have been shared only by those few of his contemporaries who were both well-educated and widely-travelled, and certainly not by those Northumbrians who contemptuously rejected the papal letters which Wilfrid brought from Rome in the expectation that they would ensure his immediate restoration to favour.[14] In one of his commentaries Bede asked his readers not to be critical because he had written so much that he had learnt from ancient authors about the nature of trees and aromatic herbs. He had not done so out of conceit, but out of regard for the ignorance of himself and his fellow-men who had been born and bred in an island of the Ocean far outside the world. How else were they to learn about what happened in Arabia and India, Judaea and Egypt, save through the writings of those who had been there?[15]

There was one very real sense in which Bede did indeed live, if not outside, at least on the edge of the world. Some two and a half miles away from his monastery towards the north-east, on a low bluff commanding the entry to the Tyne, there lay the abandoned Roman fort of *Arbeia* (now South Shields), and a similar distance to the west, but on the north bank of the river, was *Segedunum* (now Wallsend), the terminal fort of the great Wall built by Hadrian to run more than 70 miles from sea to sea. This famous Wall, as Bede called it, '8 feet broad and 12 feet high in a straight line from east to west, as is manifest to onlookers even to this day',[16] formed the most northerly sector of a frontier which in the time of Diocletian (284–305) embraced the whole of Europe south of the Rhine and Danube, as well as much of Arabia and north Africa. Jerome writing in his cell at Bethlehem, Paul and Antony sharing their loaf of bread in the Egyptian desert, Augustine writing of the City of God in north Africa, Cassiodorus turning from the Italian civil service to the preservation of manuscripts in Calabria, Martin born in Pannonia to become the soldier-saint of Merovingian France, Isidore the greatest scholar of Visigothic Spain – all these men in their different ways and ages, however much they strove to withdraw from the classical world, were, nonetheless heirs to a common imperial tradition which lived long after the death of Bede, even though its nature and strength became varied by continuing change and development.

At the beginning of the fourth century the most westerly parts of the empire, including Spain, Gaul and Britain, constituted four dioceses under the terms of the administrative reforms put into effect during Diocletian's reign. When Justinian died in 565, some thirty years before Pope Gregory sent Augustine to undertake the conversion of the heathen English, the whole of these four western dioceses had been lost to imperial control save for a small part of southern Spain which had recently been re-conquered and was still subject to Byzantine rule. Even Italy itself, though now regained by Justinian's general, Belisarius, had been under the rule of an Ostrogothic king for more than 30 years. The units of imperial government had been replaced by the kingdoms of the Anglo-Saxons, Franks, Lombards, Sueves, Visigoths and Ostrogoths, with Justinian's empire nowhere extending north of the Alps.

All that we know of the defences of Britain late in the fourth century suggests that, had they been adequately manned, they would have been capable of protecting the country against the most vigorous assaults. But it was Britain's misfortune to lie at the edge of the world, and so to seem less and less important in the eyes of those who saw Milan under siege by Alaric or the Visigothic king, Radagaesus, leading his barbarian troops through Italian countryside, and even Rome itself sacked by barbarians in 410. In times like these the defence of a remote island could have no major place in the strategy of the generals employed by Rome. Britain ceased to be part of the empire not because the defences, behind which her citizens had enjoyed remarkable security for nearly four centuries, were overthrown in battle, but because the troops manning those defences were gradually removed either to meet more pressing needs elsewhere or to support rebels seeking to win control of the Gaulish prefecture. The sanction of effective Roman government was only intermittently at work in Britain during the years between 383 and 410, and after that date it ceased to exist. Whatever beliefs or hopes may have been held in Rome, it was never restored.

REFERENCES

1   *HE* V, 24.
2   *Ep. Egb.* § 1.
3   *BVC Prol.* and *c.* XVII.
4   *Gesta Regum, RS* I, 62–3. For later *Lives* of Bede see T. D. Hardy, *Descriptive Catalogue, RS* I, i, 450–4.
5   *OE Bede*, p. 480. *Eng. Place-Name Soc.*, **XXVI**, 168.
6   Below pp. 249–50.
7   Below pp. 305–6.
8   *Ep. Cuthb. de Ob. Bed.*, ed. E. van K. Dobbie, 120–1.
9   Below pp. 170–2.
10 *HE* V, 23.
11 *In I Sam.* p. 24, *lines* 540–44.
12 *Gesta Regum, RS* I, 59.

2

Bede's View of Britain

Bede regarded Britain (*Brittania*), which he distinguished from Ireland (*Hibernia*), as an island rich in natural wealth.[1] With an abundance of crops and trees, it was well-suited for the grazing of sheep and cattle, and in some places there were vineyards. There were many kinds of birds, and it was notable for its plentiful springs and its rivers which abounded in fish, especially salmon and eels. Seals, whales and porpoises were very frequently caught round its coasts, and there were many kinds of shell-fish, including mussels which often contained the finest pearls, red, purple, amethyst or green, but most often white. There was a great abundance of cockles used to make a scarlet dye which never faded in the sun or rain, but grew ever more beautiful with age. There were salt springs, and also springs of hot water from which flowed rivers furnishing hot baths in various places suitable for people of all ages and both sexes. It was Bede's belief that the water received its heat from fire burning in the inner parts of the earth, and that when the heated water came into contact with certain metals, it was raised to boiling point and so brought to the surface of the earth.[2] Ores of copper, iron, lead and silver were plentiful, and there was an abundance of jet. Bede does not say where the ores were being worked in his day, nor does he mention tin, gold or coal. He is likely to have known about the deposits of jet at Whitby which the nuns used for making small pendant crosses,[3] whether or not they also used it for frightening snakes.

That Bede ever visited Ireland seems unlikely. He shared the geographical belief of the times that its southern shores lay far to the south of Britain, reaching down towards the north coast of Spain, and he believed that it was greatly superior to Britain in the healthy mildness of its climate. Snow seldom lay there for more than three days, and no one troubled to make hay in the summer or to build stalls for their cattle as a protection against the winter. No snakes could live there, and whenever it chanced that a snake was taken to Ireland on board a ship from Britain it died as soon as it breathed the Irish air. Moreover, almost everything that came from Ireland – and doubtless Bede did not mean to include certain Irish opinions about the proper date for the celebration of Easter – was efficacious against poison. We have seen some, Bede wrote, who after being bitten by a snake and then given a drink in which scrapings from the leaves of books brought from Ireland had been immersed, were immediately able to expel the poison of the bite from their bodies. We may smile at Bede's credulity, and reflect how little times have changed. Ireland was indeed for Bede a land of milk and honey, rich in vines, fish and fowl, and especially remarkable for its deer and goats.

Just as Bede thought it important to give in his biblical commentaries information about the far-distant lands of the south and east, so he evidently thought that there would be some among the readers of his *History* who did not know that because of Britain's geographical position, there was much greater variation in the hours of light and darkness between winter and summer than was experienced in Armenia, Macedonia, Italy and other countries of similar latitude. He knew that the variation was caused by the sun seeming to pass beneath the earth nearer to the pole in the summer and much further to the south in the winter, though of course he supposed that the movement was of the sun travelling round the earth. The symbolical significance of darkness and light is a commonplace of Biblical exegesis, yet there is at least one passage in Bede's writings which still conveys to us a vivid sense of his own personal meditations while he watched the northern stars. He conceived the shadow of the earth at night as narrowing and sharpening into a pyramid as it reached out into the void. Sometimes that shadow fell across the moon, but when it did no other star was eclipsed because the splendour of the sun spreading beyond the boundaries of the earth shone freely upon the more distant stars. 'When you look around you amid the surrounding darkness of the night, away from burning torches, you do not doubt that there are some places illuminated by the light of those torches, even though with the darkness of the night standing in your way, you cannot see more than the flames of the torches themselves. Even so (men say) that most pure place which is nearest to the void of the heavens is always full of light from the flames of the stars which spread about on all sides.'[4] A little strangely perhaps, in view of his great interest in the subject, Bede said nothing in his chapter of his *History* entitled *De Situ Brittaniae* of another natural feature of the island which would have interested many, the great rise and fall of the tides. Yet on this topic, from his own observations and from the remarks of his countrymen, Bede was able to question the view that the ebbing and flowing of the ocean took place everywhere simultaneously, as if it were one immense river. 'For we who live along the shores of the sea of Britain know that when the tide has begun to flow at one point, it is at the same time beginning to ebb at another.'[5]

Bede's conception of Britain was a geographical conception of two large islands, *Brittania* and *Hibernia*, not of four distinct countries – England, Wales, Scotland and Ireland – diversified by distinctions of race, language and institutions. During Bede's lifetime Ireland had no unity save that of its physical shape, and none of the other three countries yet existed in a form which would have enabled him or his contemporaries to recognise them as distinct national entities. In Bede's sight it was not nationalism that gave unity to *Brittania*, but the fact that the people who lived in the island all studied and professed the same knowledge of the sublime truth, in other words that its inhabitants were all Christians. He expressed his recognition of racial diversity in *Brittania* by saying that, in accord with the five books in which the divine law had been written, the Scriptures were now being studied in the languages of five different peoples – the English, the Britons, the Scots, the Picts and the Latins. He added that the language of the Latins had become common to the other four peoples named through the study of the Scriptures.[6] We ought not to infer from this remark that Latin was still being spoken in everyday life by ordinary people, but only that it was the language in which all men studied the Scriptures whatever their vernacular tongue. It would be correct to make the further inference that the Scriptures were not generally known to these peoples in either their Hebrew or their Greek forms, even though there is evidence that part at least of the Greek New Testament was known to Bede at Jarrow.[7]

Popular origins are a common form of antiquarian speculation and the story-tellers of Britain were no less fertile in their imagination than the compilers of genealogies. Bede naturally recorded something about the origins of some of the people who lived in the two islands of Britain, but he was careful to distinguish popular traditions from what he believed to be historical fact, and it almost seems as if the traditions which he chose to record were those whose credibility received some support from the circumstances of his own day. He thought, for example, that the first inhabitants of *Brittania* were the *Brettones* and he recorded a tradition that they had come to *Brittania* from Armorica. Later sources elaborate a legendary tale which derived the name *Brittania* from a certain Brutus who was associated with Aeneas and the Trojans and who eventually reached Britain after many adventures, including a stay in Gaul where Brutus supposedly built the city of Tours. The story of Romulus and Remus was known in Northumbria and it would be rash to assume that the legend of Brutus was not already current in Bede's day. If he rejected its greater extravagances, but reported a tradition that the *Brettones* had come from Armorica in Gaul, he may have done so because the Armorica of his day was indeed so completely British in race, language and social organisation that a movement from Armorica into Britain would be entirely credible. Similarly with the Picts of whose legendary origins Bede wrote at greater length. They had come, so men said, from Scythia, a land which in another context he associates with Thule and the midnight sun.[8] After being driven in their ships beyond *Brittania*, they reached the northern coast of *Hibernia*. The *Scotti* who lived there would not allow them to settle but told them that there was a bigger island not far away which they could often see on a clear day. The Picts accordingly sailed to *Brittania* and occupied the northern part of the island, since the Britons already held the southern part. Because the Picts had no wives they asked the Scots if they could have some of their women in marriage and the Scots agreed, but only on condition that whenever any doubt arose the Picts would choose a king from the female rather than from the male stock. It is well-known, wrote Bede, that this custom is still observed among the Picts to this day. And herein for Bede lay the *rationale* of the whole story. He evidently knew that the form of succession practised by the Pictish rulers differed in some way from that familiar to him in his own society and he found a credible explanation of an unusual custom in the story of the Scottish wives, which he may well have learnt from the Pictish emissaries sent by their king to discuss ecclesiastical topics with Abbot Ceolfrith at Jarrow *c*. 710. We do not know how the Pictish law of succession was practised. There is no evidence that the kingdom was ruled by a queen, nor is there any instance before Bede's death of the direct succession of a father by his son to the rule of the kingdom. The succession of a brother was common, but it seems unlikely that this was the peculiarity upon which Bede was commenting, since the succession of a brother was common in the Anglo-Saxon kingdoms, and particularly so in seventh-century Northumbria.

We do not know whether Pictish was ever a written language. Books written in Latin were certainly in use at Pictish ecclesiastical centres during Bede's lifetime, but no fragment of any such book now survives and we have no means of knowing whether the intellectual interests stimulated by the study of the Scriptures led Pictish ecclesiastics to record any aspect of their own history, other than the mere names of their kings and the number of years that each of them reigned. We can learn from Bede that on the eastern side of Britain the southern boundary of the Pictish kingdom lay on the Firth of Forth,[9] and that at least during the last twenty years or so of Bede's life its people lived on terms of friendship with the English who were their southern neighbours across the Forth. But this had not always been so. Shortly after the middle of the seventh century, perhaps some twenty years before Bede was born, the English of Northumbria conquered part of the Pictish kingdom and held it in subjection until 685. On the western side of Britain the southern boundary of the Picts, separating them from the Britons, had at one time been marked by the Firth of Clyde, but this was no longer so in Bede's time owing to the occupation of former Pictish lands in this area by people who had migrated from *Hibernia*. Before this migration, so far as we know, the whole of Scotland north of Forth and Clyde, and including the Orkneys, was Pictish.

Bede made a distinction between the lands of the northern Picts and those of the southern Picts which were separated from one another by steep and rugged mountains.[10] Early writers distinguish two major features in the Scottish mountains, the *Dorsum Brittaniae* or Spine of Britain, known also as Druimalban, running in a long gentle curve from Cape Wrath to the Clyde, and the Mounth, running east and west and corresponding with the Grampians. It is certainly to the latter that Bede was referring, but it is very doubtful whether the distinction which he made between northern and southern Picts was meant to imply anything more than a merely geographical distinction. Certainly there is no evidence from his time for the division of the Picts into two distinct kingdoms, even though we may think it unlikely that any king of that age would have been able to exercise effective control over a country whose physical geography has made its people notoriously resentful of central authority throughout their history. What particularly interested Bede in making this distinction was his belief that the northern and the southern provinces of the Picts had been brought to Christianity at different times. He thought that the northern provinces had been converted by Columba who came to Britain when Bridei was ruling the Picts and who received the island of Iona from the Picts. Bede, who dates the arrival of Columba to 565, seems to be implying that at that date Iona was part of

Bridei's Pictish kingdom, an implication not supported by Columba's biographer, Adomnan, who wrote as though he believed that the lands west of the Spine had already ceased to be Pictish in Columba's time. Bede's source of information is again likely to have been the Pictish visitors to Jarrow. But, according to common report, the conversion of the southern Picts had taken place much earlier. The tradition known to Bede, and recorded by him as a tradition, was that the southern Picts had abandoned heathenism long before Columba's arrival, and that they had been converted by a British bishop called Nynia whose 'bishopric, distinguished by the name of bishop St Martin, and by a church where he himself lies buried with many other holy men, has but lately come into the possession of the English'.[11] Bede adds that Nynia's church was in a place called *Ad Candidam Casam* (now known as Whithorn in Wigtownshire) and that it lay in that part of the Northumbrian kingdom called Bernicia. St Martin is thought to have died *c.* 397, but the chronology of his life is by no means clear and there is nothing to show whether Bede knew the date of his death. That some at least of the Picts had been converted by *c.* 450 is implied in a letter written at about that time by St Patrick who in the course of the letter twice refers to certain 'apostate Picts'. Columba's biographer, Adomnan, believed that Columba made only one journey into the kingdom of the Picts and that journey, which took him across the Spine to Loch Ness and towards the fortress of King Bridei near the river Ness, brought him into direct contact with Pictish paganism.[12]

The arrival of the British and the Picts in Britain was followed later, Bede writes, by the settlement of a third people. Coming from Hibernia under the leadership of a chieftain called Reuda, either by friendly negotiation or by force of arms, they occupied certain lands which they still possessed and which had formerly belonged to the Picts. 'They are still to this day called *Dalreudini* after the name of their leader, for in their language *daal* means "part".'[13] For Bede and other writers of his age the *Scotti* were primarily the inhabitants of *Hibernia*. The migration of some of the *Scotti* from *Hibernia* to *Brittania* and the later development of a strong kingdom of *Scotti* in *Brittania* made it necessary for both Irish and English writers to distinguish between the homeland and the offshoot and this they did by using such expressions as *Scotti Brittaniae* or, in Irish sources, *fir Alban* (men of Britain). Bede could call Ireland either *Hibernia* or *Scottia*, but he did not need any name by which to distinguish the whole of what is now Scotland from the rest of *Brittania* since such a distinction had no reality for his age.

The witness of Ammianus Marcellinus, of late Roman fortifications, of inscriptions using the distinctively Irish alphabet known as *ogam* and of Irish traditions, all testify to close connections between Ireland and western Britain beginning before the Roman occupation had come to an end and continuing through the following centuries.[14] In some areas, notably in the peninsulas of south-west and north-west Wales, there is good evidence for intensive Irish settlement, but in the outcome these settlements were absorbed in the Welsh kingdoms and never became of any lasting political significance. The settlement to which Bede refers was of vastly greater importance since it was the embryo of the kingdom of Scotland, though conception was not brought to fruition until long after Bede's death. He himself refers neither to the place nor to the date of the settlement of those known in his day as the *Dalreudini*, and it is evident from his uncertainty whether the settlement had been peaceful or warlike that he knew nothing of the circumstances in which it had taken place. Like Isidore of Seville, though with more restraint, Bede was fascinated by the etymology of names. If we are bound to regard *Reuda* as a fictitious chieftain, comparable with the Brutus who supposedly gave his name to *Brittania*, we must accept Bede's contemporary witness that at the time when he was writing his *History c.* 731 the Scots settled in Britain were known simply as *Dalreudini*. Bede's name is to be associated with the Irish *Dal-Réti*, signifying 'division of Rete', and later developing into Dalriata. *Réte* is the tribal name of the people from whom the historical kings of the Scots who settled in Britain derived their descent. We find them living in Argyllshire and also in the northern part of Ireland. According to Irish

tradition the *Dal-Réti* were said to have migrated from the
counties of Kerry and Cork in time of famine and to have
founded new settlements, some of them going to Britain and
some of them to north-eastern Ireland.[15] We have no contemporary evidence for this movement, but it is thought that the
settlement of *Scotti* which grew into the kingdom of Dalriata
took place near the middle of the fifth century, and that
geographically it embraced the islands and the western mainland northwards from the Firth of Clyde towards Loch Linnhe.
Whatever the circumstances of its origin, the kingdom of
Dalriata was in conflict with the Picts by *c.* 550, and during the
next half of the century the authority of its rulers was spreading
eastwards across the more southerly of the Pictish provinces.[16]

In the year 603 Aedan, king of the Scots of Dalriata, suffered
a disastrous defeat at the hands of Æthelfrith king of the English
of Northumbria. The battle was fought at *Degsastan*, a place
which cannot now be identified, but which probably lay somewhere to the south of the Firth of Forth. In Bede's judgement it
seemed a battle of particularly great significance, because, as he
wrote, from that day to this no king of the Scots in Britain dared
to come to battle against the English.[17] The defeat of the Scots
of Dalriata by the English of Northumbria in 603 was indeed of
lasting significance in the shaping of political boundaries, but of
even greater significance for the world in which Bede lived was
the flight into exile of the sons of Æthelfrith following the
latter's death in battle in 616. These sons, and others of the
Northumbrian nobility, all still pagan, found refuge some with
the Picts and some with the Scots. Augustine reached Canterbury six years before Æthelfrith's victory over Aedan at *Degsastan* and while Æthelfrith's sons were living as refugees and
being converted to Christianity by priests of the Columban
church, the mission of Paulinus reached Northumbria from
Canterbury.

Bede's almost idyllic picture of *Hibernia* was perhaps coloured
by his knowledge that Ireland had been at once the source of so
much Christian teaching among the English, and the inspiration of so many Englishmen who had gone there to be taught

by Irish scholars at a time when no such teaching was to be had in England. He recorded no legend about the origins of its inhabitants, the *Scotti*, nor did he ever refer to any legendary or mythical episodes in their history while they were still pagan. He shows us Ireland as a wholly Christian country, and he recorded, in a passage borrowed from Prosper of Aquitaine, his belief that in 432 Palladius had been sent by Pope Celestine as bishop to those of the Irish who were already Christian.[18] With not only the sea, but also the British kingdoms of western Britain separating the Irish Scots from the Anglo-Saxons, there was never any occasion for military conflict between the two peoples at the time when much of Britain was passing under English control. In 684 when Bede was aged about 13, Ecgfrith, king of Northumbria, sent an army to attack Ireland, and when Bede came to write of this incident in his *History* about half a century later, he was very severe in his condemnation of this attack against a people who had caused no offence but had always been very friendly towards the English, and he recorded the belief of those who saw the vengeance of God in Ecgfrith's death in battle the following year, a severe condemnation indeed for the king who had but lately given the land upon which the monasteries at Wearmouth and Jarrow had been founded.[19]

Bede shows us Ireland in the pages of his *History* as above all a land fertile in missionaries and scholars, by no means all of them Irish. It was the home not only of Columba who carried Christianity thence to the northern Picts, and later through his successors to Northumbria, but also of Fursey who established a monastery among the pagan English of East Anglia. Agilbert, though himself of Gaulish origin, came to preach among the pagan West Saxons after spending a long time studying the Scriptures in Ireland. An Englishman, Wihtberht, had lived for many years in Ireland before setting out on a mission to the pagan Frisians, and two other Englishmen, known from the colour of their hair as Black Hewald and White Hewald, also lived for a long time in Ireland before going to preach to the Old Saxons among whom they both suffered martyrdom. At about the middle of the seventh century, as Bede records, there were many Englishmen, not only of the nobility but also of the ordinary people, who had gone to Ireland either to study the Scriptures or for the sake of a more enclosed life. Some of them became monks while others preferred to devote themselves to study, moving about the country from one teacher's cell to another[20] – a land of milk and honey indeed – for so it must surely have seemed to Bede.

Lying wholly outside the empire, Ireland had never experienced Roman civilian institutions, whether political, legal or social. There were many kings, but no conception of a king of Ireland until long after Bede's day. The basis of society was aristocratic and tribal, and the maintenance of order rested with the individual nobleman and his kindred each in their own locality, rather than with any centralised authority. Though fighting was honoured in poetry, and frequent in practice, any conception of an Irish army going to war against Britons or English would be completely foreign to the age. What gives unique interest to this society when viewed against the background not only of the vanishing western empire, but also of pagan Scandinavia, is its intense individualism and its very high powers of self-expression, characteristics which remain familiar in many parts of Ireland today. Wholly untouched by Roman influences, Irish pagan society, which paid high honour to lawyers and poets schooled to their professions by rigorous intellectual training, passed directly into a Christian society which preserved and developed, as it were, an aristocracy of the intellect and the arts, an aristocracy which found outlets for its talents in scholarship, poetry, calligraphy and the working of metal and stone, and which through its missionary zeal carried its influence across England, to northern Gaul, Switzerland and Italy.

REFERENCES

1   *HE* I, i.
2   *In Genesim*, i, 2, ed. Jones *CCSL* CXVIII A, 5.
3   *Archaeologia* LXXXIX (1943), 68–70.

4   *BdTR c.* VII, *lines* 22–6.
5   *BdTR c.* XXIX, *lines* 62–6.
6   *HE* I, l.
7   See below p. 234.
8   *In Regum Lib. XXX Quaest.* ed. Hurst *CCSL* CXIX, 317, *lines* 19–27. Bede remarks that he had learnt about Thule and the midnight sun both from books and from 'men of our own time' who had come from those parts.
9   *HE* IV, 26.
10 *HE* III, 4.
11 *Ibid.*
12 *AdVC* II, 32–5.
13 *HE* I, l.
14 For an account of the emergence of the Celtic kingdoms see M. Dillon and N. K. Chadwick, *The Celtic Realms*, London 1967, especially *chaps.* 2–4.
15 *AdVC Intro.* pp. 35–6.
16 For the early history of the kingdom see *AdVC Intro.* pp. 30–66.
17 *HE* I, 34.
18 *HE* I, 13.
19 *HE* IV, 26.
20 *HE* III, 27.

Saxons then living in Britain, he names Frisians, Rugians, Danes, Huns, Old Saxons and *Boructuari* (these last known from other sources to have lived in Westphalia). His interest in the Frisians, *Boructuari* and Old Saxons was occasioned mainly by the activities of Anglo-Saxon Christian missionaries among them late in the seventh century, notably the Northumbrian Willibrord who founded a monastery on an island in the Rhine later known as Kaiserswerth, and to whom Pippin gave the old Roman fortress at *Traiectum*, now Utrecht, as a base for an episcopal seat. But Bede's comments on the pagan races of Germany are not confined solely to the work of missionaries. He notes, presumably as a distinguishing peculiarity, that the Old Saxons had no king, but were subject to a large number of chieftains of whom one was chosen by lot as leader at the outbreak of war. After the war all the chieftains once more became equal in power.[2] And he also recorded more specific information about the origin of the Germanic peoples who were living in Britain in his day. They came, he believed, from three of the more powerful races of Germany – the Saxons, the Angles and the Jutes. He located them geographically by naming the country from which the Angles came as *Angulus*, and by placing the Jutes to the north and the Saxons to the south of them. He had heard it said that after the migration of the Angles to Britain, their country had remained deserted to the present day.[3] The survival of the place-name *Angulus* as the modern Angeln, and a variety of written and archaeological evidence ranging in date from Tacitus to Alfred the Great, enable us to locate the homelands of the *Angli*, or *Engle* as they called themselves, close to the neck of the Jutland peninsula, in the neighbourhood of Schleswig and in the islands to the east of Schleswig.

Bede's account of the history of Britain between the sack of Rome by the Goths in 410 and the start of Augustine's journey to England in 596 was derived mainly from two sources, the work of Gildas, a British monk who is generally thought to have been writing *c.* 550, and a *Life* of one of the Gallo-Roman bishops, Germanus, who held the see of Auxerre and who is known to have visited Britain in 429. The *Life* would be of particular interest to Bede because he knew that the prime purpose of Germanus's visit to Britain had been to combat the Pelagian heresy and bring the British church back to the fold of orthodoxy. The amount of material which Bede took from these two sources indicates the importance which he attached to this period of Britain's history and likewise suggests that he regarded them as the best sources available for his purpose. Apart from his account of the continental origins of the Angles, Saxons and Jutes, he was able to add the names of one or two places and people, and also to give some chronological precision to Gildas's narrative by correlating some of its stages with particular years of the Christian era. But basically Bede saw the conquest of Britain by the Anglo-Saxons in the same light as Gildas saw it – the vengeance of God justly falling upon a people who, though Christian in name, had been brought to corruption and all manner of evil by wanton and luxurious living.[4] Bede could borrow from Gildas a passage lamenting that not only were all bonds of truth and justice overthrown, but that also there were very few people left who knew that such virtues had ever existed.[5] And he could add to the list of unspeakable crimes described by their own historian, the further crime that the Britons never preached the Christian faith to the Angles and Saxons living among them in Britain.

Almost in the last chapter of his *History* which, it must be remembered, was an ecclesiastical history, Bede repeated this charge of neglect, remarking that just as the Britons had been unwilling to teach the Christian faith to the pagan English, so now, when the English were in all ways instructed in the catholic faith, the Britons stubbornly persisted in their old errors.[6] Bede was here referring to the fact that in 731 the British clergy, unlike the English, the Picts and the Scots, still observed certain usages which in his view placed them beyond the pale of catholic orthodoxy. It is difficult to escape the conclusion that in using for his account of the conquest of Britain the works of Gildas and Constantius, the one bitterly attacking the British clergy as well as the laity and the other representing the victory of catholicism over Pelagianism, Bede was himself influenced by his deep, even passionate, devotion to the catholic faith. He may even have seen the continuance of the British clergy in error, and therefore sin, long after the Irish had become orthodox, as just retribution for the failure of the British to preach to the pagan English.[7] Yet it is hardly to be thought that Bede could have written an account of the Anglo-Saxon settlements in Britain even had he wished to do so. No written records were kept by either of the two sides engaged, and even if we are right to accept the narrative of Gildas as having been written c. 550, it provides contemporary evidence only for a limited part of the sixth century.

British tradition, represented by Gildas and accepted by Bede, regarded as the central episode a fatal invitation, given by men in authority in Britain, to Saxons to come and settle in the island as hirelings to do battle against the enemies of their employers. It was as a consequence of the rebellion of these settlers that most of Britain eventually came under Saxon domination. Reflecting upon the situation in which the Romano-Britons found themselves after being left to look to their own defence, and upon the many parallels to be seen in other parts of the empire, we may think it likely that this tradition faithfully reflects an episode of major importance in the conquest of Britain by the English. It is probable that the British leader mainly concerned in this episode was Vortigern, a man whom we may conceive as born into the Romano-British aristocracy and as acquiring, perhaps c. 425 or a little later, a position not unlike that of the former military governors of Roman Britain. The rebellion of his mercenaries and the beginning of a long period of warfare probably occurred c. 450. Yet we would surely be wrong to regard Vortigern's plantation of Saxons in Britain as more than an important episode in a long process by which the shores of Belgium and Gaul were affected almost as much as those of Britain. It was inevitable that later historians, and particularly Bede with his orderly mind and profound interest in chronology, should have looked for an exact point in time from which the beginnings of the English occupation of Britain might be reckoned. Yet even Bede was always careful to indicate that what he called the *adventus Saxonum* was no more than an approximation. The evidence of some pagan Saxon cemeteries, particularly those found in close proximity to Romano-British towns, may well suggest that there were parts of the country in which peaceful Saxon settlements were being made while Roman imperial government was still effective. Although the interpretation of this and other archaeo-logical evidence raises many controversial problems, there is much to suggest that the Saxon conquest of Britain was a slow piecemeal process, probably achieved by small bands of men of mixed racial origin and serving under leaders who attracted followers by their prowess in war and their generosity with the property of their defeated enemies. It was a settlement in no way comparable with the conquest of Britain by the Romans or of England by the Normans.

Although there was no Romano-British bishop to describe the siege of Pevènsey by the Saxons, as Sidonius described the siege of Clermont by the Visigoths at about the same time, surviving Anglo-Saxon heroic poetry contains accounts, albeit allusive and fragmentary, of two incidents located in the lands from which many of the settlers in Britain originally came. We can be reasonably sure of the historicity of one of them, but both seem to give a faithful reflection of the kind of incident which may well have recurred many times on both sides of the North Sea in this age of migration. The earlier of the two, known to us in part from the fragmentary *Fight at Finnsburg* and in part from *Beowulf*, has for its theme the tragic consequences of a feud between Danes and Frisians. We know nothing of the origins of the feud. A company of Danes, 60 strong and led by their king Hnaef, are visiting Finnsburg, the stronghold of Finn, king of the Frisians. Because of the loss of the earlier part of the poem we are led abruptly into a scene in which the Danish warriors, sleeping in the hall of Finn, are suddenly called to arms by their leader:

> This is not dawn,   nor flying dragon,
> Nor fire burning   the horns of this hall,
> But men in armour!   The eagle will scream,

The grey wolf howl,   and the war-wood whistle,
Shield answer shaft!   Now shines the moon
Through scudding cloud.   Dire deeds are come
Bringing hard battle   and bitter strife.
Awake my warriors!   Grasp your shields![8]

For five days the battle continued as Hnaef and his warriors
held the door against the enemy, but there unhappily the poem
breaks off before the tale is near complete. The story was used by
the poet of *Beowulf*, and although his allusive manner of telling
it raises great difficulties of interpretation, we can learn from
him that Hnaef was eventually killed and that after his death
Hengest succeeded as leader of the Danes. Hengest and his
surviving companions made a truce with Finn by whose terms
both sides would bury their dead in a great ceremonial funeral,
and Hengest and his followers would remain at peace with Finn
in Frisia throughout the winter. But when the spring came the
feud broke out again and Finn was killed. Hengest and his
victorious men then returned to their own country laden with
Finn's treasures, and taking with them as well, Hildeburh, the
Danish queen of the dead Finn.

The Finn episode in *Beowulf* is presented as part of an
evening's entertainment of song and music in Hrothgar's hall in
celebration of the slaying of Grendel. Whatever may have been
the poet's motive for introducing this particular story, his manner of presenting it assumes that it would be familiar to those
likely to hear the poem. That Bede himself, with his known
interest in vernacular poetry, knew some version of the Finn
story cannot be proved, but the possibility that he did is
strengthened by his report of a tradition that one of the leaders
of those who came to settle in Britain at Vortigern's invitation
was called Hengest, and by his statement that there was still in
Bede's own day a monument in eastern Kent bearing the name
of his brother Horsa who had been killed in battle by the
Britons.[9] There are grounds for something more than a suspicion that the Hengest who figures in Anglo-Saxon heroic
tradition is the same man as that Hengest who figured in the
tradition known to Bede and who is represented in the *Anglo-*

Saxon Chronicle as playing a major part in the conquest of Kent from the Britons at about the middle of the fifth century.

The second incident belongs historically to a later time and concerns Hygelac, who is shown in *Beowulf* as king of the Geats and uncle of the hero himself. During the entertainment which followed the recitation of the lay about Finn, Beowulf was rewarded with many costly gifts, among them a magnificent jewelled collar whose splendour was comparable only with the renowned necklace of the Brisings. The poet tells how this necklace had been worn by Hygelac on a fatal expedition to Frisia where he was killed by Franks who took possession of his body, his armour and the famous necklace. There are other references to this expedition in the poem and from one of them we learn that Beowulf himself contrived to escape with his life by plunging into the sea, bearing on his arm thirty suits of battle armour, and swimming away. Again the poet, concerned with entertainment and not with history, assumes that his audience will know about the famous necklace of the Brisings and also about the disastrous expedition itself.

The expedition of Hygelac, mentioned only in allusive fashion and embroidered with an appropriate measure of fantasy, is the only incident in *Beowulf* which can also be seen through the eyes of a writer concerned with history rather than with entertainment. Gregory of Tours, the Frankish historian, records it thus.

Afterwards the Danes, with their king called Chlochilaichus, set out by ship across the sea to attack Gaul. After disembarking, they lay waste and take possession of a district belonging to the kingdom of Theuderich, and with their ships laden with captives and other spoils of war they seek to return to their own country; but their king remained behind on the shore until the ships were dragged into the water, intending to follow afterwards. When Theuderich learnt that his land had been laid waste by foreigners he sent his son Theudebert thither with a powerful force and a great array of arms. After slaying the king, Theudebert overthrew the enemy in a naval battle and made good all the plundering of his land.[10]

There is no doubt about the identity of Gregory's *Chlochilaichus* with the Hygelac of *Beowulf*. Theuderich, son of Clovis, succeeded his father as king of the Merovingian Franks in 511 and died in 534. The raid cannot be dated exactly but probably occurred *c*. 520. Gregory's account of the raid is commonly regarded as providing trustworthy independent support for the historicity of the *Beowulf* version. Gregory's *History* was known in England during Bede's age and was used by Bede himself, though it may not have reached him till late in his life. Bede, and no doubt others as well, will have read Gregory's account of the raid.[11]

REFERENCES

1   *HE* V, 9.
2   *HE* V, 10.
3   *HE* I, 15.
4   *HE* I, 14.
5   *HE* I, 22.
6   *HE* V, 22.
7   I am indebted to Professor Whitelock for this point.
8   Translation by C. W. Kennedy, *The Earliest English Poetry* (Oxford 1943), 42–3.
9   *HE* I, 15.
10 Gregory, *Hist.* III, 3.
11 For a discussion of the Hygelac raid see D. Whitelock *The Audience of Beowulf* (Oxford 1951), 39–50.

4
English Foundations

The impression conveyed by the story of the fight at Finnsburg and of Hygelac's raid on Merovingian Gaul is of a society which would have seemed anarchical to any Roman provincial governor of the fourth century. The many homes and farmsteads which have been excavated on some of the larger Baltic islands, notably Bornholm, once the home of the Burgundians, reflect small communities supporting themselves by agriculture and no doubt living peaceably for much of their lives with only periodic outbreaks of violence. Similarly the many pagan Saxon cemeteries widely distributed over the English lowlands, and sometimes counting many hundreds of burials, testify to the settlement of the newly-won lands by small village communities, again supporting themselves by agriculture. But this foundation of the Germanic society of north-west Europe remains inarticulate and is to be known only through some of its former possessions, which have indeed much to tell of its craftsmanship and material skills, whether in the handling of wood for building ships whose quality could not easily have been bettered for the needs they were intended to meet, or in the use of metal and precious stones for their arms and their jewellery. In a society such as this, uncontrolled by any occupying military power, and knowing nothing of any universal system of law, taxation or schooling, the security of the individual did not lie within any conception of a state, but within the much smaller unity of the kin. Any movement away from fragmentation towards larger political entities had its roots in the war band held together by a successful leader – such a man perhaps as Hengest.

When the Romans invaded Britain in A.D. 43, they did so

with a highly-trained professional army of some 40,000 men, perhaps more than five times as many as William the Norman was able to put into the field at Hastings in 1066. But English traditions about the origins of some at least of the Anglo-Saxon kingdoms tell, not of large organised armies, but of chieftains coming to land with three, four or five ships: and if they were ships comparable with those found at Nydam near Schleswig or at Sutton Hoo in East Anglia they may have carried some fifty fully-armed men apiece. A seventh-century law code from Wessex defines a group of up to 7 men as thieves, from 7 to 35 men as a band, and any number more than 35 as an army (*here*).[1] By this definition the 60 warriors who went to Finnsburg would certainly have been regarded as an army. This is not to deny that there were occasions when substantially larger forces were assembled for battle, especially by the seventh century when the extreme fragmentation following the breakdown of Roman authority was beginning to give way before the emergence of larger units. Something of the way in which individual groups of settlers took possession of areas of land in Britain which were smaller than the modern English counties, but substantially bigger than even a large parish, seems to be reflected by a widely-distributed type of English place-name. *Rēada*, *Haesta*, *Angenmaer* and *Hrotha* are names of individual people now preserved in the place-names Reading, Hastings, Angmering, and the Rodings of Essex. We know nothing about them as historical people, but we can envisage them as leaders of small groups of settlers or colonists who took possession of such land as they needed and who, if the bond of kinship doubtless united some of them, were held together mainly by the common need of security in a newly-conquered land where there was no central government to maintain law and order.

Tacitus regarded the typical inhabitant of *Germania* as a wild, blue-eyed man with reddish hair and a huge frame. Well able to endure cold and hunger, though not heat and thirst, he was a courageous fighter capable of great exertions, but impatient of sustained hard work. To throw away his shield in battle was to incur the supreme disgrace, and defeated survivors often preferred to end their shame by hanging themselves. Their leaders won and maintained their position by their example rather than by their authority. When a young man seemed likely to make good, he was equipped with shield and spear at a public gathering and became attached to a group of older and more mature leaders. Within the band of companions so formed there was great rivalry for the first place beside the leader and great competition among the leaders for the largest band of companions. On the battlefield it was a disgrace for the chief to be outstripped in valour by his companions and for the companions to be less valiant than their chiefs. To leave the battle alive after the chief was dead was to incur lifelong infamy and shame. Whilst the chief fought for victory, his companions fought for their chief, and sometimes if there was a long period without fighting, the young men would leave their homelands and seek some other place where there was war afoot.[2] Tacitus fully understood that a society such as this depended for its nourishment upon continuing warfare and violence. The followers of the chiefs made demands upon them which could only be met by success in war which itself tended to increase the size of the chieftain's following.

Although Tacitus was writing some six hundred years before Bede's time and drawing upon only a limited knowledge of the *Germania* of his day, much of what he says about the Germanic warband – the *comitatus* – is characteristic of Anglo-Saxon society not merely in the age of migration and settlement, but still in much later times. Under the Roman occupation the religious cult of the deified Roman emperor may have been intended to serve as the focus of loyalty towards the universal Roman state, but in Anglo-Saxon England loyalty was personal and not to any remote abstract conception. The strength of the personal bond between a man and his lord, whose meaning was often as much human as material, the value attached to personal allegiance, and the resultant attitudes towards the virtue of loyalty and the infamy of treachery are recurrent themes of Anglo-Saxon history and literature. Bede gave expression to these themes when he told of the devotion of King Edwin's thegn, Lilla, who, with no shield to protect him, leapt between his lord the king and the assassin's poisoned dagger, when he condemned the infamous conduct of Hunwald in betraying to his death a trusting king who had sought refuge with him in time of need, and when he showed Raedwald, king of East Anglia, resisting the pressure of bribery and the threat of war to keep faith with an exile to whom he had promised friendship and a safe place of refuge.[3] Even as late as the time of Æthelred the Unready, when preachers and historians alike lamented the current evil of treachery, the old Germanic code of the *comitatus* as Tacitus describes it, finds its most powerful expression in the whole range of Anglo-Saxon literature in the poem describing the defeat of the English by the Danes in the battle at Maldon in 991. When Brihtnoth himself lay dead and his army had been turned in flight, his personal retainers fought on in determined fulfilment of their vow to their lord that if they could not ride home with him in safety they would lie with him on the field of battle.

Britain in the centuries following the Roman collapse abounded with those whom the records call kings. Some of them ruled native British principalities in the north and west – among them Strathclyde with its capital at Dumbarton, Rheged with lands lying on either side of the Solway, Gododdin in the eastern Scottish lowlands, Elmet in part of western Yorkshire, Gwynedd including Anglesey and part of north-west Wales, Powys along what was to become the borderland between England and Wales, Dyfed in south-western Wales and Dumnonia in Cornwall and Devon. Others, even more numerous, ruled in the east and south. When Edwin, king of the Northumbrians, led an expedition against the West Saxons in 626 he is said to have killed five kings there. When Saberht, a king of the East Saxons, died *c*. 617 he was succeeded by his three sons, and other incidents in the history of the East Saxons suggest that joint rule by two or more kings was common among them. When a king of Kent died in 725 he left three sons as heirs to his kingdom, and in later years, after Bede's death, a ruler in Kent could describe himself as *rex dimidiae partis provinciae Cantuariorum*.[4]

There is similar evidence of joint rule by more than one king among the South Saxons. And to these we may add the kings who ruled in East Anglia, in Lindsey, in different parts of the midlands and also in Deira and Bernicia, the component parts of the kingdom of Northumbria. To any Roman historian who had known the provinces of Britain as constituting a diocese within the western empire, such a multiplicity of kings could hardly have seemed less than complete anarchy, and to any modern historian whose conception of Germanic kingship is based on such men as Gaeseric the Vandal, Theodoric the Ostrogoth or Clovis the Frank, the petty princelings of Britain after the collapse of the western empire may seem very little more than the chieftains described by Tacitus in his *Germania*. Hengest in Kent, Ælle besieging the Britons in the Roman fort at Pevensey, Cerdic and Cynric from whom the later kings of the West Saxons claimed descent, and Ida who established a pirate stronghold on the great rock at Bamburgh were surely in their own age merely the leaders of war bands who had attracted followers to their service and who by their success were able to reward them with treasure or land or both. Doubtless there were many other leaders who remain unknown to us, partly because they did not succeed in founding a dynasty in whose genealogy their memory might be enshrined and partly because no chronicle records a single episode in the settlement of the whole of eastern Britain between Thames and Tyne during the fifth and sixth centuries.

If we interpret the scanty records correctly British opposition to Anglo-Saxon expansion was strong both in the south and in the north. Gildas recorded a great British victory – strangely described as the siege of *Mons Badonicus* – which seems to have led to a period of equilibrium, if not of British ascendancy, in the southern part of Britain for about half a century from *c.* 500. Shortly after the middle of the sixth century a series of Anglo-Saxon victories finally extinguished all British rule east of the Trent and the lower Severn. In the north the British kingdoms were still dominant over wide areas when Augustine reached Canterbury in 597, but the situation changed radically during the reign of Æthelfrith, the last of the pagan rulers of the Northumbrians, whom Bede compared with Saul for the ferocity of his attacks against the British and to whom he thought might fitly be applied the words of the patriarch when blessing his son in the person of Saul – 'Benjamin a ravenous wolf, in the morning shall eat the prey, and in the evening shall divide the spoil'.[5]

The warfare of Britain in the seventh century, when the settlement itself had been largely, if not wholly, completed, is a reflection partly of the continuing British struggle against the growing domination of the English north of Humber, and partly of the attempts of one or other of the English kingdoms south of Humber to establish supremacy over its neighbours. Bede records a list of seven kings whose position was distinguished by their ability to exercise some form of authority over an area extending far beyond the bounds of their own kingdoms.[6] The first four of them were Ælle, king of the South Saxons, whose dates are uncertain but who was ruling late in the fifth century, Ceawlin, king of the West Saxons who is said to have died in 593, Æthelbert, king of Kent, who was reigning when Augustine reached Canterbury and who died c. 616, and Rædwald, king of the East Angles, who died about the same time as Æthelbert but is said to have been winning the leadership for his people during Æthelbert's lifetime. We know next to nothing in detail about the nature of the *imperium* exercised by these kings who are known in a ninth-century source as Bretwaldas, but their emergence marks a stage in the return from fragmentation towards the unity which Britain had known under Roman rule. The next three kings in the list were all rulers of the Northumbrians – Edwin, Oswald and Osuiu. The seventh and last in the list, Osuiu, died in 671, perhaps the year in which Bede was born. The *imperium* exercised by the three Northumbrian kings came near to extending over the whole of Britain, since it included not only all the kingdoms of the English, but also a large part of the lands still held by the Britons, the Picts and the Scots. But the Northumbrian supremacy did not last. When Bede was writing the last chapter of his *History*, some sixty years later, all the kingdoms of the English south of the Humber were subject to Æthelbald, king of the Mercians, a representative of the only one of all the Anglo-Saxon royal families whose descent can, it is thought, be traced from men who ruled near Schleswig before the migration of the English to Britain. Mercian domination was confirmed and strengthened by Æthelbald's successor, Offa, who began to reign in 757, twenty-two years after Bede's death, and who in his later years styled himself *rex Anglorum* or *rex totius Anglorum patriae* in some of his charters. In 794, two years before Offa's death, Bede's church at Jarrow was sacked by Viking raiders.

REFERENCES

1 *Laws of Ine* 13, 1.
2 *Germ. cc.* 4, 6, 7.
3 *HE* II, 9; III, 14; II, 12.
4 W. de G. Birch, *Cartularium Saxonicum*, No. 194.
5 *HE* I, 34.
6 *HE* II, 5.

PART TWO

Towards Christianity

5

The Initiation of a Mission

There is no episode in the history of the English in Britain of a significance comparable with the mission of St Augustine about which we can learn so little from contemporary written sources. The contemporary evidence amounts only to some thirty letters written by Gregory, and many of these are mere letters of commendation to bishops and lay rulers through whose lands the travellers were expected to pass. The account of Gregory's tenure of the papacy in the *Liber Pontificalis* contains only a short reference to the mission. There are no surviving letters written by Augustine or any of his companions, nor by any of the bishops whom they will have met on their journey from Rome to England. A sixth-century copy of the Gospels of Mediterranean origin is associated with St Augustine by good tradition and is likely to have been in use in Canterbury in Augustine's time. Apart from a code of law, now preserved only in a twelfth-century manuscript but believed to be a genuine code issued by Æthelbert *c.* 602, there are no other Canterbury records of any kind dating from the period of the mission itself. There are several forged charters purporting to belong to the reign of Æthelbert, but the oldest unquestionably genuine Kentish charter belongs to the time of archbishop Theodore who did not reach England until more than sixty years after Augustine's death. The most valuable supplement to these scanty written records is to be found in the surviving remains of some of the oldest Canterbury churches. When considering the history of the mission in Kent, and of other missionary activities in other parts of England, we must realise that when Bede was writing his *History* more than four generations had passed since Augustine's arrival and several traditions had become crystal-

[41]

lised. There was no topic concerning the ecclesiastical history of the English which so profoundly interested Bede, yet as late as 725 it seems that he did not even know the date of Augustine's arrival in Britain and that he was only able to learn it after an English priest had gone to Rome some years later to search the papal registry for documents about the mission.

Gregory's Italy was a land brought near to exhaustion first by the wars of Justinian seeking to rescue it from Gothic domination and then by the ravages of the Lombard invasions. When we recall not only his own physical ill-health, but also the hardships and insecurity of life in a country ravaged for the best part of a century by almost ceaseless warfare, we ought perhaps to be struck more by the fact that a mission was sent at all to such a remote corner of the world than by the scantiness of the contemporary records about it. Although in the sixth century the western countries, saving only England, were dominantly Christian, there were still many pagan survivals. We can see from Gregory's letters his concern with the eradication of paganism from Sicily and Sardinia, and other sources tell of surviving heathen practices in Spain and Gaul. But there was a profound difference between these countries, including even the more heavily barbarised parts of northern Gaul, where rural populations living amid a long-established Christian society indulged in what was little more than superstitious nature-worship, and the situation in Anglo-Saxon England where the roots of paganism were widespread and deep. However much we may argue about the survival of Romano-British influences upon Anglo-Saxon England, here at least is one sphere in which the break was absolute. In those parts of Britain which had been settled by the English before 597 Christianity was totally obliterated and was replaced by Germanic paganism. Christianity survived only in those parts of the country which lay beyond the range of Anglo-Saxon settlement.

Gregory's letters suggest that it may have been his deep interest in the affairs of the church in Gaul that first brought him some knowledge of the pagan English and prompted him to consider how their conversion might be achieved. The earliest of the many letters in his Gaulish correspondence was written in June 591, a bare year after his election to the papacy, to Vergilius, formerly a monk of Lérins but at that time archbishop of Arles, in response to complaints reaching Gregory in Rome that certain Jewish merchants in Marseilles were being subjected to persecution by excessively zealous Christian Franks.[1] Gregory would not have had any occasion to refer to the English in this letter, nor in the series of letters which he wrote four years later to Vergilius of Arles, to the bishops in Childebert's kingdom and to King Childebert himself.[2] In the letters of this group he was concerned with explaining the new position which he had conferred upon Vergilius as his representative in Childebert's kingdom. But among Gregory's other Gaulish concerns he showed great interest in the administration of certain papal estates which lay in south-eastern Gaul and whose income was used to support the poor. It is in this connection that he first refers to the English. In 593 the papal patrimony in Gaul was being administered by Dynamius, a Frankish nobleman who was in effect the governor of Provençe,[3] and in April of that year Gregory wrote thanking him for the 400 *solidi*, representing rents from the estates, which had reached him in Rome,[4] but in that same year Childebert deprived Dynamius of his office and it became necessary for Gregory to take fresh action for the security of the papal patrimony. In 594 he wrote to the managers of the Gaulish estates saying that he had decided to send someone from Rome who could protect and govern them, but that as the winter made travelling difficult they were to submit themselves in the meanwhile to Arigius, the new civil governor. The rents which accrued were to be entrusted to one of their number chosen by themselves and he was to hand them over to Gregory's emissary when he arrived from Rome.[5]

The man chosen by Gregory as governor of the patrimony was a priest called Candidus who would no doubt be fully instructed in his duties before leaving Rome for Gaul. In September 595 Gregory wrote a letter to Candidus which seems from the style of its address to have been sent in pursuit of

Candidus when he had already left Rome, and from its content to embody as an afterthought some modification of Gregory's original instructions. The purpose of the letter was to tell Candidus that he was to spend locally any income that he received from the estates in Gaul because Gaulish *solidi* would not pass as currency in Italy. He was to use the money in two ways – for buying clothes for the poor and for buying English youths of the age of seventeen or eighteen so that they might be given to God in monasteries for their own well-being. And if Candidus was able to recover any of the revenues which had been wrongfully diverted, he was to use this money too for the same purposes. 'But because those who can be found there are pagans, I want a priest to be sent across with them,' wrote Gregory, so that if any of them were to be taken ill on the journey and seemed likely to die, the priest could baptise them.[6]

When Gregory sent Candidus to the patrimony in Gaul he gave him letters of commendation addressed to King Childebert (i.e. Childebert II, 575–96) and to his redoubtable mother, Brunhild, the Visigothic princess who, after her marriage to one of the grandsons of Clovis, became a dominant figure among the Merovingians for some thirty years until her death in 613. Gregory explained that he was sending Candidus to take the place of Dynamius and asked the king and his mother to give him what help they could, particularly in securing the restoration to the estates of any just dues of which they might have been wrongfully deprived.[7] Gregory made no reference to the purchasing of English boys in either of these two letters which Candidus would carry with him when he set out from Rome. There was no particular reason why he should have done so, but if, before Candidus had left Rome, Gregory had already thought of using the Gaulish *solidi* for buying English youths, it would not have been necessary for him to send a special letter in pursuit of Candidus telling him that the money was to be used in this way. In other words, although we may certainly infer from the letter to Candidus that by September 595 Gregory knew something about the pagan English and was considering how to secure the conversion of at least a few of those whom he

[44]

expected Candidus to find in Gaul, the letter offers no evidence of a long-premeditated plan for the conversion of the Anglo-Saxons as a whole.

The purchase of these youths was quite incidental to Candidus's prime duty of acting as rector of the Gaulish patrimony, and Gregory's instruction is to be set in the context of other letters sent by him to Candidus in Gaul: one asking whether he could find for a priest called Aurelius an oratory or some other place on the Gaulish papal estates which lacked a priest or an abbot and which Aurelius could serve, and another asking him to look carefully into the case of four Christians who, after being redeemed from captivity among certain Jews, were still being held in the service of those same Jews at Narbonne.[8] It is all too easy for the reader to jump to the romantic conclusion that the boys whose purchase was envisaged by Gregory were English slaves on sale in a market-place. We ought to remember the four Christians held in the service of Jews at Narbonne and to reflect that there may very well have been English youths similarly held in service elsewhere. Equally they may have been prisoners of war, mercenaries fighting in the service of the Merovingians, or merely young men in some way bound to the soil on Merovingian estates. If Candidus acted on Gregory's instructions he would have had no difficulty in finding young men of Anglo-Saxon race in Gaul at this time. The closeness of relations between the two countries, attested historically by Procopius[9] and by the marriage of a Kentish king with a Frankish princess, is an archaeological commonplace of the fifth and sixth centuries.

Candidus's duties as rector of the patrimony lay in Provençe, and we have seen Gregory asking him to look into the matter of the Christians held in Narbonne. The letters which he had for Childebert and Brunhild would help to smooth his path among local civil governors, those of them at least who were well disposed to the Merovingians, but we are not bound to suppose that they were ever delivered to the king or his mother in Paris or anywhere else in Gaul, a point relevant to conjecture on the whereabouts of the monasteries into which the English youths were to be placed for their education. A journey on which it was thought that some of them might die was likely to be a long one. In the letter to Candidus, Gregory wrote about the English youths *volo ut cum eis presbyter transmittatur* and in the slightly earlier letter to the managers of the Gaulish papal farms he referred to the man whom he will send them from Rome (Candidus) in the words *quem a latere nostro transmiserimus*.[10] It is difficult to know how far we can press the force of the prefix *trans*, but the most natural inference is that Gregory was expecting Candidus to find the English youths somewhere in Provençe or near by, and that the journey he envisaged was between Gaul and Italy, certainly a dangerous journey in the prevailing conditions.

Candidus would no doubt do his best to carry out Gregory's instructions, but there is no other reference in Gregory's correspondence to the purchase of English youths, and we are left to conjecture whether Gregory's decision to send a mission to England was the outcome of a meeting with some youths bought by Candidus and sent by him to monasteries in Italy. Whether or not Brunhild and Childebert ever received the letters of commendation written by Gregory for Candidus in September 595, Brunhild and Gregory were certainly corresponding with one another in the following year when letters were carried between them by a priest Leuparicus,[11] but there is no reference to the English in these letters. The earliest direct evidence of the reasons which prompted Gregory to send a mission to England is found in two of the group of letters of commendation given by Gregory to the missioners for use on their journey across Gaul. The whole group of letters was written in July 596, and the two of immediate concern were addressed the one to Brunhild and the other to her infant grandsons, Theuderich and Theudebert, who had succeeded to the kingdom after the death of their father, Childebert II, earlier in the same year.

Writing to the two young princes Gregory said that he had come to form great expectations of them because they desired their subjects to be completely converted to the faith which they, their rulers, professed. He continued: 'And so it has come to our ears that by the mercy of God the English race earnestly desire to be converted to the Christian faith, but that the priests in the neighbourhood are indifferent and do nothing to inflame their desires by their own exhortations.'[12] The letter seems to imply Gregory's belief that the English who wished to become Christians were subjects of the Frankish princes, but the point ought not to be pressed too hard since Gregory was certainly not well-informed about the political relations between the Anglo-Saxons and the Franks. In his letter to Brunhild Gregory included a similar phrase, remarking that he had heard that the English nation wished to become Christian 'but the priests who are in the neighbourhood show no pastoral concern for them'.[13]

Although Gregory is quite explicit both about the wishes of the English and about the negligence of the nearby priests, we can only speculate about the source of his information. He never himself says that he ever met any people of English race, though he may have done so. A likely source whence information about the English could travel to Gaul and thence to Italy would be the court of the Kentish king, Æthelbert, whose wife, Bertha, was Frankish. Bertha's father was Charibert who, as one of the four sons of Chlotar I, began to reign on his father's death in 561 and who himself died in 567. Her mother was Ingoberga who died in 589.[14] Gregory of Tours, the earliest authority to refer to the wedding, does not say when the marriage took place and may not even have known the name of Bertha's Kentish husband. Bede says that Bertha's parents agreed to the marriage on condition that she was allowed to practise her faith unhindered, but it is doubtful whether we can press Bede's reference to her *parentes* as meaning that the marriage took place before the death of her father in 567. But at least it seems a safe assumption that Bertha and Æthelbert were married before Gregory became pope in 590 and that the Frankish bishop, Liudhard, who accompanied Bertha to Kent, will have kept in touch with some at least of his colleagues in Gaul.

There is no other contemporary evidence touching upon the preliminaries to the English mission save for a remark by Gregory in a letter which he wrote to Syagrius, bishop of Autun, in July 599. The letter was primarily concerned with the hierarchical relations of the sees of Autun and Lyons, but in the course of it Gregory thanked Syagrius for the help he had given at the time when Gregory, after long thought (*diu cogitans*) had decided to undertake the task of preaching the gospel to the English 'through Augustine who was then prior (*praepositus*) of my monastery, and is now our brother and fellow-bishop'.[15] There is no profit in speculating about the exact meaning of *diu cogitans*, but the passage is valuable in telling us all that we know about the antecedents of the man chosen by Gregory to lead the mission. The monastery of which Augustine had become prior by 596 lay on the *Clivus Scauri*, a declivity on the eastern slopes of the *Mons Caelius* on the southern side of Rome. Dedicated to St Andrew, it was next to the church of SS John and Paul, and not far away from the Circus Maximus, the Colosseum and the arch of Constantine.

REFERENCES

1   *GE* I, 45.
2   *GE* V, 58, 59, 60.
3   Gregory of Tours, *Hist.* VI, 7, 7.
4   *GE* III, 33.
5   *GE* V, 31.
6   *GE* VI, 10.
7   *GE* VI, 5 and 6.
8   *GE* IX, 221; VII, 21.
9   *Wars* VIII, 20.
10 *GE* VI, 10; V, 31.
11 *GE* VI, 55.
12 *GE* VI, 49.
13 *GE* VI, 57.
14 Gregory of Tours, *Hist.* IV, 26; IX, 26
15 *GE* IX, 222.

respectively to Stephen, abbot of the monastery of Lérins in the bay of Cannes, Protasius, bishop of Aix-en-Provençe, and the patrician Arigius, the civil governor of Provençe. These three letters have one distinguishing feature in common, that not only is Augustine named as the bearer of the letters, but also in each case Gregory refers to news which he has had about their recipients from Augustine. Writing to Abbot Stephen of Lérins Gregory told of his joy at hearing from Augustine how the priests, deacons and the whole congregation were living peacefully together and he thanked Stephen for the gift of spoons and plates which he had sent for the use of the poor.[2] In the letter to Protasius, Bishop of Aix, Gregory referred incidentally to news which he had received about him from Augustine, though the letter was primarily concerned with asking Protasius to do what he could to ensure that Vergilius, Bishop of Arles, sent on to Rome the payments from the papal estates which his predecessor had for many years wrongfully retained for his own use.[3] In the third letter, to Arigius, the civil governor, Gregory referred to the good reports which Augustine had brought about him and expressed the hope that Arigius would give such encouragement as Augustine and his companions might need.[4] Unfortunately we know nothing at all about Augustine's life before 596, by which date he had become prior of the Roman monastery. It is possible that he may have made some earlier unrecorded journey to Provençe on Gregory's behalf, but in view of the bulk of Gregory's Gaulish correspondence, it seems likely that we should have heard something of it had he done so. The most probable inference from these three letters and from the letter to the missioners written during Augustine's absence is that after leaving Rome they had reached Lérins, probably Arles, the seat of the civil governor, and the see of Protasius at Aix, and that having travelled so far, they were faced with the difficulties which caused Augustine to return to Rome, whence in due course he set out again carrying the letters for Abbot Stephen, Bishop Protasius and the patrician Arigius, as well as a further series of letters for use on the later stages of the journey.

The remaining letters in the series are all addressed to Gaulish bishops. Most prominent among them was Vergilius, the metropolitan of Arles, and here Gregory had to exercise his tact. He commended Augustine and his companions, but said nothing explicit about the purpose of their journey, remarking that Augustine would be able to explain this himself. In the second half of the letter he turned to the difficult matter of the income from the papal estate in Gaul, commending Candidus, commenting on the way Vergilius's predecessor had wrongfully retained the income and remarking how detestable it was that bishops had diverted what kings had preserved.[5] In this, as in other letters of the series, Gregory shows himself quite as much concerned with the Gaulish patrimony as with the mission to the English, and if we are looking for an explanation of his reference to the tongues of evil-speaking men and of his appointment of Augustine as abbot, we may conjecture that perhaps it lay somewhere in the relations of Rome with the Gaulish church, particularly the metropolitans of Arles. The duty of obedience to Augustine which Gregory laid upon his followers suggests that after the missioners had entered Gaul, Augustine's authority may have been questioned in such a way as to cause disunity among the group.

Augustine was also the bearer of letters to Serenus of Marseilles, Aetherius of Lyons and Pelagius of Tours. All were written in identical terms, commending Augustine, saying that he would himself explain the circumstances of his journey in detail and commending Candidus.[6] Other letters were addressed to Desiderius of Vienne and Syagrius of Autun, again commending both Augustine and Candidus, but not giving any additional information. These commendatory letters leave no doubt that the route followed by Augustine was the one along the Rhône valley and not the transalpine route across the great St Bernard pass which was used in later days by travellers between England and Rome. They may have gone to Lérins either direct by sea from Rome or else by road to the mainland opposite the islands. Thence they would go to Marseilles, Aix, Arles, Vienne, Lyons and Autun. If they used the letter to Pelagius of Tours, and we do not know whether they did or not, they might have continued northwards to Auxerre and then west to Tours, a diversion which would have taken them well away from the most direct route between Rome and Canterbury.

Augustine would certainly have seen the wisdom of using the letters to Brunhild and the two young princes across whose lands he was travelling and whose protection he would certainly need. We know that he met Brunhild and, although proof is lacking, it seems likely that he would visit the courts of Theudebert and Theuderich. There are several places at which such meetings could have taken place, among them Chalons-sur-Saône, Orleans, Rheims, Metz and Paris. Whether or not the travellers visited Tours, it seems likely that, rather than embarking at the mouth of the Seine for what would have been a long sea-crossing to Kent, they would have continued north-eastwards to the port known to Bede as *Quentavic*, now Étaples at the mouth of the Canche. Though later blocked by silt, this was the main port for the crossing to England in Bede's day, and was the one from which Theodore set sail on his journey from Rome to Canterbury in 668–9.[7]

The letters which Gregory gave Augustine on his second departure from Rome were all written in July 596. A little more than a year later, in September 597, Gregory sent a long and detailed letter to Brunhild written in answer to a request for the bestowal of the pallium upon Syagrius, bishop of Autun, and explaining why he had not been able to meet this request sooner.[8] There are two points in this letter incidental to its main purport but relevant to the English mission, first Gregory's expression of gratification at the good report which had reached him about Syagrius, especially from John, one of Gregory's *regionarii* who had recently visited Gaul, and at hearing about what Syagrius had done 'for our brother Augustine'; and second his expression of thanks to Brunhild for the help which she herself had given to Augustine 'our brother and fellow-bishop' about which he had received reports from a number of the faithful. This letter is the first evidence we have for Gregory's knowledge about the progress of the travellers. It is also the first source to call Augustine a bishop. Its references to John, the *regionarius*, that is to say one of the deacons or sub-deacons concerned with the seven regions or wards of Rome, as bringer of news, and to the reports of the faithful, indicate the means of Gregory's contacts with Gaul. If by this date, September 597, Gregory knew that Augustine had already reached England it seems probable that he would have said so. Brunhild herself would certainly have been interested because Bertha, the Kentish queen, was her niece, though Gregory probably did not know this.

The first evidence of Gregory's knowledge that the mission had reached England and met with success is contained in a letter which he wrote to Eulogius, the patriarch of Alexandria on 29 July 598. The messenger who had brought letters from Eulogius found Gregory ill and left him still ill on his return to Alexandria carrying Gregory's reply. Although afflicted by bodily and spiritual troubles, Gregory wrote to say that he had been greatly cheered to hear of the success of Eulogius in winning back heretics to the Church and so bringing an increase of spiritual crops to the celestial granary. And he continued:

Forasmuch as I know that, doing good yourself, you rejoice to hear of it in others, I bring you in turn news not unlike your own. The English race who live in a corner of the world have until now remained unbelieving in the worship of sticks and stones, but aided by your prayer and prompted by God, I decided that I ought to send a monk of my monastery to preach to them. With my permission he was made a bishop by the bishops of the Germanies and with their help he reached the aforesaid people at the end of the world and now letters have just reached me about his safety and his work. He himself and those who went with him shine with such miracles among that people that they seem to imitate the virtues of the apostles in the wonders they display. At the feast of Christmas last, in this present first indiction, more than 10,000 Englishmen are reported to have been baptised by our brother and fellow-bishop.[9]

The whole tone of this part of Gregory's letter, no less than the particular phrase *iam nunc ... ad nos scripta pervenerunt*, conveys a strong impression that this good news had only just arrived at the time of writing, 29 July 598. The Christmas at which large numbers of the English had been baptised – and we need not interpret 10,000 literally – was the Christmas of 597, and with this additional date we now have four fixed points for the chronology of the mission: the second departure of Augustine from Rome in or after July 596, his meetings with Syagrius of Autun and Brunhild at a date soon enough to allow Gregory to hear about them by September 597, the baptism of many of the English at Christmas 597, and finally the arrival of letters in Rome just before 29 July 598 reporting the success of the mission. It would be a mistake to think in modern terms of a journey between Rome and Kent taking in all circumstances much the same sort of time. A large company, pausing on the way to visit bishops and royal courts, would obviously take much longer than a courier with letters making his best speed, and we can readily contemplate a variation between twelve months or more for a leisurely journey with frequent halts, and five or six weeks for a fast journey in favourable conditions. On the whole it seems probable that Augustine and his companions would pass the winter in Gaul and arrive in Kent in the spring or summer of 597.

The other point of particular interest in Gregory's letter to Eulogius is the statement that Augustine had been consecrated a bishop *a Germaniarum episcopis*. When Augustine left Rome for the second time, in or after July 596, he did so as an abbot, but when Gregory wrote to Brunhild in September 597 he referred to Augustine as fellow-bishop (*co-episcopus*), so that his consecration evidently took place between these two dates. If we keep rigidly to the sense of Gregory's letter to Eulogius we cannot easily escape the inference that Augustine's consecration as bishop preceded his arrival among the English. The letter states quite explicitly that Augustine had been consecrated by the bishops of the 'Germanies' with Gregory's permission and that with their help he reached the English. It is difficult to know how far we can press the meaning of Gregory's *Germaniae*. In the context of Diocletian's empire the two German provinces, *Germania Prima* and *Germania Secunda*, lay along the left bank of

the Rhine from near the modern Swiss frontier to the North
Sea, but it would be unwise to assume that Gregory was
referring thus precisely to former provinces which had long
ceased to exist. His use of *Germaniae*, rather than *Gallia*, perhaps
suggests no more than the northern rather than the southern
parts of Gaul.

Why did Gregory adopt this procedure rather than himself
consecrate Augustine in Rome before he set off? Lacking direct
evidence, we cannot do more than conjecture, but perhaps there
is a hint to be found in the letter which Gregory sent to Brunhild
in July 596, a letter of which Augustine himself was the bearer,
as monk and abbot, but not then bishop. In all of Gregory's
correspondence relating to the mission, this is the only letter
which reveals something of his thoughts about the immediate
objective of the mission. Clearly it was his hope that the English
would be converted, but he explained to Brunhild that, having
heard that the English wanted to become Christians, he was
sending Augustine and his companions 'so that through them I
can learn something more about their wishes and with your
help take thought for their conversion to the best of my powers.
I have told them that for carrying out this task they are to take
priests from the neighbourhood with them.'[10] This passage
suggests that Gregory envisaged Augustine's first and immediate
task as that of undertaking a preliminary exploration. Gregory
himself can have known little or nothing about the situation in
England, but as Augustine moved further north, he would be
likely to gather fresh information, and he would surely have
learnt at Brunhild's court that her niece was married to the
Kentish king and that there was a Gaulish bishop at her court
ministering to her spiritual needs. Without going beyond the
evidence of Gregory's letters, it seems fair to conjecture that
Gregory would have envisaged the possibility that Augustine
might find the circumstances to be wholly unfavourable and
that he might never be able to reach England. Taking the
possibilities of success or failure into account, Gregory may have
given Augustine written authority (*licentia*) to receive episcopal
consecration at the hands of the bishops in northern Gaul if,

[55]

when he got there, the conditions seemed favourable. And Augustine himself would surely see the need for using this permission when he learnt that there was already a bishop in Kent.

There is no hint in Gregory's correspondence or in any other contemporary source of the scene of Augustine's consecration. The most northerly of the bishops to whom he carried commendatory letters were those of Autun and Tours, but there were several places further north – Auxerre, Paris, Rheims, Metz – where he could have been consecrated. Following the letter of September 597 to Brunhild, there is a gap of two years in the Gaulish correspondence and it is not until July 599 that we have a further considerable batch of letters. They were carried by Cyriac who had succeeded Augustine as abbot of the monastery of St Andrew in Rome, and were addressed to, amongst others, the bishops of Marseilles, Arles, Vienne, Lyons and Autun, as well as to Brunhild, Theudebert and Theuderich.[11] Apart from the letter to Serenus of Marseilles which contains an interesting expression of Gregory's views on the use of statues and paintings in churches,[12] the letters show Gregory's concern with remedying various abuses which he had heard were prevalent in the Gaulish church, notably simony, and too rapid promotion of untrained laymen to the priesthood and the episcopate, and the habit of priests living with women. He urged the holding of a synod to remedy these abuses and he sent a pallium to Syagrius of Autun, but it was not to be bestowed upon him until he had summoned the suggested synod and remedied the abuses to the best of his powers. In all these letters Gregory's prime concern was with the Gaulish church, and the only reference to the English mission in the whole group is in the letter to Syagrius of Autun in which he represents the sending of the pallium as an expression of his gratitude for the help which Syagrius had given to Augustine on his journey. Although it was now three years since Augustine had left Rome and probably two since he had reached England, there are no letters to Augustine himself from this period, though we know from Gregory's letter to Eulogius that there had been correspondence from Augustine's side. In fact it is not until 601, five years after Augustine's final departure from Rome that we can at last learn something about the English mission in the context of letters sent by Gregory to the missioners in England itself.[13]

REFERENCES

1 *GE* VI, 50[a].
2 *GE* VI, 54.
3 *GE* VI, 53.
4 *GE* VI, 56.
5 *GE* VI, 51.
6 *GE* VI, 50.
7 *HE* IV, 1.
8 *GE* VIII, 4.
9 *GE* VIII, 29.
10 *GE* VI, 57.
11 *GE* IX, 218 *et seq.*
12 See below pp. 173–4.
13 Gregory kept a *Register* of the letters which he wrote and this *Register* is now our prime source of information about them. He did not keep any record of the letters which he *received* and hence it is no cause for surprise that we know nothing about the other side of the correspondence. None of Gregory's letters survive as the original documents sent to Gaul, England or elsewhere, though, as we shall see, Bede was able to secure copies of some of them.

7

Gregory's English Correspondence

There is a group of some fifteen letters all written by Gregory in the summer of 601 and arising in part from the more detailed information about the progress of the mission which some of Augustine's monks had brought back from England. We do not know when these monks went back to Rome and the fact of their journey can be established only from Gregory's references to it, not from any letters carried from England by the monks themselves. The great majority of the relevant letters written in 601 by Gregory were addressed to bishops in Gaul and in some instances his references to the English mission form no more than a closing paragraph in a letter otherwise concerned primarily with the affairs of the church in Gaul, and particularly with the synod whose calling he had previously urged but which had not yet met. Among the bishops to whom these letters were addressed we find, as in 596, the holders of the more southerly sees of the Rhône valley – Marseilles, Vienne and Lyons, as well as the metropolitan of Arles[1] – but in addition we find also a group of more northerly sees – Toulon, Chalons-sur-Saône, Angers, Metz, Paris and Rouen.[2] Again there are letters to the lay rulers Theuderich and Brunhild and also this time one to Chlotar.[3]

Despite their numbers, the letters written to recipients in Gaul add only a small, though highly important, amount of factual information, since the letters to several of the bishops are couched in identical terms, while some of the others show only minor variations. The letters reveal that some of Augustine's monks had gone from England to Rome and had told Gregory that because so many of the English had been converted there were not now enough missioners to carry on the work and Gregory had therefore decided to send others to help them. The purpose of his commendatory letters was to further the journey of the new group whom he was sending. Among this new group he mentioned two by name, a priest called Lawrence and an abbot called Mellitus. Nothing is known about the previous history of either of these two. Only one of the relevant Gaulish letters of 601 is of substantially different content. It was addressed to Vergilius, the metropolitan of Arles, and in it Gregory said that if it should happen that Augustine came to see him, Vergilius was to receive him with affection and brotherly love, and in particular if Augustine should come to see him about the delinquencies of priests or of others, the two of them were to sit together and examine each case in detail.[4]

Finally there is a group of six letters all despatched in the summer of 601 and all relating directly to the work of the missioners in England. The recipients of these six letters were Augustine, to whom three of them were addressed, King Æthelbert of Kent, Bertha his consort, and Mellitus. This last was sent from Rome in July 601 in pursuit of Mellitus and his companions who had already begun their journey to England. One of the three letters to Augustine[5] represents Gregory's response to news which he has had, seemingly from Augustine himself, about the success of the mission, news which led Gregory to open and close his letter with the joyful message of the angelic host to the shepherds watching their flocks on the night of Christ's birth. But the letter itself was a long and stern warning to Augustine that, although he could rightly rejoice that outward miracles had drawn the souls of the English to inward grace, he must equally fear lest he himself, forgetful that he was no more than the agent of God, might be led into sin through vainglory and boastfulness. 'I say these things', wrote Gregory, 'because it is my desire to prostrate the soul of my hearer in humility.' The tone of the letter, with its reminder of the fault of Moses committed 38 years before coming to the land of promise, may seem to us severe when we recall the dangers which Augustine had faced and overcome, but we do not know what were the circumstances which evoked Gregory's warning.

Gregory's letters to King Æthelbert and Bertha must always have a particular interest not only because of their content, but also because, as the first letters to be addressed to the rulers of an English state, they mark the beginnings of the change from barbarism to a literate civilisation among the Anglo-Saxons. Bertha herself would have been able to read Gregory's letter and probably to write her own reply in Latin, for, as Gregory himself remarks, she was an educated woman. Perhaps there was an element of flattery in the claim made by the poet Fortunatus that Bertha's father Charibert spoke Latin as fluently as his own language, but one of her uncles, Chilperic, knew enough Latin to be able to compose hymns in imitation of Sedulius and also to write a treatise on the Trinity.[6] Gregory told Bertha of his pleasure at having heard through the priest Lawrence and the monk Peter of the help which she had given to Augustine, comparing her part in the conversion of the English with the part played by Helena, mother of Constantine the Great. He then rebuked Bertha for not having a long time ago turned the mind of her husband towards the Christian faith which she herself held, both for his own sake and for the salvation of his people. Being strong in the faith herself and learned in letters, this ought not to have been a difficult task. Now that a fitting moment had come she must set to work and make good in greater measure what she had neglected in the past. She was to confirm her consort in the Christian faith and inflame his soul for the complete conversion of the people who were subject to him. Her excellent qualities were known not only in Rome where prayers were said for her, but also in many other places, even to the emperor himself in Constantinople, and now she was to give her whole-hearted support to Augustine and his fellow-workers.[7]

Writing to Æthelbert, whom he addresses as *Rex Anglorum*, Gregory told him that he had been brought to the office of ruler in order that he might give to his fellow-subjects the blessings bestowed upon him. He was to be heedful in keeping the grace

[60]

given to him by God and eager in spreading the Christian faith among his subjects, redoubling his zeal for their conversion. He was to attack the worshipping of idols and to overthrow the heathen temples, and, like the emperor Constantine, to turn his people to the worship of the true God. He was to pay close heed to the advice given to him by Augustine, a man well-instructed in the rule of monastic life and learned in Holy Scripture. There were many impending signs – terrors from Heaven, disordered seasons, wars, famines, plagues, earthquakes – all telling of the approaching end of this world, but if any of these things occurred in Æthelbert's own country he was not to be troubled in his mind. Such signs were sent so that man might not be taken by death unawares. 'I have spoken these things now in a few words, my illustrious son, to the end that when the Christian faith shall have increased in your kingdom, our discourse with you may also become more abundant.'[8]

Nowhere in Gregory's correspondence, our only contemporary source, is there any direct reference to King Æthelbert's conversion, but scholars generally have regarded this letter as one which could only have been written to a man who was already a baptised Christian and who was being urged to redouble his efforts to achieve the conversion of the remainder of his subjects. It seems scarcely credible that Gregory could have written in such terms as these to one who was still a pagan. Had this been the case he must surely have made a direct reference to Æthelbert's pagan beliefs at some point either in this letter or in the letter to Bertha. The rebuke to Bertha was not because her husband was still pagan in 601, but because in all the years of her marriage to him she herself, an educated Christian, had not brought about his conversion long before Augustine's arrival.[9]

One of the three remaining letters, addressed to Augustine and dated 22 June 601, contains advice about the organisation of the new church of the English.[10] Gregory authorised Augustine to use the *pallium*, but only for the celebration of mass, and he also gave him permission to ordain in various places twelve bishops who were to be subject to his authority, 'since the bishop of the city of London ought always in the future to be consecrated by his own synod, and may receive the pallium of honour from this holy and apostolic see.' Gregory went on to express his wish that Augustine send to the city of York a bishop whom he might think fit to ordain, and if York and the places nearby were to become Christian, he himself (i.e. the bishop of York) might ordain twelve bishops and enjoy metropolitan honour. Gregory expressed his intention of giving the pallium to the bishop of York who was nevertheless to remain subject to Augustine's direction. After Augustine's death, the bishop of York was to be independent of the bishop of London, and in the future the relationship between the two was to be such that whichever had been ordained first was to take precedence over the other. But in the meanwhile Augustine himself was to have authority not only over the bishops ordained by himself and by the bishops of York, but also over *omnes Brittaniae sacerdotes*.

Gregory seems to have been seeking in this letter both to deal with immediately current problems and to take a much longer view of the newly-developing church. He was not ordering Augustine to proceed at once to the organisation of two metropolitan areas, each with twelve bishops, but merely authorising him to ordain more bishops as the need arose. His only directly expressed wish is that a bishop should be appointed to York. There can be no doubt that had Gregory wished to do so he could have learnt much about the organisation of Roman Britain from materials preserved in Italy, and probably Rome itself, among them for example the *Notitia Dignitatum* or the materials from which the *Ravenna Cosmography* was compiled in the seventh century. And it would not have been difficult for him to discover that London and York had been the two major cities of Britain during the Roman occupation, or that during part of that occupation there had been bishops in both of them. On the other hand there is no hint in his letters that he regarded the mission as the winning back of a lost imperial province. What concerned him was not the pagan past but the *nova Anglorum ecclesia*. One of the most striking features of this letter is its implication that at this date Augustine was exercising his episcopal functions in London, and that Gregory expected his successors to remain there. Gregory could not foresee the future, but we cannot dismiss as ignorance his evidence about the immediate past of his own day. However little he may have known about Anglo-Saxon England as a whole in 600, he had not only had letters from Augustine by July 598, but he had also had the opportunity of hearing a firsthand account from Peter and Lawrence who went back from England to Rome at a date which cannot be determined exactly but which must be after July 598 and before June 601. We seem bound to suppose either that Augustine was then in fact in London or that he was planning to go there, and that Gregory's knowledge of the situation was derived from Peter and Lawrence. We ought not to overlook the fact that London was the only place in England with which Gregory associated Augustine. Moreover it seems easier to suppose that Gregory thought York to be a suitable place for a bishop because Augustine had told him so (through Peter and Lawrence) rather than because he had found the name in some documents in Rome.

Abbot Mellitus and his companions presumably left Rome late in June 601. On 18 July Gregory sent a letter in pursuit of Mellitus expressing his anxiety at not having had any news about their journey, and asking him to convey to Augustine his further thoughts about the treatment of pagan temples in England.[11] The temples were by no means to be destroyed, but only the images which they housed. If the temples were well built they were to be consecrated to the service of God so that the people might continue to worship in familiar places. They should not be deprived of their customary sacrifices of oxen, but on appropriate days they should build wooden booths in the neighbourhood of former temples, now converted to Christian use, and celebrate with religious feasting, their animals no longer sacrificed to devils, but killed for their own food with thanksgiving to God. Gregory seems to be supposing in this letter that Augustine would find solidly constructed stone buildings such as existed in Rome, but this would only have been the case in England with any still-standing stone temples of Romano-British construction.

[63]

Finally there remains a long document which in its present form consists of a series of questions posed by Augustine with answers written by Gregory – a document commonly known as the *Libellus Responsionum*. Although the authenticity of this work has been questioned, partly on the ground that it was not copied into Gregory's register, as his letters were, and could not be found in the papal archives when search was made for it *c.* 735, Bede accepted it as genuine and most modern historians have done likewise.[12] Apart from matters touching ritual purification, no longer of great interest, Augustine sought advice on various problems concerning the organisation of the new church, its attitude towards certain social problems and its relations with the bishops of neighbouring churches. Augustine was naturally concerned about the means of life to be adopted by himself and his clergy and with the ways in which they were to use the revenues derived from offerings. Gregory's reply shows that he did not expect Augustine, even though he had been trained under a monastic rule, to live apart from his clergy, and he envisaged that there would be some of the clergy in the lower orders who would be married and for whom a stipend should be provided. It would be right, in this newly-founded *ecclesia Anglorum*, to follow the customs of the first Christians, possessing nothing of their own, but sharing all things in common. A way of life such as this, though doubtless influenced by the monastic training of its head, was indeed communal, but not strictly monastic.

On his journey from Rome to England Augustine had noticed variations of liturgical practice in the Roman and Gaulish churches, and when he raised this question Gregory's reply was that Augustine himself was to select whatever might seem best from the usages of the Roman, the Gaulish or any other church, and so himself to shape a *consuetudo* for the English church. We may wonder if Benedict Biscop was influenced by Gregory's advice to Augustine when he was himself drawing up his rule for Wearmouth and Jarrow some 70 years later. The consecration of bishops raised a practical difficulty for Augustine. Could he consecrate a bishop without the presence of other bishops? Gregory recognised that Augustine could not avoid doing so, at least initially, since it was not to be expected that bishops would come frequently from Gaul to act as witnesses. But he was to consecrate bishops in places near enough to each other to allow ease of meeting, and when there were enough of them three or four were to assemble for each new consecration. Finally, and perhaps most important of all, there was the question of Augustine's relations with the bishops of Gaul and Britain. Gregory's reply was firm and unambiguous. He was to have no authority over the bishops of Gaul. The bishops of Arles had received the pallium from his predecessors and they were not to be deprived of this distinction. On the other hand, if Augustine ever had occasion to go to Gaul, he was to act together with the bishop of Arles in the correction of any faults that might be found in the bishops (presumably the Gaulish bishops) not as possessing any jurisdiction among them, but merely as acting in fulfilment of his Christian duty, and so that the relationship between them might be free from doubt, Gregory had written himself to the bishop of Arles. Touching the bishops of Britain, Gregory wrote: 'We entrust all the bishops of Britain to you so that the ignorant may be taught, the weak strengthened by persuasion, the perverse corrected by authority.'

This document and the letter to Mellitus dated 18 July 601 are the last of the Gregorian documents relating to the English mission. Gregory himself died on 12 March 604. Before we turn to other evidence, it will be convenient to summarise the facts which seem to be established by these letters. We know that the mission was led by Augustine and there is an inference that the priest Lawrence and the monk Peter were among his companions, but no other names are known from the first group. We do not know when they left Rome, but not later than July 596 they had reached Lérins, Aix-en-Provençe and probably Arles, Augustine had gone back to Rome and had set out for the second time. Not later than September 597 they had met Syagrius, bishop of Autun, and also Brunhild, but in neither case do we know where the meeting took place. Also by this date

Augustine, appointed abbot on his return to Rome, had been consecrated bishop by some of the bishops of northern Gaul (so interpreting Gregory's reference to the *episcopi Germaniarum*). We do not know either the scene of his consecration or the date, save within the limits of July 596 and September 597. We do not know when Augustine reached England, but many of the English were baptised at Christmas 597. Written news of these baptisms reached Gregory in or shortly before July 598. At some date after July 598, but before June 601, the priest Lawrence and the monk Peter travelled from England to Rome, but we cannot date their journey more precisely. After 22 June but before 18 July 601 a second group of missioners left Rome. Among them were the priest Lawrence and the abbot Mellitus. The monk Peter is not mentioned. We do not know when this second group reached England. Gregory, writing after the arrival of Peter and Lawrence from England, supposes that Augustine is in London and that his successors will remain there. The crucial gap in this chronological summary is our ignorance of the exact date when Augustine reached England. All we know for certain is that it was before Christmas 597, but a rapid journey could have taken him to England by the late autumn of 596. From this doubt there arises a further doubt – we cannot from the evidence of the letters be certain that Augustine was consecrated in Gaul before reaching England, and that he did not first visit England and then go to Gaul for his consecration.

REFERENCES

1   *GE* XI, 34, 38, 40, 45.
2   *GE* XI, 41.
3   *GE* XI, 47, 48, 51.
4   *GE* XI, 45.
5   *GE* XI, 36.
6   P. Riché, *Education et Culture*, 268–9.
7   *GE* XI, 35.
8   *GE* XI, 37.

9 The attempt of S. Brechter, *Die Quellen zur Angelsachsen-mission Gregors des Grossen*, 240–8, to show that Æthelbert was still pagan in 601 and that Bede deliberately suppressed the relevant letter has been effectively countered by R. A. Markus, *Journ. Eccles. Hist.* XIV (1963), 16–30, with whose opinion I am in complete agreement.

10 *GE* XI, 39.

11 *GE* XI, 56.

12 See P. Meyvaert, *Rev. d'hist. ecclésiastique*, LIV, 879–894, with references to earlier discussions by other writers. The document was reproduced by Bede in *HE* I, 27.

8

Bede's Account of the Mission

Gregory's letters have the same kind of value as evidence for the mission to England as do the letters of Sidonius Apollinaris for conditions in fifth-century Gaul. They are not the letters of a man looking back with hindsight on distant events but of one currently playing a major part in an undertaking whose outcome could not be foreseen, giving instruction for what was to be done in the future, not recording what had happened in the past. When Bede came to write his account of the mission and of the conversion of the English as a whole, events which for Gregory still lay in the future had receded for a span of 130 years into the past. How did Bede learn about the mission? In trying to answer this question we need to remember how many questions remain unanswered even for the few years covered by Gregory's letters, lest over the long retrospect from the present the more distant years become foreshortened. The earliest reference to the conversion in Bede's writings is found in his treatise *De Temporibus* written in 703 when he was a little over thirty. The closing chapters of this work were devoted to the six ages of the world and its final section contained a brief chronicle of events which had occurred in the still-current sixth age and which were arranged chronologically not by the years of the Christian era, but by the emperors in whose reigns they had occurred. For the reign of Maurice (582–602) Bede recorded only *Gregorius Romae floruit episcopus*, but for the reign of his successor Phocas (602–10) he recorded *Saxones in Britannia fidem Christi suscipiunt*.[1] The entries in this chronicle are so brief that we must be cautious in making inferences, but it seems that at this date (703) Bede did not know that Christianity had reached Britain in the reign of Maurice and we must hold it to be at least doubtful whether he knew anything about Gregory's connection with the mission or about Augustine.

In the second of his chronological works, the *De Temporum Ratione* which was written in 725, Bede greatly enlarged the chronicle of the sixth age. He removed the entry about the conversion of the English back from the reign of Phocas to that of Maurice, and in the entries which he made for Maurice's reign, and that of his predecessor, he reveals the use of a number of sources which had reached him ultimately from Rome – Gregory's *Commentary on Job*, his *Dialogues*, the *Liber Pontificalis* and one of Gregory's letters to Augustine. On the English mission Bede wrote as follows: 'He [*sc.* Gregory] converted the English to Christ after sending to Britain Augustine, Mellitus and John, together with many other God-fearing monks. And Æthelbert, being presently [*mox*] converted to the grace of Christ with the people of Kent over whom he ruled, gave to the neighbouring provinces his own bishop and teacher Augustine, as well as other holy bishops with an episcopal see. But the races of the English living on the north side of the Humber under their kings Ælle and Æthelfrith had not yet heard the word of life. Gregory, writing to Augustine in the 18th year of Maurice and the 4th Indiction, decides that when they have received the pallium from the apostolic see, the bishops of London and York are to be metropolitans.'[2] The first sentence of this entry is derived from the brief life of Gregory contained in the *Liber Pontificalis*, whence comes the name John, not hitherto mentioned. We may assume that Bede's knowledge about Æthelbert's conversion was derived from Kent. The final sentence refers to the letter which Gregory wrote to Augustine on 22 June 601.[3]

How much are we entitled to infer from this entry about Bede's knowledge of the mission at this date (725)? Did he know the date of Augustine's arrival? At least he knew that it had been in Maurice's reign and not the reign of Phocas, as he had thought in 703. Did he suppose that Augustine and Mellitus had travelled together or did he know that there had been two separate missions? Was Gregory's letter to Augustine about the

[69]

metropolitans of London and York the only letter of Gregory's which Bede had, or did he choose to refer to that one alone because of its reference to the metropolitan status of York, which had not yet been achieved by 725, but which we know was of great interest to Bede? We do in fact know that Bede already had one other document of Gregory's – the *Libellus Responsionum* – because he refers to it in the *Life of Cuthbert* which he had written *c.* 720.[4] In the remainder of the chronicle at the end of the *De Temporum Ratione*, covering the years 603–*c.* 720, there are only six items relating to the church among the English – including references to the arrival of Theodore and Hadrian, to Audrey and the founding of Ely, to Willibrord and to Cuthbert. Since it is certain that in these later entries Bede was in no way seeking to record all that he knew, we ought perhaps to be cautious before we assume that in his entry about the conversion of the English Bede was trying to do anything more than make a very brief summary of salient events which had occurred – or in the case of Northumbria had not occurred – during the reign of Maurice.

Since it can scarcely be open to dispute that Bede, like any other historian, was selective in the use of his materials, it will never be possible to trace the growth of his historical knowledge in detail or to determine exactly what materials were available to him at particular times. There were many occasions on which materials could have reached him, even from Rome itself. We shall consider later the several journeys made to Rome by monks from Wearmouth and Jarrow, but meanwhile we may note the comment which Bede made near the end of this chronicle of the sixth age in his *De Temporum Ratione*. 'In these times', he wrote, in a context of *c.* 720 and in a way showing that he was looking back over several years, 'many of the race of the English, suffused with divine love, used to go from Britain to Rome, noblemen and common people, men and women, officers of government and ordinary citizens.' It would be surprising if none of these travellers brought back information – for example the epitaph on Gregory's tomb in Rome – which ultimately found its way to Jarrow, and especially so if the monks of Wearmouth and Jarrow who carried to Rome the great pandect which we now know as the Codex Amiatinus came back empty-handed.[5]

Bede's account of the Gregorian mission occupies eleven consecutive chapters of the first Book of his *Ecclesiastical History*. Rather more than two-thirds of the entire content of these eleven chapters are derived in direct quotation from Gregory's letters, while the remainder consists of narrative. We know from Bede's own words that it was Albinus, abbot of the monastery founded by Augustine in Canterbury who urged Bede to write the work and who was also Bede's chief source of information about the beginnings of Christianity in Kent and the neighbouring parts. Since Albinus became abbot *c.* 710 and was still alive in 731, it seems likely that he would be about the same age as Bede. Although they never met, they corresponded with one another, but there survives only a single letter from Bede to Albinus. Bede's debt to Albinus is expressed in the *Preface* to his *History* in terms which are a witness no less to his generosity than to the pains he took in his search for historical truth. He records how Albinus 'diligently investigated either from written records or the traditions of the elders all the things that were done in that same province of the people of Kent or also in the regions adjacent to it, by the disciples of the blessed Gregory; and who sent to me by the pious priest of the church of London, Nothhelm, those of them which seemed worth recording, either in writing or by word of mouth of the same Nothhelm. Nothhelm afterwards went to Rome, and with the permission of Pope Gregory who is now set over that church [i.e. Gregory II, 715 to 11 February 731] searched into the archives of the holy Roman Church, and found there some letters of the blessed Pope Gregory and of other pontiffs. And, returning home, he brought them to me by the advice of the aforesaid most reverend Father Albinus, to be inserted in my history.'[6]

The material which reached Bede from Canterbury consisted in part of written documents and in part of local tradition. It is worth recalling that Abbot Albinus had been educated in the school established in Canterbury by Theodore and Hadrian who reached England in 669 and who were both men of intellectual distinction. Gregory the Great was still alive when Theodore was born (*c.* 602), and so also was Augustine. Albinus himself, Bede wrote, knew not a little Greek and was as familar with Latin as with his native English. [7] With this background it seems likely that unwritten traditional information reaching Bede from Canterbury would be well-founded. We know from Bede's letter to Albinus that there were two separate occasions on which material was brought from Canterbury to Jarrow. On the other hand after the death of King Æthelbert there was a strong pagan reaction and the church in Kent came near to total extinction. There are some grounds for thinking that Bede may already have largely completed the writing of his *History* before he received the letters of Gregory which Nothhelm brought him from Rome. We have seen that in all there were some 30 relevant letters, but although Bede used only 8 we do not know whether they were all that he had or merely a selection from a larger total. In the *History* as we have it now, we find that sometimes Bede reproduces the text of letters, with no more than a brief introductory comment, while at other times he seems to be making inferences from their content. He states explicitly that the reason why Augustine returned to Rome was that the company had been 'struck with a cowardly fear, and considered returning home, rather than proceeding to a barbarous, fierce and unbelieving nation, whose very language they did not know'. [8] Was this an inference from Gregory's letter of encouragement, or current Canterbury belief? Bede also says that Gregory had appointed Augustine to be consecrated bishop if he should be received by the English and in a later chapter he adds that, at some unspecified date after his arrival in England, Augustine went to Gaul and was consecrated by Etherius, the archbishop of Arles. [9] In one detail we know that Bede here fell into error since the archbishop of Arles was Vergilius, not Aetherius who was bishop of Lyons, but it was an error very easy to make. Yet, as we have seen, Gregory's letter to Eulogius says that Augustine was consecrated 'by the bishops of the Germanys' and seems to imply that the consecration took place before Augustine reached England. Bede knew that Gregory had told the archbishop of Arles to give Augustine any help he might need and he may also have had, though he did not quote it in the *History*, the letter in which Gregory envisaged the possibility that Augustine might have occasion to visit the archbishop in Arles. But it seems almost certain that Bede did not know about the vital letter from Gregory to Eulogius. If this letter had been known either to Bede or in Canterbury it seems scarcely credible that the incident of mass baptisms among the English on Christmas Day of 597 would not have had its dramatic potentialities exploited to the full. It is possible that Bede was right in saying that Augustine was consecrated in Arles, though not by Aetherius, but even if he was wrong, and the letter to Eulogius is cogent evidence, we can very easily see how the inadequacies of his sources might lead him to make a wrong inference.[10]

The account of the mission which Bede derived from Canterbury through the agency of Nothhelm forms two consecutive chapters of the *History* (I, 25–6) entirely without quotations from documentary sources, and may be summarised thus. Augustine and his companions, reported to have numbered nearly forty men, landed in Thanet and made their presence known to King Æthelbert through interpreters from Gaul. The king ordered them to remain there while he considered what should be done with them, since he had heard something about the Christian religion from his Christian wife, Bertha, and her bishop, Liudhard. Some days later he went to the island and met the missioners, in the open air, as a protection against magical devices. They approached carrying a silver cross with an image of the Lord painted on a board and chanting litanies. They preached to the king whose answering words, given in direct speech, were that he could not abandon his old ways, but that he wished them no ill and would allow them to continue their preaching. He gave them somewhere to live in Canterbury and as they approached the city they sang in unison the litany: 'We beseech thee, O Lord in all thy mercy, that thy wrath and thy indignation be turned away from this city, and from thy holy house, because we have sinned. Alleluia.' After they had entered Canterbury they began to live after the fashion of the primitive Christians, with prayer and preaching, and after a while several people (*nonnulli*) believed and were baptised. Near to Canterbury, on the east side, there was a church dedicated to St Martin and built while the Romans were still in Britain, where the queen was accustomed to pray, and they too began to hold their services in the same church. After the king had been converted, they were allowed to preach more widely and to build more churches. People came in greater numbers to be baptised and abandoned their heathen practices. It was not long before the king gave them a place for an episcopal seat in Canterbury.[11]

This marks the end of the narrative and in the following chapters Bede recorded Augustine's visit to Arles for consecration and then returned to the Gregorian letters.[12] One or two additional items of information which may have been derived from Canterbury tradition are recorded in later chapters. Bede named the leaders of the mission of 601 as Mellitus, Justus, Paulinus and Rufinianus, but the last three of these names are not known either from Gregory's letters or from the *Liber Pontificalis*. They are said to have brought with them sacred vessels, ornaments, vestments, relics and a large number of books. He concluded his account of the mission with references to the restoration of another church in Canterbury believed to have been built by the Romans, and to the building of a monastery within which, at Augustine's instigation, King Æthelbert built a church dedicated to SS Peter and Paul. The church was consecrated by Augustine's successor Lawrence, and the first abbot of the monastery was the priest Peter who was later drowned while crossing the sea on a mission to Gaul.[13]

We ought not to be sceptical about the general veracity of this Canterbury account of the beginnings of Christianity in Kent. The church of St Martin still survives and among a hoard of coins found nearby was one inscribed with the name of Bishop Liudhard. The church dedicated to SS Peter and Paul has been excavated and the tombs of the early archbishops have been located. The third church has not been identified because its site lies beneath Canterbury cathedral.[14] But equally we ought not to ignore the differences in kind between the Gregorian letters looking towards the future and the Canterbury tradition enshrining in its memory the dramatic moments which in retrospect were rightly held to be of such great consequence. Bede's problem was whether to amalgamate these different kinds of evidence into a single narrative or to present them separately for what they were. He would certainly realise, as should we, that the Canterbury tradition gave no answers to several questions that a historian would naturally ask. When did Augustine land in Kent? When did he first go to Canterbury? Did he go anywhere else? When was King Æthelbert converted? When was the building of the monastery begun? When and where was Augustine consecrated bishop? Knowing Bede's deep interest in chronology, we may be sure that all these questions would have occurred to him, but so far as we can tell now, he had no other evidence about the chronology of the mission save the dating clauses of Gregory's letters, and with scholarly caution he did not attempt to answer questions when he had no evidence, save on the place of Augustine's consecration and on this point we cannot be sure that he was wrong.

Bede concluded Book I of the *History* with a Northumbrian episode not related to the conversion but placed at what seemed to him the chronologically appropriate point.[15] He opened Book II with a reference to the death of Gregory in 605 and devoted the remainder of the first chapter to a long account of Gregory's life and works. This account, mostly derived from Gregory's biography in the *Liber Pontificalis* or from certain autobiographical passages in Gregory's own writings, is accompanied by a survey of most of these writings, including the *Commentary on Job*, the *Pastoral Care*, the *Homilies*, the *Dialogues* and, of lesser works, the *Libellus Responsionum* and the *Libellus Synodicus*. After commenting on Gregory's character, his achievement in securing the conversion of the English and his liturgical reforms, Bede followed a short reference to his death and burial with the epitaph inscribed on his tomb in Rome in 16 lines of elegiac couplets.

The epitaph might well have seemed to Bede an appropriate ending to his account of Gregory's life, but he chose instead to add a tale about a supposed incident belonging to a time before Gregory had become pope. He wrote: 'A story about the blessed Gregory which has been handed down to us ought not to be passed by in silence. They say that one day . . .'[16] Part of the story which follows is familiar to many who perhaps know nothing else about the Gregorian mission. It tells how when Gregory was looking at the merchandise for sale in a market-place, he saw some handsome boys for sale. He learnt that they came from Britain and that they were still pagans. He asked what was their race and when he was told that they were *Angli*, he replied: 'Good, for they have angelic faces.' On learning that the people of their province were called *Deire*, he answered: 'Good – Deire – snatched from wrath (*de ira*) and called to the mercy of Christ.' And when they told him that their king was called Ælle, he replied: 'Alleluia, the praise of God the Creator ought to be sung in those parts.' Gregory then went to the bishop of the Roman see and asked him to send preachers to the English, saying that he was ready to go himself. This he was unable to do because, though the pope was willing the citizens of Rome would not let him go. Bede ended the story with these words: 'We have thought fit to insert these matters into our ecclesiastical history according to the story which we have received from our ancestors.'

The opening and closing words of this story make it clear beyond dispute that Bede learnt it from current English tradition, not from documents or oral reports reaching him from Rome. Its association with Deira suggests furthermore that its source was Northumbrian and not Kentish tradition, a suggestion which receives confirmation from a variant version of the same tradition found in the Whitby *Life of Gregory* which was written perhaps as much as 30 years before Bede's *History*.[17] The Whitby version of the meeting with the English boys differs only in some minor details from Bede's, but in the second part it differs fundamentally. According to the Whitby version the pope did give Gregory permission to go to Britain, a decision which greatly angered the citizens of Rome, and the story continues: 'So when it was announced that permission had been given, they divided themselves into three groups and stood along the road by which the Pope went to St Peter's Church; as he passed, each group shouted at him, 'You have offended Peter, you have destroyed Rome, you have sent Gregory away'. As soon as he heard their dreadful cry for the third time, he quickly sent messengers after Gregory to make him return. But Gregory, with holy insight, had already learned of this repeated call for his return through the inward promptings of the Lord and by means of a locust. For after a three days' journey, while they were resting in a certain place as travellers are accustomed to do, a locust [*locusta*] settled on him while he was reading. At once he recognised from the name of the insect that he was, as it were, being told to stay in the place [*Sta in loco*]; nevertheless he quickly urged his comrades to move on. But as he was doing so, he was forestalled by the messengers and he and his companions were brought back to Rome.'[18] Recalling the three puns of the first part of the story, we may note the saying divided into three parts and the three days spent on the way. In a later passage the same Whitby writer, associates the three syllables of King Edwin's name (Latin *Edwinus*, OE *Eadwine*) with the mystery of the Trinity.[19] This is surely no more than a Northumbrian folk-tale. Bede was certainly familiar with it, but he chose not to repeat it, nor did he repeat the Whitby writer's heavily laboured explanation of Gregory's three puns. We have seen how Bede distinguished carefully between the evidence of Gregory's letters and the evidence of Canterbury tradition, but he was surely well aware that, considered in terms of value as historical evidence, what Albinus reported to him about events in Canterbury was in quite a different category from what floating Northumbrian tradition reported about events in Rome. It would have been easy for him to have inserted this story at the chronologically appropriate place either in his account of the mission or in his

16 *HE* II, 1.
17 *C.* 9.
18 *C.* 10, tr B. Colgrave.
19 *C.* 14.

9

The First Archbishops of Canterbury

The dating clauses of Gregory's letters gave Bede a firm foundation for chronological inferences, but there was no similar foundation in Anglo-Saxon tradition whether the source was Canterbury, Wessex or Northumbria, and it is this gap which creates for us, as it did for Bede, many obscurities in the history of Christianity among the Anglo-Saxons in the decade following Gregory's death in 604. Bede knew that in 604 Augustine consecrated two of his companions as bishops – Mellitus and Justus – but we do not know whence he derived the date and can only guess that it came from Canterbury. He also knew, from the epitaph inscribed on his tomb, that Augustine himself died on 26 May during the reign of King Æthelbert, but he did not know the year. Accepting that Augustine was still alive in 604, we know that he was dead by 610 when Pope Boniface IV addressed letters to his successor, Archbishop Lawrence.[1] Later sources guess at different dates, but Bede did not go beyond his evidence, nor did he attempt to be chronologically precise about a tradition which had reached him of Augustine's relations with some of the bishops of the British church.

The tradition tells how, with the help of King Æthelbert, Augustine summoned the bishops and teachers from the nearest British province to a conference at a place which in Bede's day was called Augustine's Oak and lay on the borders of the Hwicce and the West Saxons. Augustine tried to persuade them to join with him in preaching to the heathen English, but he failed, nor would they yield to him on any of the matters in which their customs differed from those of the catholic church. In an attempt to settle their differences by testing the efficacy of their respective prayers in healing a blind man, the British failed, but Augustine succeeded. The British clergy still refused to yield without first consulting their own people and they accordingly asked for a second meeting at a later date. The second meeting was attended by seven British bishops and a number of very learned men from the most renowned of their monasteries, called by the English *Bancornaburg*, that is Bangor-is-Coed in Flintshire. The British clergy had been advised by an anchorite that they were to follow Augustine if he showed humility by standing up as they approached. Augustine failed to rise from his chair and the British clergy charged him with pride. In his reply to the charge Augustine said that although there were many ways in which the British church acted contrary to the custom of the universal church, he and his companions would tolerate their other aberrations if they would comply in three matters – the celebration of Easter at the proper time, observance of the Roman rite of baptism and collaboration in preaching to the heathen English. The British refused and Augustine foretold that if they would not accept peace from their brethren, they would have war from their enemies. This prophecy was later fulfilled by Æthelfrith, king of the Northumbrians, who, when he was about to give battle to his enemies at Chester, saw a company of priests and monks gathered in a place apart from the opposing army. Most of them were from the monastery of Bangor. When King Æthelfrith learnt that they had come to pray for his defeat, he ordered that they should be attacked first. In the slaughter which followed it was said that about 1200 of those who had come to pray were killed and that only 50 escaped. 'And thus was fulfilled the prediction of the holy Bishop Augustine.'[2]

We know from Welsh and Irish sources that Æthelfrith who was the last of the pagan kings of Bernicia and was killed in *c.* 616, did fight victoriously at Chester against certain rulers from northern Wales, and his reputation was such that he may well have slaughtered monks, but this is the only incident in the story which we can submit to the test of trustworthy independent evidence. Yet for Bede the interest of the story is not so much in the battle, save as the fulfilment of Augustine's prophecy, as in its record of the first meeting between the new emissaries from Rome and the heirs to the old Romano-British church. Even though we cannot now identify the site of Augustine's Oak, there is enough circumstantial detail in the story to support the inherent probability that at some stage in his mission Augustine did meet some of the British clergy and discuss the problems by which both sides were faced. But we shall miss much of the significance of the story as a whole if we concern ourselves merely with the historicity of its content and do not go on to ask why it was that Bede chose to represent the fate of the unfortunate monks of Bangor as the vengeance of God upon them for the obstinacy of their predecessors in failing to meet the reasonable demands of Augustine who, by his success in bringing sight to a blind man, had shown himself qualified to bring true spiritual enlightenment to others.

As Bede tells this story, the opponents of Augustine are the enemies of the *pax catholica* and the *universalis ecclesia*, the British people are heretics and their soldiers impious. We know that the military struggle between the native British kingdoms and the English invaders was long and hard-fought, especially over what was to become the kingdom of Northumbria and it seems very probable, as Bede himself indicates, that hostility between the two nations would remain strong long after the days of open warfare were past. But to this surviving racial hostility there was added a measure of *odium theologicum* which among some at least of the supporters of Rome reached great intensity and which has undoubtedly coloured the historical writings of Bede's age. The universal church, though existing as an abstract ideal, had no historical reality in western Europe in the days of the Gregorian mission to England. We have already seen Gregory telling Augustine not to be disturbed at finding ecclesiastical practices in Gaul which were different from those with which he was familiar in Rome and advising him to make his own choice of whatever liturgical practices he found best.

Of much greater moment than varying liturgical practice was

the problem of determining the proper date for the celebration
of Easter, a problem which for long troubled the Christian
church as a whole and by no means only its western fringes. As
the continental churches moved towards unity, the Celtic
church became increasingly isolated in its practice of Easter
observance through its retention of ways of calculating the date
which had been rejected by others. When the Augustinian
mission was still in its early days in Kent, Columbanus, the Irish
abbot of the monastery at Luxeuil in Burgundy, was incurring
the hostility of the Gaulish clergy over the Easter problem and
he tried to enlist Gregory's support against the Merovingian
bishops. During the seventh and early eighth centuries different
sections of the Celtic church – the southern Irish, the northern
Irish, the Columban church, the Picts – gradually moved into
conformity with Roman practice, as did the English at the
synod of Whitby, but with increasing uniformity there arose
increasing bitterness from the Roman side towards those who in
their obstinacy refused to conform.[3] At the time when Bede was
writing his *History* only one branch of the Celtic church still held
out against Rome – the church in Wales. A measure of the
bitterness felt by some of the Romanist churchmen towards this
continuing nonconformity may be seen in the letter written by
Bede's older contemporary, Aldhelm, bishop of Sherborne, to
Geraint, king of Dumnonia, in 705. He wrote, of the Celtic
priests living beyond the Severn in southern Wales, that 'they
will neither pray with us in church, nor eat with us at table.
Worse, they throw out the food left over from our meals to dogs
waiting open mouthed and to foul pigs; they give orders that
the dishes and bowls which we have used must be scraped and
scoured with sand or with cinders before they are fit to be placed
upon their tables'.[4] Although Bede did not write in quite such
pungent terms, he leaves us in no doubt at all about the strength
of his own views. We may note his acid comment on the attempt
of Archbishop Lawrence, Augustine's successor, to bring the
British clergy into the *unitas catholica:* how in his account of the
synod of Whitby, Wilfrid, spokesman of the Roman party, is
represented as saying that those who rejected the Apostolic

decrees undoubtedly committed sin; and how in the penulti-
mate chapter of the *History* he described the British as not only
opposing the English with their personal hatred, but opposing
also the appointed Easter of the whole catholic church by their
wicked customs.[5] We may find Bede's attitude towards the
Easter question less attractive than the more tolerant ways
adopted by some at least of the Celtic supporters who could
argue that there was room for more than one point of view, but
for Bede it was not merely a matter of chronology, a subject on
which he could certainly speak with the greatest authority. It
was also a question of heresy and sin, and here there could be
no compromise. It is against this background of unyielding
dogmatism that we must set Bede's account of Augustine's
relations with the British clergy and of the divine vengeance
which fell upon the monks of Bangor. Perhaps Bede did not
foresee how Augustine himself would suffer from the mistaken
use of this tradition as evidence for his own character.

Of the two bishops consecrated by Augustine in 604 we know
from Roman sources that Mellitus had left Rome in 601 as
leader of the second group of missioners, while Bede believed
that Justus, who is not mentioned in Roman sources, was also a
member of this group. Mellitus was sent to preach to the East
Saxons whose kingdom was then ruled by a nephew of King
Æthelbert of Kent and was subject to his over-riding supremacy. The success achieved by Mellitus led King Æthelbert to
build in London, the East Saxon capital, a church which was
dedicated to St Paul and may be presumed to have lain on the
site now occupied by St Paul's cathedral, although no traces of
any remains have been found. It was intended that London
should be the episcopal seat of Mellitus and his successors.
Justus was to remain in Kent with his seat at Rochester in a
church built for him by Æthelbert and dedicated to St Andrew.
The remains of this church are thought to be represented by the
foundations of a small rectangular nave and a chancel with a
stilted apse lying partly beneath and partly outside the west end
of the present cathedral. Some traces of a second seemingly early
church have also been found near by.[6]

Augustine was succeeded in the archbishopric by Lawrence whom he himself had consecrated as his successor. Augustine's action, though uncanonical, was no more than prudent and Bede could find a precedent in the action of St Peter himself who was said to have consecrated Clement as his successor. Lawrence, coming first to England with Augustine on the journey of 596 had later gone back to Rome with letters from Augustine for Gregory and then returned to England in 601. Bede's account of his tenure of the archbishopric which may have lasted ten years or more, is marked by information on three topics: relations with the Celtic church, the sending of an embassy to Rome and a pagan reaction which followed the death of Æthelbert and came near to destroying all that the mission had achieved in south-eastern England.

Bede gives as his source of information on the first of these topics a letter whose protocol represents it as having been written jointly by Lawrence, Mellitus and Justus and addressed to their brother bishops and abbots throughout Ireland (*Scottia*). He informs his readers that he is quoting only the beginning of the letter and in the extract from it which he gives there is no dating clause. The extract tells how when the writers were first sent to Britain they held both the British and the Irish (*Scotti*) in great veneration, believing that both walked in the ways of the universal church. On coming to know the British, they thought that the Scots were better. 'But now we have learnt from Bishop Dagan, coming into this aforementioned island, and from Columbanus, abbot in Gaul, that the Scots in no way differ in their manner of life from the British. For when Bishop Dagan came to us, not only did he refuse to eat with us, but he would not even take his food in the same house.' After ending his quotation from the letter, Bede added that Lawrence and his fellow bishops sent letters to the British priests, appropriate each to his own degree, in an endeavour to strengthen them in the catholic faith – 'how much profit he gained by doing this, these present times still declare'.[7] There were only two possible sources from which Bede could have acquired this letter, either the Canterbury archive through the agency of Nothhelm, or one of the recipients, but in either case it is the first and only surviving document apparently emanating from the Canterbury church earlier than the days of Archbishop Theodore. Its form seems ill-calculated to win the support of the Irish clergy, but perhaps the complete letter would have conveyed a different impression from that given by the extract, and its reference to the great veneration formerly felt by its writers for both the British and the Irish churches seems a little at variance with the apparent ignorance of Roman churchmen about the condition of the Celtic church in Britain at the time of the Gregorian mission.

The embassy to Rome was led by Mellitus whose purpose was to consult with the Pope, Boniface IV (608–15), about the needs of the English church, and whose arrival chanced to coincide with a synod of Italian bishops assembled to discuss the regulation of monastic life. Mellitus attended the deliberations of this synod which met on 27 February 610, and brought back with him a copy of its decrees as well as letters for Archbishop Lawrence and King Æthelbert. None of these documents has survived, but later forgeries purporting to represent their content were used by William of Malmesbury. Nothing more is known about the fortunes of the mission until after the death of its patron, King Æthelbert, which Bede believed to have occurred on 24 February 616. Æthelbert's son, Eadbald, who is said to have suffered from fits of madness, married his father's widow – not Bertha who had pre-deceased Æthelbert – and relapsed to paganism. This disaster in Kent was paralleled among the East Saxons whose Christian ruler, dying at about the same time, was succeeded by three pagan sons. Mellitus was driven out of London and after conferring with Archbishop Lawrence and Justus of Rochester all three agreed that they had better abandon the mission and return to Italy. Mellitus and Justus went to Gaul and Lawrence was about to follow them when some change of fortune persuaded him to alter his decision. Bede hints that the change was wrought by the death in battle of some of the pagan rulers who had opposed the mission, but he reported a Canterbury tale which told how Lawrence had received a visitation and a severe scourging from St Peter and how, when King Eadbald saw the marks, he thought it wise to abjure the idols, put away his unlawful wife and receive baptism. When the king had been won over Mellitus and Justus returned, but the people of London refused to have Mellitus back and both they and the East Saxons as a whole were to remain pagan for some 40 years to come. Lawrence died on 2 February, seemingly in 619, and was succeeded by Mellitus who himself died on 24 April 624. Bede speaks in high praise of the achievements of Mellitus, despite his being severely afflicted with gout, but we know nothing in detail, save that he received letters of exhortation from Pope Boniface V and that he was instrumental in saving the church of the Four Crowned Martyrs from destruction when the city of Canterbury was ravaged by fire. [8]

Altogether we know the names of eight men, all of them presumably Italian, who were associated with the mission in the years from 596 to 624. Augustine, Lawrence and Mellitus, the first three archbishops, were now all dead. So also was Peter, if we are right in identifying him with the first abbot of St Augustine's monastery who was drowned while crossing the sea to Gaul. Two of the remaining four, John who is mentioned in the *Liber Pontificalis*, and Rufinianus who is named by Bede, are mere names of whose history we know nothing. The two who were still alive in 624 were Justus who was then bishop of Rochester, and Paulinus. Both of them had first come to Britain in 601. Justus became the fourth archbishop and held the see for three or four years, but although Bede knew the day of his death, 10 November, he seems not to have known the year. Paulinus survived till 10 October 644.

Where the evidence is so slight and so many questions remain unanswered, it is difficult to estimate the achievement of the Gregorian mission in these years. The history of three great churches – the cathedrals of Canterbury, Rochester and St Paul's in London – begins in this age, and we know that in addition to the church of St Martin used by Bertha, there were at least three other churches built in Canterbury. Two of them, dedicated respectively to SS Peter and Paul and to St Mary,

were built the one by King Æthelbert and the other by his
successor, King Eadbald, and lay within the precincts of St
Augustine's monastery. The church of SS Peter and Paul came
to house the tombs of the first eight archbishops, and although
the relics were translated to a new church late in the eleventh
century, the remains of some of the tombs can still be seen. Of
the church of the Four Crowned Martyrs we know nothing
beyond its name. Within the kingdom of Kent the mission
introduced the Roman fashion of committing the law to writing,
and Æthelbert's code, written not in Latin but in English,
marks the first attempt to assimilate the bishops and the lower
orders of the clergy to Anglo-Saxon society. There is no evidence
that the missioners penetrated beyond the confines of Kent,
save momentarily into London and Essex, nor even within Kent
itself were they able to secure the banning of idol worship by
royal edict. On the other hand, attempts seem to have been
made to enter into relations with both the British and the Irish
clergy. This achievement, though geographically limited, will
seem by no means negligible, not at least to those with sufficient
knowledge and historical imagination to enable them to visualise
some of the formidable difficulties which were faced and
overcome by a small group of Italian monks.

REFERENCES

1 *HE* II, 3–4.

2 *HE* II, 2.

3 See K. Hughes, *The Church in Early Irish Society* (London 1966),
   103–110, and for a detailed discussion of the whole Easter
   problem C. W. Jones, *Bedae Opera de Temporibus* (Cambridge,
   Mass., 1943), 6–104.

4 Ed. R. Ehwald, *Aldhelmi Opera, MGH Auct. Ant.* XV, 484. See
   also E. S. Duckett, *Anglo-Saxon Saints and Scholars* (New York
   1947), 79.

5 *HE* II, 4; III, 25; V, 23.

6 *TASA* II, 518–19.

7 *HE* II, 4.

8 *HE* II, 5–7.

and the kings of Kent through his marriage with Æthelberg, daughter of King Æthelbert. When Edwin first sent suitors to ask for her hand her brother, Eadbald, was reigning in Kent and Edwin was told that a Christian maiden could not be given in marriage to a pagan. Edwin replied that he would not oppose the religious practices either of Æthelberg or of any others who might come with her, and furthermore that he would not himself refuse to accept her religion if after examining it his councillors should find it good. Æthelberg was accordingly sent to Edwin accompanied by Paulinus who had been consecrated bishop, as Bede believed, on 21 July 625.[2] In the following year the king of the West Saxons sent an assassin whose attempt on Edwin's life was frustrated by the loyalty of one of Edwin's thegns, who interposed himself between the king's body and the assassin's poisoned dagger. The assassin himself was then killed by another of the king's thegns. On the night of Easter in that same year, i.e. 20 April 626, Æthelberg gave birth to a daughter who was called Eanflæd. While the king offered thanks to his pagan gods, Paulinus gave thanks to Christ and assured Edwin that it was his prayers which had brought about the happy issue. Edwin promised that he would accept Christianity if he were victorious against the king who had sought to have him assassinated, and in pledge for fulfilment of his promise, he allowed the infant Eanflæd to be baptised. Her baptism took place at Pentecost, and with eleven other members of her household, she became the first of the Northumbrians to receive Christianity. Edwin then led an expedition against the West Saxons and won a great victory, but he still hesitated to receive baptism, preferring to learn more about the new religion from Paulinus and to discuss the problem with his councillors. At this point in Bede's narrative there follow the two letters from Pope Boniface.

After giving the text of the two letters, Bede then recorded how Edwin was influenced in his decision by an experience when, during the reign of Æthelfrith, he was living as a refugee at the court of Rædwald, king of the East Angles. On discovering where Edwin was, Æthelfrith, by bribery and the threat of war, persuaded Rædwald to betray Edwin to him. As he was brooding over his misfortunes, Edwin was approached during the night by a stranger who sought from him a promise that he would submit in all ways to the teaching of that man who should succeed in delivering him from his present calamities and restoring him to his kingdom. Edwin gave the promise and the unknown visitor then placed his right hand on the king's head and told him that he was to fulfil his promise when that sign should be given to him again. With that the mysterious visitor vanished. In the sequel Rædwald, at the persuasion of his wife, determined not to betray Edwin, but to go to war against his enemy, Æthelfrith, whom he defeated and killed in a battle fought near the river Idle. And thus Edwin was restored to his kingdom. One day when Paulinus was preaching and Edwin was still hesitating, he approached the king and laying his right hand on his head asked him whether he remembered the sign. Agreeing that he was now both willing and in duty bound to accept Christianity, Edwin decided to summon a meeting of his councillors so that he might ask each of them in turn what he thought of the new faith. Coifi, the chief of his priests, adopted the worldly view that, though none had worshipped the gods with greater zeal than he, there were many others who enjoyed greater prosperity and honour.

Another of the councillors replied with a speech which has rightly become the most familiar passage in the whole of Bede's writings:

Thus, O King, the present life of men on earth, in comparison with that time which is unknown to us, appears to me to be as if, when you are sitting at supper with your ealdormen and thegns in the winter time, and a fire is lighted in the midst and the hall warmed, but everywhere outside the storms of wintry rain and snow are raging, a sparrow should come and fly rapidly through the hall, coming in at one door and immediately out at the other. Whilst it is inside it is not touched by the storm of winter, but yet, that tiny space of calm gone in a moment, from winter at once returning to winter, it is lost to your sight. Thus this life of men appears for a little while; but of what is to follow or of what went before, we are entirely ignorant. Hence, if this new teaching brings greater certainty, it seems fit to be followed.[3]

After some further discussion Edwin formally renounced paganism and accepted Christianity, whereupon Coifi, arming himself with sword and spear and mounting one of the king's stallions, rode off to profane the pagan temple which he then ordered his followers to destroy by fire. Bede records that the site of the temple was still shown a little way to the east of York beyond the river Derwent at a place which in his day was called *Godmunddingaham* and is now called Goodmanham. Edwin was baptised on Easter Day, 12 April 627 in a wooden church dedicated to St Peter and hastily built while, as a catechumen, he was being prepared for baptism. He gave Paulinus an episcopal see in York and immediately after his baptism he began to build, under Paulinus's instructions, a larger stone church in the midst of which the wooden oratory was to be enclosed. Before the church was complete Edwin was killed in battle, but for the six years between Edwin's conversion and his death Paulinus continued to preach.

Apart from the two letters to Boniface, there can be no doubt that Bede derived the substance of his account of Edwin's conversion from Northumbrian tradition. As he himself wrote in the *Preface* to the *History:* 'As for what was done in the Church through the various regions in the province of the Northumbrians, from the time when they received the faith of Christ until the present, I learnt it not from any one authority, but by the faithful testimony of innumerable witnesses, who might know or remember the same; besides what I had of my own knowledge.' It seems probable that much of this tradition reached him from Whitby. The infant Eanflæd, the first of all the Northumbrians to be baptised, was presiding, jointly with her daughter, over the monastery at Whitby in 685 when Bede was already aged about 14. She will surely have learnt about the circumstances leading to the baptism of her father, Edwin, the more so as he too was buried at Whitby. The story of Edwin's exile in East Anglia, of the attempted assassination, of the debate among the councillors and of the destruction of the heathen temple were incidents whose dramatic force was the greater for being associated with the first Christian ruler of

Bede's own kingdom. If we recognise, as of course we must, that their content is traditional, nonetheless traditions so well-founded have a historical value of an order quite different from that of the Northumbrian tale about Gregory and the English slaves in Rome.

While Edwin of the Deiran royal family was reigning, the sons of Æthelfrith of Bernicia were in turn driven into exile. During the six years of his mission Paulinus was active both in the southern and in the northern half of Northumbria, basing his operations on royal estates where he would enjoy the king's support and protection. In addition to his work at York, his episcopal seat, and the estate near Goodmanham in the East Riding, he baptised many of the people of Deira in the river Swale close to Catterick, the site of a small Romano-British town whose occupation continued well into the fifth century, and a place known to have been of some importance in the seventh and eighth centuries. On another royal estate, said by Bede to have been in *Campodono*, Paulinus built a church which was afterwards destroyed by the pagans who killed Edwin. The altar of the church survived the fire because it was of stone and in Bede's day it was still preserved in Abbot Thrythwulf's monastery in Elmet.[4]

Accompanied by Edwin and his queen, Paulinus visited the royal estate at Old Yeavering in Bernicia and he is said to have spent 36 days there teaching the people who came to him from the nearby villages and baptising them in the river Glen. The site of this royal estate, first located by aerial photography and subsequently excavated, lies among the northern foothills of the Cheviots some 15 miles inland from Lindisfarne and from the rock stronghold at Bamburgh where the beginnings of the kingdom of Bernicia had been established nearly a century earlier in 547. The excavations at this site, which unlike York and Catterick has no Romano-British history, have yielded the remains of a series of timber halls whose association with Edwin and his successor Oswald has been clearly established. Of particular interest are the remains of a wooden church, yielding a suggestion that it may at one time have served as a heathen temple, and the remains also of a timbered auditorium which is thought to belong to the time of Edwin and may well have been used by those who came to listen to the preaching of Paulinus himself. Since all the buildings on the site were of timber, their forms can only be reconstructed from the holes and trenches formerly occupied by posts and beams long since decayed.[5]

The seeming contrast between the success achieved by Paulinus over a large area of northern Britain and the much more limited attainment of Augustine in Kent may perhaps be explained by the different backgrounds of the two missions. There can be no doubt that the English settlement of Kent and Essex had been thorough and that paganism was deeply rooted. Moreover the south-eastern part of Britain had been firmly under Germanic control for about 150 years before Augustine's arrival. In northern Britain there had certainly been some intensive settlement in the East Riding of Yorkshire, but beyond this area to the north, where now lie the northern English and southern Scottish counties, the authority of the native British kings was only just beginning to be challenged as Augustine was arriving in Kent. So far as we know these northern British kingdoms were themselves Christian, and indeed a late Welsh tradition claimed that Edwin himself had been baptised by the son of one of these British rulers. In the south-east Augustine found himself attacking heathenism, as it were from the edge, with a deep belt of paganism stretching westwards into Wessex, across the midlands into Mercia and northwards across Essex, East Anglia and Lindsey to the Humber. The position of Paulinus was almost exactly the reverse. Pagan Bernicia lay on the edge with a Christian hinterland stretching across the British kingdoms to the Scottish and Irish churches. At the time when Paulinus was preaching at Old Yeavering it seems very likely that there would be Christian communities living in the valley of the Tweed and its tributaries.

Paulinus came to England in 601 and if he did not go to York till 625, there is a long period for which we have no good evidence to show where he was or what he was doing. Lacking such evidence we may wonder how much conjecture can fairly be based on the story of the mysterious stranger who visited King Edwin while he was an exile in East Anglia. In Bede's version of this story the stranger is not named, but it is Paulinus who places his right hand on Edwin's head and asks him if he recognises the sign. In the earlier version of this story which is found in the Whitby *Life of Gregory* the night visitor is specifically identified with Paulinus.[6] We know that Rædwald, king of East Anglia, visited Kent where he was baptised and although we do not know the date of his visit, it seems likely that he would meet Paulinus when he was there. On returning to East Anglia Rædwald was seduced from his new faith by his wife and certain perverse teachers, so that in a temple, whose remains were still visible in Bede's day, he kept one altar for Christian worship and another for sacrifices to devils.[7] In addition to the link between East Anglia and Kent on the one side and between Northumbria and Kent on the other, we know also that after Rædwald's death Edwin secured the conversion of his son, Eorpwald. Recalling that the Whitby writer identified the night visitor with Paulinus, we may at least wonder whether at some date during Rædwald's reign, Paulinus had been on a mission to East Anglia and had been present at Rædwald's court when Edwin was in exile there.

After Edwin's conversion, but not more closely dated by Bede, Paulinus led a mission to Lindsey which lay across the Humber on Northumbria's southern border. He secured the conversion of the *praefectus* of the city of Lincoln and built there a stone church whose walls were still standing in Bede's time, though the roof had fallen in. Bede learnt about the Lindsey mission in part from the abbot of Partney in Lincolnshire who himself had the account from an old man who was baptised in the Trent with many others in the presence of King Edwin himself. Littleborough in Nottinghamshire is believed to have been the scene of these baptisms. It was from this source that Bede was able to describe Paulinus as 'a man tall of stature, a little stooping, with black hair and a thin face, a hooked and thin nose, his aspect both venerable and awe-inspiring'.[8] One of the companions of Paulinus in Lindsey was James the Deacon who played an important part in the later history of the Roman mission in Northumbria and was still living in Bede's day. When Justus moved to Canterbury to become its fourth archbishop, he was succeeded at Rochester by Romanus of whom we know nothing save that, being sent on a mission to the pope in Rome, he was drowned in the Mediterranean. Archbishop Justus died on 10 November, probably in 627. He was succeeded as fifth archbishop by Honorius whom Bede calls 'one of the disciples of the blessed Pope Gregory'.[9] With London still pagan and both Rochester and Canterbury now vacant, Paulinus was the only other bishop in the *ecclesia Anglorum*, and this more than 30 years after Augustine had first set out from Rome. Honorius accordingly went to Lincoln and was consecrated there by Paulinus in the newly-built church.

Bede closed the chapter in which he had recorded the Lindsey mission with a comment on the state of peace which then prevailed wherever Edwin's dominion reached, so that 'as is proverbially said to this day, if a woman with her new-born babe chose to wander throughout the island from sea to sea she could do so without molestation'.[10] He then devoted three consecutive chapters to the content of certain papal letters before resuming his narrative with an account of Edwin's death and the ensuing disasters. Two of the letters were addressed by Pope Honorius I who had succeeded Boniface V in 625, the one to Edwin and the other to archbishop Honorius of Canterbury.[11] The former is undated, but the latter has an elaborate dating clause which is given in full by Bede and shows that it was written on 11 June 634. It appears from the letters that Pope Honorius has had news of the success achieved by Paulinus and now, amid general exhortation, he urges King Edwin to employ himself in reading the works of Pope Gregory, evidently supposing that Paulinus would be able to give him copies of some at least of them.

The main point of the two letters was to inform both the king and the archbishop that he was sending two *pallia*, one for the archbishop and the other for Paulinus, so that when one of them died the other could consecrate someone else in his place. It seems very likely that when Paulinus sent news to Rome he would remark on the dangers of a situation in which he had found himself to be the only bishop in the English church, and that he would perhaps remind the pope that the mission had already suffered two grievous losses from the hazards of travel; Peter, the abbot of St Augustine's monastery in Canterbury, drowned while going to Gaul, and Bishop Romanus of Rochester drowned in the Mediterranean. The sending of the two *pallia* was not only in conformity with Gregory's plans for the two metropolitans, but was also a practical precaution against further misfortune.

In addition to these two letters quoted in full, Bede also knew that Pope Honorius had written letters to the Irish clergy urging them to conform with the Catholic church in the observance of Easter, but he did not quote from any of these letters. He did quote, however, some extracts from another papal letter written some six years later, between August and December 640, by Pope John IV and others at the papal curia to a number of Irish bishops, priests, abbots and teachers, several of them being named in the protocol. The extracts quoted by Bede concern the Easter problem and also the Pelagian heresy which was said to be springing up afresh among the Irish.[12] In the following chapter Bede resumed his narrative, recording that on 12 October 632 Edwin was killed and his army destroyed by Cadwallon, Christian king of Gwynedd, in alliance with the heathen Penda of the Mercian dynasty. Northumbria was ravaged and Paulinus went by sea to Kent taking several members of the Northumbrian royal family with him, including Edwin's widow, herself Kentish, and their infant daughter, as well as a gold cross and chalice which had belonged to Edwin and were still to be seen in Kent in Bede's day.

So far as we know Paulinus never returned to Northumbria. Arriving in Kent he occupied the vacant see at Rochester and remained its bishop until his death on 10 October 644.[13] He was buried in the sacristy of St Andrew's church in Rochester and we may suppose, that, having laboured among the English for more than 40 years he would be a man of great age at his death. When Paulinus died in 644 there were, as we shall see, Irish bishops working among the English, but of the Gregorian mission there remained only Honorius still in episcopal orders. As successor to Paulinus at Rochester, Honorius consecrated Ithamar who was of Kentish birth and the first Englishman to reach the office of bishop. Honorius himself survived till *c.* 653 and was succeeded at Canterbury by a West Saxon whom Ithamar had consecrated, and in due course Ithamar was succeeded at Rochester by a South Saxon, but it had needed more than half a century before men born and trained in England were able to be promoted to episcopal office.

The flight of Paulinus from Northumbria, perhaps prompted by his sense of duty towards his Kentish protegée and her infant daughter, did not lead to the complete extermination of Roman influences in the north. One member of the mission remained behind in Northumbria, James the Deacon, of whom we first hear as a companion of Paulinus on the Lindsey mission. James lived mostly near Catterick in a village which is now lost, but was still called after him in Bede's day. He spent much time teaching and baptising in York and was renowned for his skill in the Roman chant. We find him present at the synod of Whitby where he naturally adhered to the Roman cause, and, as Bede puts it, 'he survived down to our own times'.[14] If James who had been with Paulinus in Lindsey *c.* 627 was still alive *c.* 671 when Bede was born, he is likely to have been aged 70 or more when he died. We do not know the date of his death nor the date when he first came to England, but through his association with Paulinus he was but one stage removed from Gregory the Great himself, and we ought not to overlook the importance of his northern ministry as a continuing centre of Roman influence at a time when Celtic influences originating with the Columban mission were very strong.

REFERENCES

1 *HE* II, 9–14.

2 Bede's chronology of the Northumbrian mission has been criticised by D. Kirby, *EHR* LXXVIII (1963), 514–27. I hope to examine the matter in greater detail elsewhere.

3 *HE* II, 13. *Tr.* by D. Whitelock, *EHD* I, 617.

4 *HE* II, 14. Bede's *in Campodono* has commonly been associated with the Romano-British *Cambodunum*, but the two are by no means linguistically identical. In the OE version of *HE* the name is rendered *in Donafelda*. It may refer not to any specific place but only in a general way to the area traversed by the river Don. See *Eng. Place-Name Soc.* XXXVI, p. 34, n. 3.

5 For a summary of Dr. Hope Taylor's excavations see *Medieval Archaeology* I, 1957, 148–9. A full report is expected shortly.

6 *C.* 16.

7 *HE* II, 15.

8 *HE* II, 16.

9 *HE* V, 19.

10 *HE* II, 16.

11 *HE* II, 17, 18.

12 *HE* II, 19.

13 *HE* III, 14.

14 *HE* II, 16, 20; III, 25.

11

'Celtic' and 'Roman' Missionaries

The second Book of Bede's *History*, opening with the death of Gregory the Great in 605, ended with the death of Edwin and the flight of Paulinus a little less than 30 years later. The third Book is largely devoted to an account of the Columban mission to Lindisfarne and of all the consequences which flowed from the presence of Irish clergy working among the English, consequences which issued not merely in the widening of missionary work in hitherto pagan areas, but also in the resolution of liturgical conflicts between Roman and Celtic practices at the synod of Whitby which was held a few years before Bede's birth. Looking back to this generation, to which Bede's parents belonged, we need not only to discard the over-tones of modern nationalist sentiment conveyed by the inevitable use of such terms as Celtic, Irish, English and Roman, but also to remember that the English were still enemies to the British whose lands they were taking more and more into their possession. Welsh monks had been slaughtered by the pagan Englishman, Æthelfrith. The Christian Edwin had been killed by a Welshman, and the crime was no less because that Welshman was himself a Christian.

Augustine, and probably most, if not all, of his companions were Romans in the literal sense that they did in fact come from Rome itself, but by the middle of the seventh century, the *Romani* were Romans only as in the present age men may be Presbyterians, Lutherans or Roman Catholics. Parts of the church in Ireland had already moved into conformity with Rome a whole generation before the synod of Whitby, and to that extent their clergy were both Irish and 'Roman'. English-men went to Ireland to be taught by Irish scholars, some of whom may have been 'Romans' and some not. When the Irish Colman left Lindisfarne after the synod of Whitby, he took with him not only the Irish monks who refused to conform with Rome, but also some 30 English monks who agreed with them. The English monks lived a monastic life in common with the Irish monks on the island of Inishboffin off the west coast of Ireland. While it is true that they later quarrelled, the quarrel was not over doctrinal matters, but because the Irish monks went roaming through the summer and then returned in the winter expecting to share in the harvest which they had left the English to gather.[1] The quarrel was settled by the establishment of a separate monastery for the English in Mayo and the English connexion created at that time remained strong until long after Bede's death. The monastery at Gilling, in the West Riding of Yorkshire, was founded shortly after 651 by Eanflæd who had been baptised by Paulinus and remained staunchly 'Roman', though her husband, an Englishman was ecclesiastically 'Celtic'. Gilling's first abbot, Trumhere, was an Englishman who had been educated and ordained by the Irish. Its second abbot, Cynefrith, was also English by birth, but he left Gilling and went to Ireland. His brother was that Ceolfrith who taught Bede and was sole abbot of Wearmouth and Jarrow for much of Bede's life. The great Cuthbert, though English by birth, was first a monk at an Irish foundation, Melrose, governed by an Irish abbot, Boisil. Many other instances could be adduced to show how in the generation before Bede the Irish could well be ecclesiastically 'Roman', while the English could equally be 'Celtic'. Bitterness grew only when tolerance yielded to dogma, and when opposition to Roman dogma was equated with heresy and sin.

A year of anarchy followed the death of Edwin before Oswald defeated Cadwallon in a battle fought near the Hadrianic Wall, not far from Hexham, on a site which came to be called Heavenfield, doubtless because of its association with a victory won by a king whose posthumous fame as saint and martyr was widespread. Oswald's action in setting up a wooden cross before joining battle, a cross which so far as Bede had been able to discover was the first visible sign of Christianity to be set up in the lands of the Bernicians, may well mark the beginnings of the cult of the cross in Northumbria witnessed by the large numbers of sculptured free-standing stone crosses of later years. Bede is emphatic that before Oswald erected his cross there had been neither Christian church nor Christian altar anywhere in Bernicia, though of course he was not in a position to know about any wooden structures which may have been built at Old Yeavering and later destroyed by fire and the abandonment of the site.

As Edwin had lived in exile during Æthelfrith's reign, so the sons of Æthelfrith, including Oswald, had found refuge in the far north with either the Picts or the Scots. The Northumbrian and Pictish dynasties were brought temporarily into peaceful relationships with one another at this time by intermarriage, and, more important, Oswald and several of his noblemen received baptism from the Scots. We are not dependent solely on the evidence of Bede for this event which proved to be of such momentous significance for the English church. Later in the seventh century, Adomnan, abbot of St Columba's monastery on Iona, became closely associated with the Northumbrian king Aldfrith (685–705) who is known to have been an educated and learned man. We know that Adomnan visited Northumbria at least twice and that on one occasion he went to Wearmouth and Jarrow. Bede is likely to have seen him on that visit though at the time he was only a boy of about 14, but he seems not to have known that, shortly before 700, and after his North-umbrian visits, Adomnan wrote a *Life* of Columba which included an account of Oswald's victory over Cadwallon. It was said, Adomnan wrote, that Columba himself (d. 597) had appeared in a vision to Oswald during the night before the battle and promised him victory. On the morrow the king told of his vision and all his people promised that after the battle they would receive baptism – 'For up to that time all that land of the English was shadowed by the darkness of heathenism and ignorance, excepting the king Oswald himself, and twelve men who had been baptised with him, while he was in exile among the Irish.'[2] We expect the writers of hagiography to glorify the saints whose Lives they write, and it was natural that the great achievement of the Columban mission to the English should be made to redound to the credit of the saint himself. Even so, and despite his visits to Wearmouth and Jarrow, Adomnan may not have known anything at all about the Gregorian mission in Kent or about the activities of Paulinus in Northumbria itself.

Columba died on 9 June 597. It was Bede's belief that after crossing from Ireland in 565 he had received from the Picts the island of Iona where he founded a monastery which served as the base for a mission to the northern Picts. Bede also mentioned by name another monastery founded by Columba in Ireland itself. We know the place now as Durrow. Bede, with an interest in the etymology of place-names which finds frequent expression in his writings, wrote that 'because of the great number of oaks, it is called Dearmach in the Irish tongue, that is The Field of Oaks'.[3] He also knew that many other monasteries were founded both in Britain and Ireland as offshoots of these two, though for a long time it was Iona that held a position of pre-eminence both among the northern Irish and also among the Picts. We know that there were at least two Englishmen – Genereus the Baker, and Pilu[4] – living in the community at Iona while Columba was still alive, and therefore before Augustine's arrival in Kent. Neither Adomnan nor Bede state explicitly that Oswald was baptised at Iona, but it seems likely enough that he had been there some time during the years of his exile (c. 617–34) and it was to Iona that he turned for help in restoring Christianity to Northumbria.

Bede recorded a report that the first preacher sent from Iona met with no success, and that on his return to Iona he described those to whom he had been sent as wild ungovernable men of harsh and barbarous disposition.[5] This reported failure, whether designedly or not, served to show the saintly Aidan who came to Lindisfarne in 635, in all the more favourable a light. Aidan is portrayed by Bede as a man imbued with every

Christian virtue, save one. Despising wealth, charitable to the poor and filled with true humility, he was 'a man of the greatest gentleness, godliness and moderation, and possessing the zeal of God, although not entirely according to knowledge. For he was accustomed to observe the day of the Lord's Easter according to the manner of his nation.'[6] Nonetheless, Bede leaves us in no doubt at all about his own view of the importance of Aidan's arrival at Lindisfarne. 'From that time many began to come every day from the regions of the Scots to Britain, and to preach the word of faith to those provinces of the English over which Oswald reigned . . . churches were built in various places . . . possessions and estates were given by the gift of the king for the founding of monasteries; English children, as well as older people, were instructed by Scottish masters in study and observance of monastic discipline.'[7] Remembering the strength of Bede's sympathies with Rome and the dominance of Roman influences at Wearmouth and Jarrow, we must recognise the force of his tribute to the achievement of the Irish monks who came to Britain in such large numbers at this time, though in doing so we by no means belittle the achievement of the Romans in maintaining for so long a mission separated from their home-land by a journey which could take many months to complete. It was one thing for Aidan to move from one island site at Iona to another at Lindisfarne where he had the help of an English king who had already been baptised and could speak Irish well enough to act as Aidan's interpreter. It was another thing for Augustine to journey a thousand miles from Rome with no more than a Frankish queen to help him at the end of his journey in a deeply pagan land. Yet comparing the methods used by the two missions, if comparison is valid where the evidence is so slight, particularly from Canterbury, we are struck at once by the importance which the Irish attached to the teaching of both children and older people. The Irish may have lacked the skill, and probably the desire, to create an organised church such as Gregory had wanted to see, but until Theodore reached Canterbury in 669, we can find little trace among the Roman missioners of that zeal for scholarship and teaching which was so characteristic of the Irish monks and which drew so many Englishmen to Ireland in search of the learning which they could not find in their own land.

Aidan died in 651 and was succeeded by Finan, another of the monks from Iona, whose tenure of the bishopric (651–61) was marked by the first penetration of the pagan midlands and by the restoration of Christianity to the East Saxons who had reverted to paganism on the death of King Æthelbert some 40 years before. Bede's information about these new activities was derived verbally from the monks of Lastingham in the North Riding of Yorkshire where a monastery had been founded at about the middle of the seventh century by one of those chiefly concerned, Cedd. Bede's account of the first mission to the midlands recalls the earlier sequence of events both in Kent and in Northumbria – a heathen prince, Peada the son of Penda, seeks the hand of a Christian princess, Alchflæd, but her father, Osuiu king of the Northumbrians, will not give her away unless her suitor will himself become Christian. Peada's conversion was furthered by the marriage of his own sister to one of Osuiu's sons, and he was baptised with many of his noblemen on a royal estate near Hadrian's Wall. On returning to the midlands, Peada was accompanied by four priests of whom, we should note, three were English and one Irish. Penda, Peada's father, remained heathen until his death, but he did not forbid the preaching of the Gospel, and after his death, Diuma, the one Irishman among the four, was consecrated bishop by Finan of Lindisfarne for the whole midland area, including the lands of the Middle Angles as well as those of the Mercians. Diuma's successor in the midlands was another Irishman, Ceollach, who later returned to Iona, and he in turn was followed by Trumhere, abbot of Gilling and English by birth though educated and ordained among the Scots.[8] We cannot establish the dates of these bishops with any certainty nor do we know whereabouts in the midlands they were chiefly active. The monks of Lastingham upon whom Bede depended for his information seem not to have known much about them. There is no sign that they had any contact with Canterbury and we must presume that they looked to Lindisfarne, and beyond to Iona, as the mother church to whom obedience was due. But if there is no sign of relations with Canterbury, equally there is no hint of any antagonism between the English and the Irish members of this midland mission who worked together in amity towards their common end.

The restoration of Christianity to the East Saxons was brought about through the personal friendship of Osuiu, king of the Northumbrians, with Sigebert, king of the East Saxons, who was a frequent visitor to the Northumbrian court, and who at Osuiu's persuasion was baptised at the same place as Peada. Cedd, one of the four who had gone to the midlands, was recalled and sent to the East Saxons with another priest. After meeting with early success, he returned to Lindisfarne where he was consecrated bishop by Finan with two other bishops assisting him. Going back to the East Saxons, Cedd built churches in various places and ordained priests and deacons. Two of the places at which Cedd built churches were known to Bede by name, and are known to us now as Tilbury and Bradwell-on-Sea.⁹ At the latter, substantial remains of Cedd's church may still be seen where he built it among the ruins, then no doubt substantial, of the west gateway of the old Saxon Shore fort known to the Romans as *Othona* and to the English of Bede's time as *Ythancaestir*.¹⁰ At these two centres Cedd gathered groups of people together and taught them the regular monastic way of life, so far as they were capable of learning it. Again, and despite its close proximity, we have no evidence of contact with Canterbury, nor do we know anything precise about the chronology of the mission. Cedd maintained his contacts with Northumbria and it was he who founded the monastery at Lastingham where he died, probably in 664, shortly after attending the synod of Whitby.

While the monks of Iona and Lindisfarne were preaching in the midlands and among the East Saxons, there were others engaged in laying the foundations of the church in East Anglia and in Wessex. For his information about Christianity in East Anglia after the days of Rædwald, Bede was indebted in part to written sources and in part to a certain abbot Esi of whom we know nothing beyond his name.[11] There is some parallel between East Anglia and Northumbria in that, after early failures, the effective introduction of Christianity into East Anglia was largely the achievement of a king, Sigebert, who had been converted in exile, and of whom Bede tells us enough to make us wish that we knew more, particularly as he is the first English king whom we know to have been interested in scholarship and to have acquired a reputation for learning. We learn from Bede that Sigebert incurred the enmity of Rædwald and was driven out of East Anglia to seek refuge in Gaul where he apparently remained in exile during the reign of Rædwald's successor, and for a further three years after that successor's death. We cannot establish either the place of Sigebert in the genealogy of the East Anglian kings, or the chronology of his life, but so far as the evidence goes it suggests that he had lived in Gaul from before *c.* 616 when Rædwald was killed, until *c.* 630 when he returned to rule in East Anglia. It was while he was in Gaul that he was baptised and presumably during the same period that he acquired the taste for knowledge which led him to establish a school in East Anglia and enabled Bede to describe him as a very learned man (*doctissimus*). After reigning for some years he abandoned his life in the world, as many other kings and noblemen were to do in later years, and entered a monastery which he himself had founded. He had lived as a monk there for many years when Penda, king of the Mercians, invaded East Anglia and attempts were made to persuade him to leave his monastery and lead his soldiers into battle. Refusing to do so, he was led to the battlefield by force and there, still refusing to violate his monastic vows, he was killed.[12] Bede does not name the site of the monastery in which Sigebert lived, though it may have been Burgh Castle, nor does he give the date of his death, of which we can say only that it must have been before Penda's death in 654.

Before his abdication Sigebert had been greatly helped in his efforts to convert his people by Felix, a man who had been brought up and consecrated bishop in Burgundy and who, on coming to Archbishop Honorius had been sent on by him to preach to the East Angles. Felix received an episcopal see *in civitate Dommoc* which has usually been identified with Dunwich, though there is a case for thinking that it may have been the old Romano-British fort of the Saxon Shore which has now been lost beneath the sea off Felixstowe,[13] and there he remained until his death seventeen years later. In particular Felix was able to help Sigebert by supplying his school with teachers and masters in the manner of the people of Kent.[14] Save for this one reference we would not have known that there were any schools in Kent at this time, though we might reasonably have inferred that young Englishmen would be being trained for the priesthood at Rochester and Canterbury. Bede does not make it absolutely clear whether Felix got his teachers from the Kentish schools or whether he meant simply to say that Felix introduced to Sigebert's school in East Anglia schoolmasters such as were also to be found in Kent. Bede himself may not have known. Later sources represent Felix and Sigebert as having met in Gaul and travelled to England together, but this is contrary to Bede's narrative which seems to imply that Felix's journey to East Anglia had been made at the prompting of the archbishop in Canterbury. The name Felix effectively conceals the nationality of its owner, but remembering that Burgundy was the main centre of Irish missionary activity in Gaul, associated particularly with Columbanus and Luxeuil, we ought not to exclude the possibility that both Felix and King Sigebert himself had been associated with some centre of Irish monasticism in Burgundy or elsewhere in north-eastern Gaul.

Whatever may have been the antecedents of Felix and Sigebert, Bede knew that through the activities of the Irishman Fursey the church in East Anglia was brought into association with Irish monasticism both in Ireland and in Gaul in the first half of the seventh century. The source of his knowledge was a *Life* of Fursey from which he quoted extensively in his *History*.[15] Fursey is represented as going to Britain with a few companions in order to escape the crowds which came to see him in Ireland, and as being honourably received by King Sigebert who gave him a site on which to build a monastery inside a fort which the English called *Cnobheresburg*. The monastery probably lay inside one of the Roman forts of the Saxon Shore, *Garrianonum*, now Burgh Castle near Yarmouth, where a Christian cemetery and some other post-Roman remains have been found.[16] Fursey later entrusted the care of the monastry to his brother Foílléan and went himself to Gaul where he settled in a monastery which he built at Lagny on the Marne east of Paris. Dying soon afterwards, he was buried at Péronne.[17] Whether or not his East Anglian monastery was the one to which Sigebert withdrew, it was later enriched by King Anna, his successor.

The jewellery from the ship-burial at Sutton Hoo and the eighth-century *Life of Guthlac* whose author had a wide-ranging knowledge of the literature of his age, including some of the works of Gregory the Great, point to the existence in East Anglia of a civilisation which attained a very high degree of both artistic and intellectual excellence. Moreover, at Iken, near Aldeburgh, there lay at about the time of Bede's birth a monastery of which we know nothing save that its fame was great enough to attract Ceolfrith to pay it a visit shortly before he left Ripon to help Benedict Biscop with the new foundation at Wearmouth.[18] So far as we can see this East Anglian civilisation which has otherwise almost wholly vanished, had its roots in a mixture of Gaulish and Irish influences represented in the persons of Felix the Burgundian and Fursey the Irishman, with perhaps some indirect influences from Rome through Kent.

Bede's information about the conversion of the remainder of the English – the West Saxons, the South Saxons and the people of the Isle of Wight – was derived partly from Canterbury and partly from Daniel who became bishop of Winchester in 705 and who survived Bede himself by some ten years. Daniel was known to his contemporaries as a man of learning and from some of his surviving correspondence we can see that he was closely interested in the activities of the English missionaries, especially Boniface, who were working among the pagan Germans on the continent during the early years of the eighth century. He is likely to have been at pains to learn as much as he could about the beginnings of Christianity in southern England, but there is no hint that he was able to draw upon early written sources or upon local traditions such as were preserved for Northumbria at Whitby, and in consequence the account which he sent to Bede seems to have embodied no more than imprecise traditions about one or two early bishops. The first of these was a man called Birinus who is said to have come to Britain on the advice of Pope Honorius after being consecrated bishop by Asterius whom Bede calls bishop of Genoa. He had promised Honorius that he would visit the remotest inland parts where no teacher had previously been, but on reaching the island he came first to a people called *Gewisse* – the name, says Bede, by which the West Saxons used to be called of old – and since they were all pagan he decided to remain among them. The king, Cynegils, was baptised and at his baptism he was sponsored by Oswald, king of the Northumbrians, who was seeking the hand of a daughter of Cynegils in marriage. The two kings gave Birinus an episcopal seat at Dorchester-on-Thames, and there, after building churches and securing the conversion of many people, he died and was buried. Many years later, during the episcopacy of Hædde, Daniel's predecessor, his remains were translated to Winchester.[19]

We have no independent contemporary evidence against which to check this account, nor can we tell whether it reached Bede from Canterbury, from Daniel or in part from both. The translation of the relics from Dorchester to Winchester would have provided an occasion for a commemorative homily and this in turn might have given Daniel some information about Birinus. The account itself, which is entirely without dates, conveys the impression that Birinus was active among the West Saxons for many years and that his mission was successful at least to the extent of securing the veneration of his relics. Pope Honorius was in office 625–38 and was, as we have seen, in touch with his namesake of Canterbury and informed about the mission of Paulinus to Northumbria. Bede was slightly misinformed about Asterius who, though he lived at Genoa, held not the bishopric of Genoa, but the archbishopric of Milan. We know nothing further about king Oswald's visit to the West Saxons save that it could scarcely have been before his victory at Heavenfield and probably not before the arrival of Aidan at Lindisfarne in 635. These dates suggest the limits 635–8 for the arrival of Birinus, and they may perhaps be the foundation of the chronology given by the *Anglo-Saxon Chronicle* which records that Birinus preached to the West Saxons in 634 and that Cynegils was baptised in 635.

We do not know how long the mission of Birinus lasted, but despite the terms in which Bede writes of him there is little to suggest that he made more than superficial inroads on southern English paganism. Cynegils's successor, Cenwalh, remained pagan on his father's death, but was later converted at the instigation of Anna, king of the East Angles, at whose court he had taken refuge from the attacks of Penda, the pagan king of the Mercians. The chronology of these events is very uncertain, but it is probable that Cenwalh recovered his West Saxon kingdom c. 640. Perhaps some ten years later,[20] a bishop called Agilbert who was of Gaulish birth, but had spent some years in Ireland studying the Scriptures, attached himself to Cenwalh's court and began preaching to the West Saxon people. Impressed by his learning and industry, Cenwalh asked Agilbert to remain as bishop. The few recorded incidents of Agilbert's career suggest that had he found a biographer, such as his protegé Wilfrid was to find, he would be seen to have played an important part in the history of the English church at a time when the impetus of the Gregorian mission was failing and before the arrival of another Mediterranean archbishop, Theodore of Tarsus.

There is a hint in Bede's narrative that Agilbert had received his episcopal orders in Gaul, and in view of his later history we are probably right in thinking that his Irish studies had not been in the Columban church in the north, but in some more southerly part where the Irish clergy were already in conformity with Rome and to that extent were themselves 'Romans'. Bede records that Agilbert exercised his ministry for many years among the West Saxons, but he does not name the seat of his bishopric and we ought not to assume that it was Dorchester-on-Thames. After a time Cenwalh, it is said, grew wearied of his barbarous speech and secretly introduced a bishop called Wine, who had been ordained in Gaul and who could speak his own tongue. If, as we may believe, Agilbert was an educated, scholarly man sprung from the ranks of the distinguished Gallo-Roman episcopate, doubtless he too was wearied of the barbarities of a still dominantly pagan society. Not unnaturally he took offence and left Wessex to the episcopal care of Wine who was established by the king in Winchester. According to West Saxon tradition it was Cenwalh who built the church at Winchester which came later to be known as the Old Minster, but Cenwalh later expelled Wine who took refuge with Wulfhere, king of the Mercians and Christian successor to the pagan Penda. Bede states that Wine bought from Wulfhere the vacant bishopric of London and held it for the remainder of his life. According to the *Chronicle* Agilbert left the West Saxons in 660 and Wine moved to London three years later. 'And so', writes Bede, 'the province of the West Saxons was without a bishop for no little time.'[21]

It is difficult to establish the chronology of Agilbert's later career. We know that he visited Northumbria where he ordained the young Wilfrid to the priesthood in his monastery at Ripon and also that he took an important part in the synod of Whitby, but it is not clear whether he had in the meanwhile paid a visit to Gaul. He eventually became bishop of Paris and in that capacity, together with several other bishops, he consecrated Wilfrid bishop in a ceremony of great splendour at Compiègne. Shortly afterwards he was host to Theodore who passed a long stay with him while on his journey from Rome to Canterbury in 668–9. Meanwhile in Wessex, Cenwalh, harassed by many troubles, asked Agilbert to return but he refused to do so saying that he could not leave his Gaulish episcopate. Instead he sent his nephew, a priest called Leuthere whom he regarded as suitable for episcopal orders and who was eventually consecrated bishop by Theodore.[22]

Save only for the Isle of Wight, whose people were still pagan some fifteen years after Bede's birth, the kingdom of the South Saxons was the last of the English kingdoms to abandon paganism. A small community of Irish monks was living at Bosham in the seventh century, but although they were allowed to remain in peace, none of the inhabitants of the kindgom cared either to imitate their way of life or to listen to their preaching.[23] The conversion of the South Saxons was the achievement of Wilfrid who, on reaching England from Rome in 680 and finding himself again rejected in his native Northumbria, eventually returned south and settled for some years among the South Saxons on an estate given to him by their king at Selsey which became the seat of a bishopric. Wilfrid's earliest contact with the South Saxons had been some 15 years before, when his ship was blown ashore on their coast when returning from Gaul. His biographer has left us a vivid account of the scene which faced him and his companions. Driven ashore by a south-easterly gale, their ship was left stranded by the receding tide, and as a host of pagans approached, their chief priest took up his stand on a high mound 'and like Balaam, attempted to curse the people of God, and to bind their hands by means of his magical arts. Thereupon one of the companions of our bishop took a stone which had been blessed by all the people of God and hurled it from his sling after the manner of David. It pierced the wizard's forehead and penetrated to his brain as he stood cursing; death took him unawares as it did Goliath and his lifeless body fell backwards on to the sand.' The pagans then prepared for battle, but Wilfrid and his men, determined 'that none should turn his back upon another in flight, but that they would either win death with honour or life with glory', drove off three attacks, and as the pagans prepared for a fourth onslaught, the tide returned and their ship was refloated.[24] It is well to remember that this scene was enacted some 70 years after the landing of Augustine on the neighbouring shore of Kent, and only some four or five years before Bede's birth.

PART THREE

The Growth of Monasticism

Rochester, and Deusdedit (Frithonas), the first English holder of the archbishopric of Canterbury. His chosen successor went to Rome for consecration, but he was attacked by the plague there and he died together with almost all of those who had travelled from England with him.

Seen retrospectively the synod of Whitby which was held a few months before the plague struck, has acquired a decisive importance since by its decision the English church is seen to have moved into conformity with Rome, but we may suspect that it was Bede himself who gave it this importance as he looked back across the two generations which separated the holding of the synod from his writing of the *History*. There was no English church in the years about 664. We may think that Christianity had become strongly rooted among the English of Northumbria and East Anglia, and doubtless also in Kent, even though the sees at Canterbury and Rochester were vacant. Elsewhere, Sussex and the Isle of Wight were still unvisited by missionaries, Essex was lapsing to paganism. If we may judge from the density of place-names with heathen connotations, much of the land where now lie the counties of Surrey, Middlesex and Hertfordshire was still deeply pagan. And further inland we have no ground for suspecting anything more than the slightest of inroads upon the paganism of Wessex and the Midlands. There was in these areas no diocesan organisation, no regular endowment and no provision for ecclesiastical government, nor indeed any need for it since there was nothing to govern. That Christianity not only survived, but also continued to spread in this predominantly pagan society, was due in part to the missionary zeal of small communities of monks widely scattered over the country, and in part to the appointment to the vacant archbishopric of a monk who may well be regarded as one of the most distinguished holders of that see in all its history.

The last of the papal letters used by Bede was written by Pope Vitalian (657–72) and addressed to Osuiu, the Northumbrian king, in answer to letters received from him and the king of Kent which were taken to Rome by Wigheard, the Canterbury priest, whom they had sent to be consecrated bishop.[4] The letter is predominantly one of exhortation, but Vitalian told the Northumbrian king – and he may well have sent a similar letter to the Kentish king – that Wigheard had reached Rome, but had died there. Vitalian promised that he would send someone suited to the needs of the English as soon as he could find any one. The man whom he eventually chose was a distinguished Asiatic Greek called Theodore, who was then living in Rome, but who had been born at Tarsus, St Paul's birthplace on the southern shores of Asia Minor (Cilicia) and had perhaps been educated partly at Athens. As his companion – and also, as Bede would have us believe, as a watchdog, lest Theodore might be tempted to corrupt the young English church by introducing the practices of the Greek church – Vitalian chose a monk called Hadrian who was an African by origin but was at that time abbot of an Italian monastery not far from Naples. After a delay of four months, enabling Theodore's hair to grow out of the eastern Pauline form of the tonsure and receive the Petrine tonsure in the form of a crown, Theodore was consecrated bishop by Vitalian on 26 March 668 and he set off for England with Hadrian on 27 May. They reached their church at Canterbury a year later to the very day, 27 May 669. Hadrian had previously visited Gaul more than once, but they also had as guide on their journey Benedict Biscop who was to start building the new monastery at Jarrow five years later.[5] Although he was already 66 when he was consecrated bishop, Theodore held the archbishopric of Canterbury for the next 21 years. These were the years of Bede's childhood and youth, and when, late in life, he came to write the *History* he looked back on the days of Theodore and Hadrian as the happiest years since the English had come to Britain, a time when the country was at peace and when teachers were at hand to instruct all those who wanted to learn, in secular as well as in sacred letters, in Greek as well as in Latin.[6] Although Theodore acted vigorously to create a regular diocesan organis-ation and to establish an ordered system of government, both he and Hadrian were monks and it was the monasteries which were the creative centres from which there sprang with surprising suddenness a rich spiritual, intellectual and artistic life.

The arrival of Theodore and Hadrian at Canterbury acted as a potent stimulus to the already incipient movement of the Anglo-Saxons away from barbarism and towards a literate civilisation. A search for the origins of western monasticism would carry us to North Africa, the Egyptian desert, Palestine and Syria, and to times when Britain was still a prosperous and secure part of the Roman Empire. Recognising, but not examining, these eastern foundations, we ought to take account of a few of those western centres in Gaul, Italy and Spain whose influence upon the insular monasticism of Britain, and more particularly upon Wearmouth and Jarrow, can be directly traced. When Theodore reached Canterbury Pope Vitalian, like Gregory the Great some 70 years before, might still have regarded at least the English inhabitants of Britain as occupying a remote corner of the world, an *alter orbis*, but the growth of Anglo-Saxon monasticism and the development of intellectual interests which were its frequent, though not invariable, accompaniment brought at least a small section of the population into an association with western Europe which is at times surprisingly wide-ranging.

The monasteries lying in the lower part of the Rhône valley, and including the foundation at Lérins as their mainspring, constitute one of the most powerful centres of influence upon western monasticism in general and upon Wearmouth and Jarrow in particular. The monastery which is commonly known as Lérins was founded *c.* 410 – at the very time when Britain was passing out of Roman control – by Honoratus, and lay on an island which still bears his name, the Isle de St Honorat, and which is one of the group of the Isles de Lérins lying a short distance from the coast in the Bay of Cannes. Augustine and his companions were entertained there by its abbot Stephen on their journey to England and it was there that Benedict Biscop first received the monastic tonsure. Most of what we know about Honoratus and the nature of his monastery is derived from a commemorative sermon written by his kinsman, Hilary –

such a sermon as Bede later wrote to commemorate Benedict Biscop himself.

Honoratus is represented as a man born into a wealthy and distinguished Gaulish family and as having to overcome the opposition of his father who tried to dissuade him from becoming a monk. After travelling to the east and to Greece in company with a brother who died there, he returned to Gaul where he established a monastic community on an island which was 'uninhabited because of its excessive desolation, unapproachable because of the fear of poisonous beasts'.[7] Hilary's sermon, eulogistic and epideictic in character, yields very little factual information about the monastery itself, but it places much emphasis upon the ascetic nature of the life led by its members and the exceedingly severe discipline. There are no references to any form of intellectual life being practised in the monastery save for the answering of the many letters which Honoratus received there. In later years Honoratus himself moved away to become Bishop of Arles, bringing to that church an increase of discipline and a decrease of the wealth which had long been accumulating and long lying idle.[8]

The modern traveller, seeking escape from his present world, might not be appalled at the prospect of living on a small Mediterranean island close by the shores of the Riviera, and no doubt there were times when Benedict Biscop, facing the rigorous climate of the north-east coast of England, looked back with nostalgia to the two years which he spent at Lérins. Nonetheless, that Honoratus intended his island monastery to offer an escape from the luxurious living of the western empire into a world of rigorous asceticism seems to be suggested by Hilary's sermon and to be confirmed by some of the comments of Sidonius Apollinaris. Writing to Faustus, who became abbot of Lérins in 433 and later bishop of Riez in eastern Provençe, Sidonius comments on the visits which Faustus used to make to the monastery which he had once governed, remarking how, instead of using it for rest and recuperation, he would scarcely sleep at all or eat, but lived a life of complete self-denial, only enriching his long fasts with psalmody.[9] He writes also to Lupus, renowned bishop of Troyes, recalling the way he used to keep 'the laborious watches in the holy warfare at Lérins', and in a letter to Principius, bishop of Soissons, he recalls the example of Bishop Antiolus 'who was formerly an eminent head of the Lérins community, a cell-mate of men like Lupus and Maximus, striving by the lengths to which he carried abstinence to overtake the archimandrites of Memphis and of Palestine'.[10]

A few years after the settlement of Honoratus among the islands of Lérins two monasteries were founded near Marseilles by another monk, John Cassian, whose monastic experience had been gained first at Bethlehem and later in the Egyptian desert and who embodied in his writings, the *Institutes* and the *Conferences*, the severely ascetic and contemplative ideal of monasticism which he had learnt in the east, albeit with modifications adapting it to the different conditions of the west.[11] Although both Lérins and Cassian's foundations seem to have been intended as places of retreat where the warfare of spiritual asceticism might be waged on the Egyptian model and to have long remained so, they were not surrounded by the empty spaces of the Egyptian desert, but were close neighbours of what was perhaps the wealthiest and most highly cultured part of the western Empire, the old cities of the Rhône valley, where the ancient traditions of classical education were still unbroken, that kind of humanist education which could produce the learning of Sidonius Apollinaris.

When we find that among those who were associated with Lérins for shorter or longer periods there were a number of men of great intellectual eminence, we perhaps do better to think that their intellectual training, their interest in grammar, dialectic and rhetoric, was the product of continuing Gallo-Roman secular education rather than of a newly-founded place of retreat on an island previously uninhabited because of its desolation. Many of those who were at one time or another at Lérins, played distinguished parts in the Gallo-Roman church of southern Gaul, notably in the church of Arles. We have seen that Honoratus became bishop of Arles; so also did its second abbot, Hilary, whose over-ambitious defence of the metropolitan rights of his see brought him into direct conflict with Pope Leo I. Caesarius, the author of a large body of sermons and one of the most distinguished holders of the see of Arles (502–42) had also been a monk at Lérins, and at the end of the sixth century the holder of the see to whom Gregory commended Augustine and his companions, was Vergilius who had formerly been abbot at Lérins. Among others associated with Lérins in the fifth century were Eucherius, one of the most distinguished holders of the bishopric of Lyons: Lupus who became bishop of Troyes and who probably visited Britain to combat the spread of Pelagianism: Faustus, the bishop of Riez to whom Sidonius wrote and who may possibly have been a native of Britain, though perhaps more probably of Brittany: and Vincent, the distinguished theologian and exponent of the theological doctrines known as semi-Pelagianism. Lérins was also visited by many Irish monks and may have been a formative influence on Irish monasticism.

We do not know whether Honoratus composed his own written Rule for Lérins, but certainly none has survived. It would of course be foolish to suppose that the manner of life which prevailed in the fifth century still continued unchanged when Benedict Biscop stayed there in the seventh. Even so, when we find Bede describing how Benedict Biscop had compiled the Rule for Wearmouth and Jarrow from all that he had found best in seventeen of the most ancient monasteries which he had visited on his travels, we can be sure that Lérins was among these monasteries, and it seems very likely that Benedict's whole attitude towards monasticism would be greatly influenced by what he had learnt about such men as Honoratus, Hilary, Cassian and Vincent, as well as other great men who had been associated with the island. Perhaps it is to these roots, growing in that part of the western empire which had been least affected by the barbarian invasions, that we should trace Benedict Biscop's evident determination that his foundations in Northumbria should not be mere retreats for asceticism and the waging of holy warfare, but should also be seed beds for intellectual growth.

It would be surprising if, for the libraries which Benedict Biscop created at Wearmouth and Jarrow, he did not secure copies of the works of some at least of these southern Gaulish writers, the more so as we know that Vienne, in the Rhône valley, was one of the cities from which he secured books. Yet it is not surprising that they should have left little direct trace in Bede's own works. Bede used the *Collationes* of Cassian and also his *Contra Nestorium*,[12] but even if he did read the writings of Faustus or the *Commonitorium* of Vincent, he would not have been likely to cite as authorities on Scriptural interpretation the works of men who had vigorously attacked St Augustine's teaching on Free Will and Predestination. Vincent, no less than Bede, was deeply concerned with knowing how, in an age of turmoil and widespread heresy, it was possible to discern the truth of the Catholic faith from the falsity of heretical corruption. He believed that this could be done partly on the authority of Divine law and partly on the tradition of the Catholic church, the tradition of what had been believed everywhere, always and by all.[13] Bede would not have quarrelled with this view and he would certainly have approved of Vincent's own placing of Pelagius in the company of such heresiarchs as Arius, Sabellius and Priscillian.[14] Nevertheless the more liberal theology of Vincent and some other Gaulish writers involved a direct attack on some of St Augustine's teaching in a way which has led modern scholars to describe their doctrine as semi-Pelagianism. Whatever the label, Bede and Vincent would certainly have parted company on this issue, for, excepting Arianism itself, no heresy was more frequently attacked by Bede than the heresy of Pelagius. But if Vincent's *Commonitorium*, despite its condemnation of Pelagius, was the mainspring of the southern Gaulish attack on some, but only some, of Augustine's teaching, it was another one-time monk at Lérins, Caesarius bishop of Arles, who was mainly responsible for the condemnation of Pelagianism at the Council of Orange in 529.

Honoratus, the founder of the monastery at Lérins, died *c.* 430, about the time at which one of the Gallo-Roman bishops, Germanus of Auxerre, visited Britain to combat the spread of the Pelagian heresy. Some fifty years later there were born in Italy two men, Benedict and Cassiodorus, who both survived into the lifetime of Gregory the Great and who were both profoundly influential in shaping the world in which Bede lived. We know very little about the life of Benedict of Nursia (so called to distinguish him from his later namesakes Benedict Biscop and Benedict of Aniane) save that it was spent for the most part in central Italy between Nursia, his birthplace, some distance to the north of Rome, in Rome itself where his parents sent him for his education, and Monte Cassino some distance to the south. His lifetime coincided in part with the reigns of Theodoric the Ostrogoth in Italy (483–526) and Clovis the Frank in Gaul (481–511), but it was not until c. 520 that he founded his monastery at Monte Cassino after having lived for some years as a solitary hermit at Subiaco.

The immense importance of the Benedictine Rule – the Rule par excellence of European monasticism in the Middle Ages – has perhaps led to some tendency to exaggerate both its influence and the rapidity with which it spread during the sixth and seventh centuries. This was an age when there were many different rules, an age when individual founders, such men as Columbanus at Luxeuil, Leander and his brother, Isidore, at Seville, and of course Benedict Biscop himself, composed their own rules for their own foundations. As we shall see, the Benedictine Rule was certainly known in England during Bede's lifetime, though it was not the rule by which he lived at Jarrow, nor is there any evidence to show that it was the rule by which Augustine governed the monastery which he founded at Canterbury.

Cassiodorus who was born c. 485 into an aristocratic Roman family with estates in southern Italy, lived to within less than twenty years of the arrival of the Augustinian mission in Kent. During the earlier part of his life he rose through a succession of offices to the rank of praetorian prefect, and as a result of his close association with Theodoric and his Ostrogothic successors he developed a great admiration for the Goths which found expression in a history of their nation designed to reconcile the

Romans to being ruled by those whom they regarded as barbarians, and to show that the Goths were worthy to be ranked with the Greeks and the Romans. Unfortunately this work is known to us only through a résumé made by Jordanes. It had at one time been the intention of Cassiodorus, when Agapetus was pope, to establish a school of Christian studies in Rome itself, on the model of the school at Alexandria, but the plan came to nothing and towards the middle of his life – the date is uncertain but it was perhaps *c.* 540 or a little later – he withdrew from public office and retired to his family estates at Squillace in Calabria. Here he founded two monasteries of which one, known as Vivarium, from the fishponds which were among its delights, was designed partly as a theological school, partly as a great library and partly as a scriptorium where monks could be trained in the copying of manuscripts. Work of this kind was being done on a small scale elsewhere in Italy at this date,[15] and in Gaul at a considerably earlier date there were scribes among the monks of St Martin's monastery at Marmoutier near Troyes, but what gave particular distinction to the school at Vivarium was the insistence with which Cassiodorus impressed upon his monks the importance of studying secular Greek and Latin literature as a preparation for the study of the Scriptures.

At about the middle of the sixth century Cassiodorus wrote the *Institutiones*, a work which was intended to introduce the monks at Vivarium to their course of study and to guide them in their approach to a number of practical problems which would confront them in the scriptorium. The second of the two Books into which the work is divided was concerned with the seven liberal arts of secular studies, comprising grammar, rhetoric, dialectic, arithmetic, music, geometry and astronomy, and it is for the most part a mere compilation from other sources. The real interest of the work lies in the first Book, the *Institutiones Divinarum Lectionum*. Here Cassiodorus discussed such practical matters as punctuation and the emendation of corrupt texts. In punctuation there was a choice between the classical method used by the secular grammarians, comprising a variety of stops not fundamentally different from the modern system, and the different system which had been advocated by Jerome and was known as writing *per cola et commata*. In this system, which we find in a number of Northumbrian manuscripts, notably the Lindisfarne Gospels and the Codex Amiatinus, the text was copied so that the lines, always rather short, were of varying length and corresponded as closely as possible with the phrasing of the words themselves, thereby facilitating the task of those who were not skilled as readers. Cassiodorus accepted the authority of Jerome on this point.[16]

A chapter[17] was devoted to advising scribes how to deal with the difficult problems presented by seemingly corrupt texts, particularly sacred texts. Minor errors, arising, for example, from confusion between such letters as *b* and *v*, *o* and *u*, or *n* and *m*, might be corrected, but where sacred texts contained usages at variance with contemporary accepted usage, the texts were not to be altered. The inflexion and character of nouns and verbs could not always be suited to human rules and there were times when the idioms of human speech should be overlooked in preference for the criterion of divine communication. A phrase known to have pleased God was not to be enfeebled by the influence of human desire. But when corrections did have to be made to manuscripts, the scribe was to make the corrections with such care as to deceive the reader into thinking them to be the work of the original scribe. In the eyes of Cassiodorus the work of the scribe was indeed deserving of the highest praise since every word of the Lord which he wrote was a wound inflicted upon Satan.[18]

Yet the larger part of the first Book of the *Institutiones* was devoted to discussion of more general matters affecting Biblical studies – an account of the way in which the various books of the Old and New Testaments were divided among the nine volumes of the monastic copy of the Bible, references to other divisions made by Jerome or Augustine or in the Septuagint, remarks about the best commentaries on the different books of the Bible, and so forth. Although there can be no doubt at all about the magnitude of the debt owed by posterity to the work done by Cassiodorus and his scribes at Vivarium, work which included not only the copying of manuscripts, but also the translating of Greek works into Latin as well as Biblical exegesis, Book I of the *Institutiones* does not itself seem to have enjoyed a wide circulation and in particular there is no certainty that Bede himself knew it. Yet we are not likely to be mistaken in supposing that the libraries at Wearmouth and Jarrow, through their possession of works which might not otherwise have survived, would be substantial, if indirect, beneficiaries of the work done at Vivarium. We can, however, go beyond the general to the particular, since we know that Bede himself not only made considerable use of some of the writings of Cassiodorus – notably his *Commentary on the Psalms*, of which a manuscript made at Jarrow in the eighth century still survives – but also used a Bible which had once belonged to Cassiodorus himself. In the *Institutiones* Cassiodorus described three Bibles which were in the library at Vivarium, one which consisted of nine separate volumes, a second which he described as a pandect (that is, a complete Bible) in smaller writing, and a third which he called 'a larger codex written in clearer script'. This latter, commonly known as the Codex Grandior, was illustrated with pictures and diagrams to which Cassiodorus himself had contributed what he described as an accurate drawing of the Tabernacle and the Temple.[19] Bede refers on two separate occasions in his commentaries to a drawing of the Temple which he himself had seen in a pandect which had belonged to Cassiodorus.[20] We are certain that Bede never went to Italy and we cannot doubt that the pandect to which he was referring was the Codex Grandior which had once belonged to Cassiodorus at Vivarium and which had subsequently reached Northumbria. After the death of Cassiodorus *c.* 580, aged about 95, we soon lose sight of Vivarium. A few years later, Gregory the Great received a deputation of its monks, but with the Lombards moving as far south as Calabria conditions were not favourable for continued study. The great library was later dispersed and no doubt its books were widely scattered, to the benefit of other libraries elsewhere.

REFERENCES

1   *De Nat. Rer. c.* xxxvii.
2   *HE* III, 27.
3   *HE* III, 23.
4   *HE* III, 29.
5   See below, pp. 175–6.
6   *HE* IV, 2.
7   *Vit. Hon. c.* 3 (15).
8   *Ibid. cc.* 4 (22), 5 (28).
9   *Carm. Sid.* XVI, 104–15.
10 *Ep. Sid.* VI, i, 3; VIII, xiv, 2.
11 For Cassian see W. O. Chadwick, *John Cassian*, 2nd ed., Cambridge 1968.
12 *In I Sam.* ed. Hurst, p. 194, *lines* 2461–2; *BdTR* p. 190, *lines* 107–10.
13 *Vinc. Comm. c.* 2.
14 *Ibid. c.* 24.
15 P. Riché, *Education et Culture*, 201-4.
16 *CI Praef.* 9.
17 *CI* I, xv.
18 *CI* I, xxx, i.
19 *CI* I, v, 2; xi, 3; xii, 3; xiv, 2.
20 *De Temp. Sal.* 16, *PL* 91, col. 775; *De Tab.* 2, 12, *PL* 91, col. 454.

13

Spanish Influences

The last decade or so of the sixth century was a time of profound importance for western Christianity, but we should lose sight of much of the significance of these years if we were to look at them only in terms of Gregory the Great and Augustine's mission to the English. At about the time when Cassiodorus died, Gregory, then one of the seven deacons of Rome, was sent as papal representative to the court at Byzantium and it was there that he met the Spaniard Leander. Gregory went back to Rome to become abbot of the monastery where Augustine was already then or soon afterwards a monk, and Leander returned to Spain to become bishop of Seville *c.* 584. Augustine reached England in 597 and three years later Leander was succeeded in the bishopric of Seville by his brother, Isidore, on the walls of whose library there might be seen the effigies of Gregory and Leander side by side.[1] That part of Spain to which Leander and Isidore belonged by adoption though not by birth, resembled Bede's part of Northumbria in the sense that both were frontier areas lying between two different cultural worlds. The Spanish conquests of Justinian's mercenaries which brought much of Baetica under Byzantine control stopped only a little short of Seville. Isidore's Seville was well-placed for communicating across Visigothic Spain by land to Saragossa and thence into the former Gaulish Narbonensis (now likewise Visigothic) and the cities of the Rhône valley. Yet Baetica also had both an Atlantic and a Mediterranean seaboard which enabled the Seville of Leander and Isidore to play what may well have been a role of vital importance as the link between the late classical antiquity of North Africa and Byzantium and the growth of learning in Irish and Anglo-Saxon monastic centres. Within the

more limited western sphere we know that Gregory the Great
sent a copy of his *Cura Pastoralis* as well as part of his *Moralia* to
Seville. Bede was of course familiar with both of these works and
it was the belief of Alfred the Great who later had the *Cura
Pastoralis* translated into English, that this work had first been
brought to England by Augustine himself. We know that there
were also in the Seville library some of the works of southern
Gaulish writers, among them being Cassian and Eucherius, one
time monk at Lérins and later bishop of Lyons.

Although it is certain that there were both monks and nuns in
Spain in the earlier part of the sixth century, it was the conversion of King Reccared to catholicism and the resultant
unification of a hitherto divided church that gave fresh impetus
to the development of Spanish monasticism. It is from Spain
that we have some of our earliest information about an aspect
of monasticism which became of great importance in both Gaul
and England in the seventh century, namely the part played by
women in monastic life. Among the important documents of
sixth-century Spanish monasticism is the Rule which was
composed by Leander, brother of Isidore, for their sister
Florentine. In a long introductory passage Leander contrasts
the behaviour which he commends to his sister with the
behaviour of worldly women – those who adorn themselves
with splendid clothing, scent themselves with strange perfumes,
change their eyes with paint, cover their faces with white
powder, load their arms with gold bracelets, put rings on their
fingers till their hands glitter like stars with their assortment of
jewels, weigh down their ears with metal rings, hide their necks
with a collar of pearls and other jewels, and wear a gold head
dress. Leander comments: *Certum, inquam, est hanc non esse castam*,
and he urges upon Florentine complete withdrawal from this
world.[2]

Florentine and her fellow nuns are to have nothing to do with
married women nor with men, even though they are holy men,
and if they must avoid the company even of holy men, how
much the more care must they take to avoid even the sight of
young men, lest the virgin be tempted to think during the night

[131]

of those upon whom her eyes have rested during the day. They were not to eat more than was needed to sustain life and they were never to talk singly with one another, but only in the company of two or three others. Reading and prayer were to be their chief occupations, their day being so divided that after they had prayed they were to read and when they had read they were to pray; but when they were reading in the Old Testament they were to remember that certain things were allowed in those days which were not allowed in these, nor were they to interpret the Song of Songs only according to what they heard with their ears. Other chapters of Leander's Rule dealt with fasting, the use of wine, bathing, not to be indulged in for pleasure but only when required by ill health, the dangers of laughter, and so forth. Each nun must remain in the monastery which she had first entered and she must never seek to return to the world which she had abandoned.[3] These communities of nuns are also mentioned by Isidore in his *De Ecclesiasticis Officiis* which, together with his own *Regula Monachorum*, contains much of great interest about the Spanish monasticism of his age. There are, he writes, communities of women resembling those of monks in their way of life, but occupying their own dwellings built at some distance away from the monasteries of monks. No young men are allowed access to them, and even the oldest and most venerable of the monks may go only as far as the forecourt to provide them with necessities. These communities are governed by women, and they occupy themselves in weaving. They receive food from the monks in return for the clothing which they make for them.[4]

Isidore distinguished between six different kinds of monks, three of them good and three of them bad. The three good kinds comprised the coenobites who lived in communities sharing all things in common and calling nothing their own, the hermits who lived in desert places far from men, and the anchorites who, after coming to perfection in the coenobitic life, enclosed themselves in small cells and lived solely in contemplation of God. The three bad kinds were the pseudo-anchorites who left their monasteries not because they had achieved perfection in the communal life, but because they could no longer bear the yoke of humility and submission, the *Circum-celliones* who wandered about dressed as monks, parading an air of bogus sanctity, and finally the Sarabaites who built themselves small cells which they falsely called monasteries and in which they lived solely for their own gain, governed by no superior and obeying no rule. The reason why men came together in the monastic life was that they might abandon the delights of the world and live together 'in prayer, reading, discussion, vigil and fasting'. They came to enrol in a holy army, and not merely those who were born free, but also former slaves who had been freed by their masters for this purpose, as well as common labourers from the fields.[5]

In his *Regula Monachorum* which he had compiled from precepts found scattered among the writings of the fathers, Isidore envisaged a monastery as being built far from any town, entirely enclosed, with only one gate leading to the outside world and a postern leading to the garden. The cells of the brothers should be built close to the church so that they could get to the divine office the more quickly. There would be an infirmary at some distance from both the church and the cells, for the sake of greater quiet. The storehouse was to be next to the refectory and there was to be a small garden enclosed within the monastery so that when monks were working there they would have no need to go outside. While stressing the overriding importance of the spiritual life and remarking on the need for all the monks to give of their labours wherever they might be needed, Isidore certainly envisaged that the monastery would also be a place for intellectual study. All the books were to be kept in the care of the *Custos Sacrarii* and each monk might borrow one from him at the beginning of the day, but it was always to be returned after vespers on the same day. No one who asked to keep his book longer was to be allowed to do so. After the evening meal or after vespers the brothers might question the abbot about passages in the work which they had been reading and might not have fully understood. Isidore evidently envisaged that a monastic library would contain secular or heretical works, and while he did not prohibit the reading of such works, he warned the monks that they must be read with care, since it was better to be ignorant of their pernicious doctrines than to be led into the snares of error.[6]

Despite the strictness with which Leander urged the complete segregation of monks and nuns from one another, there can be no doubt that at least in parts of Spain men and women were much more closely associated with one another in the monastic life than either he or Isidore had envisaged. Some double houses, containing both men and women, did exist.[7] The contemporary *Life* of Fructuosus and his own *Regula Monastica Communis* are of considerable interest not merely for what they have to tell about this aspect of Spanish monasticism in the seventh century, but also for the curiously close parallels which they reveal with certain features of Northumbrian monasticism during Bede's lifetime. Fructuosus, born like Benedict Biscop into the aristocracy, seems to have been a younger contemporary of Isidore, but a man distinguished rather by his devotion to the contemplative than to the active religious life. He became Bishop of Dumio shortly after 653 and in 656 he was raised to the metropolitan see of Braga. The date of his death is not certainly known, but it was *c.* 660, so that he lived not only in the age of Leander and Isidore, but also survived into the age of Aidan, Cuthbert and Wilfrid, though not quite till the birth of Bede.

We first meet Fructuosus in the mountain valleys of Bierzo where his father's sheep were being counted, but after the death of his parents he received the tonsure, and in the years which followed he used his former wealth to endow a monastery at Compludo in Gallicia.[8] The *Life*, which names eight other monasteries founded by him, also shows him anxiously seeking to escape from the fame which his sanctity had brought upon him by withdrawing to wild and remote places where he could live among rocks and caves, forests and mountains. On one occasion, dressed in a goatskin, he narrowly escaped death from a hunter who mistook him for his prey and at another time, living in places accessible only to mountain goats, he trained jackdaws to find his secret retreats and so reveal his whereabouts

to those who wished to find him.[9] There is much in this aspect
of the life of Fructuosus which is reminiscent of Cuthbert's
attempts to escape the duties of public life in the remoteness of
his hermitage on Farne. But he was not only the hermit. We
know that he visited Seville and we find him travelling, on foot
as was his custom, and the custom also of Aidan in Northumbria,
from Lusitania to Baetica with a load of books carried on a
horse which was being led by a boy some way in front. Horse
and boy had the misfortune to fall into a flooded river and all
the books were tipped out of their bags into the water. Needless
to say, when Fructuosus caught up he was able to effect their
recovery undamaged. From Seville he went by boat to Cadiz
and there he founded a monastery which attracted very large
numbers of monks. The author of the *Life* remarks that a
countless army would have assembled there had there not been
an outcry demanding some restriction on the numbers seeking
to become monks lest there should be none left to go on military
service.[10] Some years after the death of Fructuosus the Spanish
king issued a law requiring all men to serve the government at
times of insurrection or invasion, and it may well be that this
law was directed at monastic communities whose members were
not liable for military service. The same problem arose in
Northumbria in the eighth century when Bede, then near the
end of his life, saw it as a major threat to the security of the
kingdom.[11]

The *Life* of Fructuosus does not contain any evidence that he
himself established any double houses for men and women, but
we are told of the virgin Benedicta for whom he built a cell in the
forest and whose example attracted so many others that a
community numbering 80 nuns was soon assembled.[12] Yet in
the *Regula Monastica Communis* which belongs to the period
when Fructuosus had become a bishop and seems to embody
episcopal regulations relating to monasteries in general, there
are a number of clauses which refer to both men and women.
The sixth chapter, itself headed, 'How men with wives and
children are to live in a monastery without danger', envisages a
situation in which entire families might come to monasteries

[135]

seeking admission and be received by the abbot. The fifteenth chapter – 'How monasteries of men and maidens are to guard themselves' – forbids the brethren to live in the same monastic building with their sisters, to share a common place of prayer or to be under the same roof. The monks themselves are not to assemble or to eat together with the sisters whom they have in their care. If both monks and nuns should be working in the common field, the two groups are to keep separate from one another, each in their own part.

There can be little doubt that, despite the strict segregation of men and women, these regulations refer to double houses, that is to say to religious foundations providing for both men and women, though, unlike the situation which we shall find in England where nuns and monks commonly lived under the government of an abbess, the Spanish double houses seem normally to have had an abbot ruling the monks and an abbess the nuns. Just as we shall see Bede echoing the fears expressed in the *Vita Fructuosi* about the excessive growth of monasticism and the shortage of fighting men, so also we shall find him echoing the remarks of Fructuosus himself about the growth of spurious monasteries. Fructuosus would not have introduced this topic into the very first chapter of his own *Regula Monastica Communis* unless the growth of such monasteries had already become a matter of real gravity. It was the custom of some, he wrote, to turn their own homes together with their wives, children, servants and neighbours into what they falsely called monasteries. 'Where you find such as these, you are to believe that they are hypocrites and heretics, not monks.' Such people were living entirely according to their own will and not in subjection to any authority. They did not give of their substance to the poor, but rather, as if they were poor themselves, they made haste to seize other people's property and so with their wives and their children to become much richer than they had been before.

The Visigothic renaissance of the late sixth and the early seventh century was rooted partly in the great episcopal centres established in towns which still preserved much of the material civilisation of the antique world, and partly in the great monasteries. It was furthered by the development of the court itself, at Toledo, into a centre of intellectual interests, particularly during the reign of Sisebut (612–621) a man of considerable talent who corresponded with laymen as well as with the clergy and who enjoyed writing Latin verse. It was at Sisebut's request that Isidore wrote his *De Natura Rerum* and when Isidore sent him a copy of the completed work in 613 Sisebut himself composed a poem on astronomy which became an inseparable part of the first edition of the *De Natura Rerum*. About seventy or more years later, at the time of the Anglo-Saxon renaissance, we find the English scholar Aldhelm citing one of King Sisebut's verses, though he thought it was Isidore's, in a letter which he wrote to the Northumbrian king Aldfrith who, though English, was renowned among the Irish as a great poet and scholar.[13] The parallel is striking. Yet the Visigothic renaissance produced no great works of theology or Biblical exegesis, and despite the presence of Greek-speaking and Jewish communities in certain parts of Spain, neither Greek nor Hebrew was studied. Spain's function was to succeed Africa as the guardian of antique culture and subsequently to hand on to the west what had been left in her safekeeping.[14]

REFERENCES

1 J. Fontaine, *Isidore de Séville et la culture classique*, II, 842.
2 For the text of Leander's *Rule* see *PL* LXXII, 874–94.
3 *Cc.* III–XI, XVI, XXI.
4 *De Ecc. Off.* II, xvi, 17, *PL* LXXXIII, 801.
5 *Ibid.* II, xvi, 2–9, 15. Cf. the four kinds specified in *BR c.* I.
6 *Isid. Reg. Mon. cc.* I, VIII, *PL* LXXXIII, 869, 877–8.
7 On double houses in Spain and elsewhere see P. S. Hilpisch, *Die Doppelkloster, Entstehung und Organisation, Beitr. z. Gesch. des Alten Mönchtums u. des Benediktinerordens*, Münster, 1928, heft 15. For early Spanish monasticism see W. S. Porter, *Laudate*, X (1932), 2–15, 66–79, 156–67.
8 *Vita Fructuosi cc.* II–III.
9 *Ibid. cc.* IV, V, VIII, IX.

14

Aspects of English Monasticism

The monasticism of Italy, Spain and Gaul developed within the framework of a diocesan organisation which was itself based upon the still-surviving urban civilisation of the later Roman empire. In the far west and north of Britain there had never been any towns, and in those parts occupied by the English there were merely the remains of towns. It would be foolish to suppose that in the sixth and seventh centuries all the former towns of Roman Britain were falling into ruins and entirely without inhabitants. In a few cases – London, Canterbury, Rochester, York, Carlisle – we know that this was not so, but it seems certain that in none of these towns did any literate civilisation, whether secular or ecclesiastical, survive beyond the Roman occupation. Whatever gossamer threads of continuity there may have been, in this respect at least the break was complete. Augustine came to England from a monastery in Rome and when he built his own monastery in Canterbury no doubt there would be many Roman buildings still standing there, in addition to the two churches mentioned by Bede. He would find in Canterbury at least the semblance of a Roman town and if it had suffered damage during the Anglo-Saxon invasions, so had many of the Italian towns during the Lombard invasions. So far as we know this was the only monastery built in England during the Augustinian mission. We hear nothing of similar monasteries at Rochester, London or York.

The further development of monasticism among the English stemmed from the arrival of Aidan at Lindisfarne in 635 and the subsequent movement of Irish missionaries into different parts of the country. It is unusual to have exact information about the dates of foundation but Bede himself refers to several monast-

eries which seem to have been founded during the fifteen years
635–50, including Melrose, Gateshead and Hartlepool in
Northumbria, Burgh Castle and an unnamed site in East
Anglia, Tilbury and Bradwell-on-Sea in Essex. No doubt if the
records had been more detailed they would have mentioned
several other sites, though it is likely that they would have been
small communities. During the period from 635 till the birth of
Bede *c.* 672, we can detect three influences which between them
made the Anglo-Saxon church predominantly monastic in this
age; the missionary zeal of the Irish monks, the influence of
northern Gaulish monasteries upon the education of Anglo-
Saxon women and the introduction of the Benedictine Rule by
Wilfrid.

The little that we know about the physical appearance of
monasteries founded on the Irish pattern among the English is
derived mainly from written sources, since the materials used in
their construction were not substantial enough to have survived
above ground and no site has yet been fully excavated. There
was a fondness for remote places, but as we have already seen
from Lérins and from the life of Fructuosus in Spain, this was not
a peculiarity distinctive of Irish monasticism so much as the
counterpart in material terms of spiritual withdrawal from the
world. Antony had wrestled with demons in the Egyptian desert
and Isaiah had prophesied that grass should be made to grow
where once only dragons had lived. Bede quoted this passage
from the prophet in describing the site at Lastingham in
Yorkshire which was chosen by Cedd who had been trained in
the Irish customs of Lindisfarne. 'It lay', wrote Bede, 'among
remote and craggy hills where there seemed rather to be lurking
places for robbers and dens for wild beasts than dwelling places
for men. In this desolate spot where there had been none but
beasts, or men living in the fashion of beasts, the fruit of good
works should be brought forth.' It is as difficult to recognise the
Lastingham of today by this description as it is to recognise the
Lérins described in similar terms by Hilary. Yet no doubt Cedd
wrestled with many terrors, both seen and unseen, while he
observed his Lenten fast at Lastingham, eating nothing all day

(save on Sundays) until the evening when he took a little bread, one hen's egg and a little milk diluted with water. He used to say that it was the custom of those from whom he had learnt the regular discipline that when a place had been newly received for building a monastery or a church, it must first be consecrated to the Lord by prayer and fasting.[1]

Three of the monasteries with which Cuthbert was associated at different times of his life – Melrose, Ripon and Lindisfarne – were all foundations on the Irish pattern, though we know very little about Ripon before the site was acquired by Wilfrid. Nowadays it is difficult to view either medieval Melrose or Old Melrose save through the romantic eyes of Walter Scott, but the monastery in which Cuthbert first lived as a monk lay on a site which was almost surrounded by the river Tweed and which was faced by lofty cliffs rising steeply from the river's outer bank. This was the setting in which Dryhthelm, a man who was believed to have returned to life on the morning after his death, used to describe his vision of hell, and his description, as Bede records it, wants for nothing in its details of the icy cold, the flaming abyss, the insufferable stench and the hideous lament-ations of souls tormented by laughing demons. The monks of Old Melrose would not have gone short of salmon, but for Dryhthelm the river was not a place for fishing, but a place for the mortification of the flesh, and as he stood in the bitter waters in winter time with blocks of ice floating about him men would say to him: 'It is wonderful, Brother Dryhthelm, that you can endure such bitter cold.' He used to answer simply, for he was a man of simple nature and sober habit, 'I have seen greater cold.'[2]

We find this – to a modern age – rather distasteful asceticism being practised by Cuthbert when he went from Melrose to visit Coldingham, a double house of both men and women. A suspicious cleric of the monastery, following him one night, was put to shame by discovering him singing psalms and walking out into the tumultous waves of a stormy sea.[3] Among the turbulent waters, the rugged cliffs, the seals, the myriad cormorants, the gannets and the eider duck, it is still possible

for the visitor to contemplate almost unchanged the surroundings in which Cuthbert moved from the coenobitic life of
Lindisfarne to the life of the hermit on Farne. Hermits comprise
the second in Isidore's categories of monks, as also in the
Benedictine Rule which was known at Lindisfarne in Cuthbert's lifetime and which describes hermits as those who, 'after
long probation in a monastery, having learnt in association with
many brethren how to fight against the devil, go out well-armed
from the ranks of the community to the solitary combat of the
desert. They are now able to live without the help of others, and
by their own strength and God's assistance to fight against the
temptations of mind and body.'[4] Both Isidore and Bede would
have agreed with the Benedictine Rule in regarding the
contemplative life of the hermit as being superior to the active
coenobitic life of the monk. It was on Farne, where scarcely any
man had been able to live alone for any length of time, that
Cuthbert built himself a small dwelling from which he could see
nothing save the heavens above.

The hermitage to which Cuthbert moved on Farne, and
where he eventually died, was a few miles south of Aidan's
foundation at Lindisfarne which remains, as it was when Bede
described it, a place which twice each day is turned into an
island by the rising tide to be joined to the mainland again on
the ebb. Bede noted that the church built there by Aidan's
successor, Finan, was made in the Irish fashion 'not of stone,
but hewn entirely of oak and thatched with reeds', and he knew
that subsequently the reed thatch was removed and the whole
fabric of roof and walls encased with lead,[5] in striking contrast
with the stone-built churches of Wearmouth and Jarrow. Yet
the point which he seems to have thought would be of particular
interest to his readers was the, to him unfamiliar, way in which
the monastery at Lindisfarne was organised as a community.
Describing Columba's foundation on Iona itself, he remarked
that the community there was always accustomed to have as its
ruler an abbot to whom the whole province of the monastery
and the bishops themselves were to be obedient, a system which
he described as *ordo inusitatus*. Commenting on the organisation

of the monastery at Lindisfarne, he wrote: 'And let no one be surprised that, though we have said above that in this island of Lindisfarne, small as it is, there is found the seat of a bishop, now we say also that it is the home of an abbot and monks; for it actually is so. For one and the same dwelling-place of the servants of God holds both. Aidan, who was the first bishop of this place, was a monk and always lived according to monastic rule together with all his followers. Hence all the bishops of that place up to the present time exercise their episcopal functions in such a way that the abbot, whom they themselves have chosen by the advice of the brethren, rules the monastery; and all the priests, deacons, singers and readers, and the other ecclesiastical grades, together with the bishop himself, keep the monastic rule in all things.'[6]

Coldingham, visited by Cuthbert from Melrose, was a house of nuns which was at that time governed by Æbbe whom Bede calls *mater congregationis*, and who is elsewhere described as 'a widow and the mother of them all in Christ', but there were also men in the community, including the cleric who spied upon Cuthbert, an Irish ascetic called Adamnan and an Englishman whom Bede calls 'my fellow-priest'.[7] We know that Cuthbert visited at least two other abbesses and we find that the contemporary sources, in contrast with the inventions of the Norman age, consistently show him as enjoying the friendliest of relations with women. Coldingham itself figures in Bede's history chiefly as the subject of a cautionary tale – both men and women were found to be indulging in sinful ways, the cells built for praying and reading had been turned into places for feasting, drinking, talking and other delights, and the nuns, despising their vows, employed their leisure in weaving fine clothing which they used either to adorn themselves like brides or to win the friendship of men from outside. Divine wrath fell upon the house and it was destroyed by fire.[8] This description of the corruption of Coldingham is significant chiefly for the contrast which it offers with almost everything else that we know about the part played by women in Anglo-Saxon monasticism in the seventh century, a contrast so strong as to give grounds for suspecting a measure of exaggeration to explain an otherwise inexplicable fire. Another one-time member of the community at Coldingham was Audrey, who was the former wife of a Northumbrian king, the daughter of an East Anglian king and herself the foundress of the double house at Ely.

The double house may be defined as a body of monks and nuns, not living in buildings physically separated from one another by a distance of several miles, but in buildings which themselves formed a single physical unit, even though the monks and the nuns lived each in their separate parts, and which also formed a single juridical unit in the sense that all the inhabitants of both sexes owed obedience to a single head. This institution seems to have been introduced into England from northern Gaul where, as in England, the arrival of Irish missionaries led to a rapid and widespread development of monasticism, though it is not to be supposed that the double house was particularly favoured by the Irish. This Irish monasticism was taking root in northern Gaul, notably at Luxeuil, founded by Columbanus, at about the same time as the Gregorian mission was embarking on the conversion of the English, but it is not until some years later, perhaps *c.* 625, that we hear of the foundation of the first nunnery, the house later known as Remiremont where monks from Luxeuil instructed the nuns in the Columban rule.[9] Towards the middle of the seventh century at a time when, as Bede writes, 'few monasteries had been founded in the country of the English, many persons were accustomed to go from Britain to the monasteries of the Franks or Gauls for the sake of the monastic life; and they also sent their daughters to be instructed there'.[10] Although in the passage which follows Bede is specific only about those monasteries in Gaul to which the women went, his comment implies that the majority of those who went were men. Some of them would no doubt remain in Gaul and we know of at least one instance of an Englishman who later became abbot of a Gaulish monastery.[11]

Bede seems to have been well-informed about the nunneries of northern Gaul and he names three in particular as places

with which English women had close associations, Fare-
moutiers-en-Brie, Chelles, and Andelys-sur-Seine. The first of
these was founded as a nunnery by Eustasius, abbot of Luxeuil,
with Burgundofara as its first abbess. Monks were sent to take
charge of the building work and also to instruct the nuns in the
Columban rule. Although seemingly founded as a nunnery,
Faremoutiers became a double house containing both monks
and nuns. It is possible that the close associations of the Kentish
and East Anglian royal families with Faremoutiers owed
something to the career of a remarkable Englishwoman,
Balthild, who, after being sold into the household of a mayor of
the palace, became the wife of Clovis II (639–57) and was not
only a great benefactress of Faremoutiers, but was also herself
the foundress of Chelles, near Paris, to which, after the death of
Clovis, she retired, living there a life which won for her a
saintly reputation.[12] We know little about the early history of
the third house named by Bede, Andelys-sur-Seine, save that it
is said to have been founded by the wife of Clovis I. Bede records
the names of three English women of royal birth who went to
Faremoutiers – Eorcengota, daughter of a Kentish king who
was remembered by Bede as the first of all the kings of the
English to order the destruction of the idols throughout his
kingdom, and Sæthryth and Æthelberg, both of whom were of
the East Anglian royal family and both of whom so distinguished
themselves in the monastic life that they eventually became
abbesses of Faremoutiers, despite their foreign origin. Hilda,
who was also related to the East Anglian royal family and is
renowned as the abbess of Whitby, had wanted to join the
community at Chelles where her sister, Hereswith, the mother
of an East Anglian king, had already gone, but she was dis-
suaded from leaving England by Aidan. According to the *Life*
of Bertila who was abbess of Chelles in the second half of the
seventh century, both monks and nuns, as well as considerable
quantities of books, were sent to England from Gaul at the
request of English kings to assist in the foundation of English
monasteries.[13]

The Kentish and East Anglian kings whose daughters were

associated with Faremoutiers, had both been ruling for some years by 650, and in default of more precise information we may suppose that the connexion with Faremoutiers had been established before the middle of the century. Bede would not necessarily have known about the earliest women's monasteries in southern England, but he believed that the first woman in Northumbria to adopt the religious life was Heiu who received the nun's habit from Aidan and founded a monastery at Hartlepool. Since Aidan died in 651 we may think it likely that Hartlepool was founded in the 640's.[14] Heiu moved later to a place which is commonly identified with the modern Tadcaster and she was succeeded at Hartlepool by Hilda. In addition to such northern double houses as Coldingham, Hartlepool and Whitby, we know that similar foundations came to be widely distributed over much of England – among them being Repton and Much Wenlock in the midlands, Partney, Ely, Barking and Minster-in-Thanet in the east, and Wimborne in the south-west. All of these houses were governed by abbesses and all of them had monks associated with them as well as nuns.

The foundation at Wimborne is described as comprising two separate monasteries, one for men and the other for women, both being surrounded by high walls. No woman was ever allowed to enter the men's monastery, nor any man the women's save only for the priests who could go to the women's church for the celebration of Mass. When the abbess had to concern herself with outside affairs affecting the monastery as a whole, she would come to a window to give her instructions. One of the abbesses, a sister of the king of Wessex, maintained such strict discipline that she would not allow even the bishop to enter the women's house, and one of the nuns who became prioress ruled the younger nuns with such severity that after her death they desecrated her grave.[15] At Barking only children were allowed to go into the women's part of the monastery, but at Ely we are told that a man described as a medicus was present at Audrey's deathbed. When her remains were translated sixteen years after her death it was the monks who were

sent to search among the Roman ruins at Cambridge for a
suitable stone coffin, and on a later occasion we find both
monks and nuns attending a service together, though each kept
to their own side.[16]

The monastery at Whitby was founded in 657 by Hilda and
under her guidance as abbess it rapidly became the most
important and influential centre of Christianity in the country.
Her parents who were related to the Deiran royal family and
who so far as we know were pagans, lived in exile in the British
kingdom of Elmet while Edwin himself was in flight from the
pagan king Æthelfrith. Although herself removed from Edwin
by two generations Hilda received baptism from Paulinus at the
same time as Edwin himself. We do not know what became of
her at the time of Edwin's death, but we find her later in East
Anglia seeking to cross to Gaul in order to join her sister who
was a nun at Chelles. She was recalled to Northumbria by
Aidan who gave her a small piece of land on the north bank of
the river Wear where she remained for a year living a monastic
life with a few companions. She moved from this place, whose
exact locality is not known, to become abbess at Hartlepool in
succession to Heiu and there she promptly began to organise
everything according to the Rule in which she had been
instructed by several learned men, Bishop Aidan among them.
Save for the Benedictine Rule itself, no monastic rule survives
from any English monastery, whether of monks or nuns, from
the seventh or eighth centuries, but since Hilda was instructed
in the monastic life by Irish men of learning, presumably the
Rule which she learnt was the Rule of Columbanus, the Rule
which was also observed at most of the women's houses in
northern Gaul. Yet we do not find in Hilda herself or in her
monastery any trace of the more ascetic forms of Columban
monastic doctrine. Although teaching the strict observance of
justice, piety and chastity, she laid particular emphasis on the
virtues of peace and charity. It was not for Hilda to look out-
wards into the world through the peep-hole of a window.
Religious men of learning were attracted to her by her wisdom,
while not only humble men and women, but even kings and

officers of government would come to her in search of advice on the problems by which they were confronted.

These qualities enabled Hilda to create what was so far as we know, the first monastic community among the English in which educational and intellectual activities came to form a major part of the spiritual life as a whole. From the first Hilda saw the importance of learning and she insisted that those under her care should devote much time to the study of the Scriptures, for it was in this way that some help could be given towards meeting one of the most urgent needs of the Anglo-Saxon church at about the middle of the seventh century – the lack of adequately trained bishops. No fewer than five men, all of them of English race, reached the rank of bishop after receiving education at Whitby. One of these five, Oftfor, after devoting himself to the study of the Scriptures both at Hartlepool and at Whitby, later took himself to Kent to work under the direction of archbishop Theodore who, though he disapproved of double houses of men and women,[17] would have been able to teach him Greek. Not content with this, Oftfor went on to Rome before returning to England to undertake episcopal duties in the western midlands. In addition to the other four – Bosa at York, Ætla at Dorchester, John at Hexham and Wilfrid II at York (not the more famous Wilfrid) – we know also of a sixth man from Whitby, Tatfrith, described by Bede as a most vigorous and learned man of excellent ability, who was elected bishop in the west midlands but who died before he could be consecrated.[18]

If there was to be an educated priesthood and episcopate in the church of this age the Scriptures, illuminated by the commentaries of the Fathers, had to be studied in Latin, but there was a further problem, that of communicating the elements of the Christian faith to the ordinary people who would have been wholly unable to read even if there had been any books available. This could be done by preaching, helped by pictorial representation, whether on paintings in churches or on sculptured monuments in the open air, but it could also be done by exploiting the native fondness for poetry and song. The story of Cædmon, gifted as a poet and singer, has long been familiar, so much so that we may lose sight of its real significance. Cædmon spent most of his life in the secular world, and the glimpse that we have of him escaping to the cow byres before his turn came to entertain the company gathered for an evening's merriment, suggests that he may have worked on one of the Whitby estates. The gift of song came to him late in life and it was the composition of a hymn in praise of creation that led his overseer on the estate to take him to Hilda. There he was examined by a number of learned men who gave him a passage from Scripture and sent him away to see if he could put it into verse. His task completed, he was persuaded to enter the monastery as a monk and he was then set to a course of study in sacred history. He evidently did not learn to read himself, but strove to remember as much as he could by listening attentively to his teachers. He would then turn all that he remembered into vernacular verse. Hilda herself and those of the monks in her monastery who were primarily concerned with its educational activities, would have seen at once the importance of Cædmon's gift as a medium for communicating the elements of the Christian faith to an illiterate and no doubt still largely pagan population. The history of Genesis and of the Exodus of Israel from Egypt, the stories of the Incarnation, the Passion, the Resurrection, the Ascension – these and other topics drawn from Scripture, as well as themes relating to the Day of Judgement (on which Bede himself composed a Latin poem) the pains of Hell and the joys of Heaven – became the subject matter of what must have been a very considerable body of vernacular religious poetry whose dissemination is likely to have been a major factor in furthering the spread of Christianity in Northumbria and beyond.[19]

Hilda died in 680, seven years after the foundation of Wearmouth and the year before the foundation of Jarrow. Bede, then aged about 9, had been in the care of Benedict Biscop for some two years. After Hilda's death Whitby was governed by Eanflæd who, like Hilda, had been baptised by Paulinus, and was indeed the first of all the Northumbrian race to receive baptism. For some years she ruled the monastery in conjunction with her daughter, Aelfflæd, who died in 713 or 714 and was commemorated by a mural inscription of which a part still survives.[20] Through the baptism of both Hilda and Eanflæd by Paulinus and the spending of Eanflæd's girlhood in Kent, Whitby enjoyed a close link with the Gregorian mission itself, a link which was strengthened by the survival in Yorkshire of one of the companions of Paulinus for many years after the death of Paulinus himself – James the Deacon, who was present at the synod of Whitby. We have already considered the significance of this link for the historicity of the traditions which Bede records about the beginnings of Christianity in Northumbria, and doubtless this same link may be held to account for the great interest taken at Whitby in Gregory the Great himself.

It was a monk of Whitby who wrote a work which is not only the oldest biography of this pope, but which is among the oldest surviving pieces of literature written by an Englishman in an English monastery. The writer of the *Life*, which was probably completed between 704 and 714 was able to use the *Liber Pontificalis*, in its second recension, and most of the major works of Gregory the Great. We may presume that these works were in the Whitby library which must also have been well-stocked with other books relating in particular to Biblical study. We have not so far been able to identify any single manuscript as coming from Whitby, nor have we any means of learning how wide was the range of other books available for the use of those who studied there or at Hartlepool which remained under Hilda's control after her move to Whitby. Of the vernacular poems attributed to Cædmon none survives save the brief *Hymn* in praise of creation, and not even that in a Whitby copy. On the other hand abundant, if tantalising, evidence of literary activity has been recovered from the ground: a number of now badly mutilated and often illegible inscriptions on stone monuments, some of them parts of free-standing crosses, some of them mural tablets, some in Latin, some in the runic alphabet; a considerable number of elaborately decorated metal tags which were evidently intended to be attached to some delicate fabric, such as a ribbon of silk, and which seem likely to have served as book-markers; several *styli* used for writing on wax tablets; and also some fragments of ornamental metal-work used for the external adornment of liturgical books.[21]

Hilda's monastery is believed to have been destroyed during the Danish invasions of the ninth century, if it had not already decayed before, and the site remained unoccupied until the late eleventh century. To the north of the existing abbey, in an area extensively used as a burial ground in the Middle Ages, there have been found some remains of an enclosing wall, as well as the foundations of several small buildings, some of which may represent the domestic quarters of the nuns, but no remains of any larger buildings or of any church have been recovered. There can be little doubt that we should visualise Hilda's Whitby, the burial-place of several members of the Northumbrian royal family, as a community of considerable size whose members, perhaps to be reckoned by the hundred, led a rich spiritual and intellectual life devoted in large part to furthering the spread of Christianity. Though it was perhaps more a place of education than of profound scholarship, Hilda's Whitby deserves to be remembered not merely as the meeting-place of a famous synod which rejected Celtic in favour of Roman liturgical practices, but also as a link in the chain which joins the Vivarium of Cassiodorus, the Rome of Gregory the Great and the Seville of Isidore to Bede's Jarrow.

The life of Wilfrid, known to us in considerable detail from his biographer Eddius, reflects much of the confused state of Christianity among the English in the seventh century. Of noble birth, and said to have been ill-used by a cruel stepmother, he had his first sight of monastic life when he went as a boy to Lindisfarne. In later years we find him, at different times, crossing Gaul, staying in Lyons, visiting Rome and more than once, back in England at York, Ripon or Hexham, preaching to heathens in Sussex or Frisia, quarrelling with kings and bishops, imprisoned in Northumbria, again in Rome seeking papal support for his claims, founding monasteries in the midlands and finally in his old age reconciled to those with whom he had earlier quarrelled so bitterly. No one can read the *Life* written by Eddius without seeing in Wilfrid a vigorous and forceful personality likely to arouse extremes of affection and hatred. Nonetheless, despite his restless travels and his violent quarrels, Wilfrid left a distinctive mark on the character of the English church in the seventh century. He was not a humble man, nor, so far as we can see, was he a man greatly interested in learning, and perhaps he would have been more at home as a member of the Gallo-Roman episcopate where the wealth which gave him enemies in England would have passed unnoticed and where his interference in matters of state would have been less likely to take him to prison.

As a boy at Lindisfarne Wilfrid would see the modest wooden church with its thatched roof, but when the time came for him to build his own churches we find him striving to introduce something of the dignity and grandeur of the Roman buildings he had seen in Gaul and Italy. When he went to York he found that the church built in the days of Paulinus was sadly decayed, with the roof leaking, no glass in the windows and the walls fouled by the birds nesting within. Not only did he put on a new leaded roof, glaze the windows and whitewash the walls, but he also equipped the church with new vessels for the service of the altar and gave it fresh endowments of land.[22] At Ripon, on the site formerly occupied by the Irish monks, he built a new stone church with columns and side aisles, vesting the altar with purple interwoven with gold. The dedication of the new church, a splendid ceremony attended by kings and other leading men, was followed by three days of feasting, and among the treasures to be seen was a copy of the four Gospels written in letters of gold on purple-dyed parchment, and with a gold case set with precious gems to contain it – 'a marvel of beauty hitherto unheard of in our times.'[23] Wilfrid's crypts still survive at both Ripon and Hexham, and at the latter enough is known about the ground-plan to enable us to visualise a basilican church of considerable dignity built mostly of stone taken from nearby Roman sites.[24] Wilfrid undoubtedly introduced a greater element of splendour and dignity into the churches of seventh-century England, yet it was perhaps a greater distinction that it could be claimed on his behalf that he had been the first to organise the life of his monastic foundations according to the Benedictine Rule. Although Eddius was not above distorting history in favour of his hero, there does not seem to be any ground for doubting his testimony on this point. Moreover, Bede himself seems to lend some support to the claims made by Eddius when he describes Wilfrid as being the first bishop among the English race who learnt 'to deliver to the churches of the English the catholic manner of life'.[25]

REFERENCES

1   *HE* III, 23.

2   *HE* V, 12.

3   *AVC* II, 3.

4   *BR* I, 3–5. *Tr.* J. McCann.

5   *HE* III, 25.

6   *HE* III, 4 and *BVC c.* XVI. *Tr* B. Colgrave.

7   *HE* IV, 25, *AVC* II, 3.

8   *HE* IV, 25.

9   *Vita Columbani*, II, 10.

10 *HE* III, 8.

11 *AVCeol* 7.

12 *HE* III, 8, *Vita Columbani*, II, 7. W. Levison, *England and the Continent in the Eighth Century* (Oxford 1946), 9–10.

13 *HE* III, 8; IV, 23. *Vit. Bertilae c.* 6, *MGH SS Rer. Merov.* VI, 106–7. See also S. Hilpisch, *Die Doppelkloster*, 39, and W. Levison *op. cit.* 132, n. 2. For an 8th – 9th century copy of Augustine's commentary on the Psalms thought to have been written by nine of the nuns of Chelles see *CLA* VIII, 1152. Several other MSS have been attributed to the Chelles scriptorium. See B. Bischoff, 'Die Kölner Nonnenhandschriften und das Skriptorium von Chelles', *Karolingische und Ottonische Kunst* (Wiesbaden 1957), 395–411.

14 *HE* IV, 23.

15 *Vita Leobae cc.* 2–4. *Tr, EHD* I, 719–20.

15

Benedict Biscop's Early Years

The founder of Wearmouth, and subsequently of Jarrow, was an English nobleman of Northumbrian birth who, while in the service of King Osuiu, had been endowed with an estate appropriate to his rank as a king's thegn, but nothing more precise is known either of the place of his birth or of the location of his estate. Although the date of his birth has not been recorded in any early source, and although we do not know how old he was when he died on 12 January 689, we can neverthe-less calculate that he was born within a year or so of Edwin's baptism by Paulinus in 627 and we may even conjecture that some unrecorded circumstances attending his birth at this particular time might account for his unusual name. He has come to be known generally as Benedict Biscop, but Eddius knew him as Biscop Baducing, and it is apparent from Bede who refers to *Benedictus* as his *cognomen*, that this name was adopted by him after his abandonment of secular life. Baducing may be taken as a patronymic, but Biscop, though susceptible to other explanations, can most naturally be associated with OE *biscop* from the Latin *episcopus*. The name, though certainly strange, is not unique, since it is found as that of a *presbyter* in the Lindis-farne *Liber Vitae* and also in the genealogy of the kings of Lind-sey.[1]

During his service at Osuiu's court Benedict Biscop would learn something of the Scottish Christian practices then favoured by Osuiu, as well as something of the Roman observances followed by Eanflæd his queen, who, though born in North-umbria, had been nurtured in Kent after her father's death in battle. For more than two generations past the *peregrinatio pro amore Dei* had been a familiar activity of Irish Christianity[2] and it may have been some Scottish or Irish example which prompted Benedict at about the age of 25 to sever all his connections with the temporalities of this world and embark on a pilgrimage to the resting-places of the saints in Rome.[3] The hundred-fold reward promised to those who, like Benedict, abandoned home, kinsmen and country for Christ's sake was the recurrent theme of the homily which Bede composed for Benedict's day many years later, at a time when his early labours had borne rich fruit at Jarrow as well as at Wearmouth. Bede wrote little about this, Benedict's first, journey though he may have known more than he chose to record. When Benedict reached Kent he found that Wilfrid who was likewise anxious to visit Rome, had been waiting there for the past year for a guide to go as a companion. Eddius claimed that hitherto no Englishman had ever made the journey to Rome.[4]

Benedict and Wilfrid were in Kent when Honorius was archbishop, and Honorius died on 30 September 653. Wilfrid had left Lindisfarne a few years after 648 and had been in Kent for a year. On this evidence we can date the journey to *c.* 652–3,[5] with Benedict then aged about 25 and Wilfrid about 18. The two, no doubt with many attendants, such as would at least ensure the safety of two noblemen, travelled in company as far as Lyons, but there they parted. Eddius would have his readers believe that they quarrelled as Barnabas and Paul quarrelled over John Mark,[6] and the terms of his reference to Benedict as a stern guide make plain his desire to absolve Wilfrid from any blame. Bede does not tell of any quarrel, even though he is likely to have known about it, but he records only that Wilfrid was kept back in Lyons by Dalfinus, while Benedict completed his journey by sea. Both Bede and Eddius mistakenly represent Dalfinus as bishop, instead of count, of the city of Lyons, but both tell how Dalfinus sought to secure Wilfrid as husband for his niece. Perhaps the resolution of Wilfrid was tested amid the unfamiliar luxury of a Roman city, and it may be that the disagreement between the older and the younger of the two companions had a more romantic ground than Eddius could well afford to admit. Benedict would continue his journey southwards down the Rhône valley either by the Roman road or else by boat down the Rhône itself past Vienne and Valence to Arles. Since we know that he completed his journey by sea we may infer that he took ship either from Arles itself or from Marseilles direct to the port for Rome at the mouth of the Tiber.

During the next fifteen years Benedict paid no fewer than five more visits to Rome, but although we can follow the course of his travels in broad outline, chronological detail escapes us. Nonetheless, it is abundantly clear that from the first Wearmouth and Jarrow enjoyed closer relations with Rome than had been experienced by any community in the English church since the days of Augustine himself in his monastery at Canterbury.

We do not know how long Benedict stayed in Rome on his first visit nor do we know anything of his whereabouts on his return to England. His second visit to Rome was to have been made in the company of King Osuiu's son, Alchfrith, who became a close friend and supporter of Wilfrid, as well as a leading protagonist in the cause of the Roman church in England, but when Osuiu intervened and ordered Alchfrith to remain at home, Benedict went back to Rome on his own. This second visit, which lasted for some months, occurred after the election of Vitalian to the papacy in 657, and was followed by an experience which is likely to have had a deep influence not only upon Benedict himself, but also upon the later spiritual and intellectual development of English monasticism in Kent as well as in Northumbria. This was his visit to Lérins. It was at Lérins that Benedict received the tonsure and took his monastic vows, and it was here, in surroundings so different from the bleak north-east coast of his native land, that he lived as a monk for the next two years, learning and practising the regular observance of monastic discipline.[7]

Whether it was that Benedict was a restless wanderer by nature or that the enchantment of Rome proved too strong for him, after two years at Lérins he seized the opportunity offered by a passing ship to visit the city for the third time, apparently with the intention of passing the remainder of his life there. His visit to Rome chanced to coincide with the arrival of the embassy from Kent whose purpose was to secure the consecration of Wigheard to the archbishopric of Canterbury. We have already seen (above p. 118) that Wigheard and almost all of his companions died in Rome and that on 26 March 668 Pope Vitalian consecrated Theodore to the vacant archbishopric. Although we do not know how long Benedict had been in Rome when the English embassy arrived, the *menses aliquot* of his second visit, the *biennium* spent at Lérins and the third visit to Rome probably fell in the years 664–8.[8] If these dates are correct, when Benedict eventually returned to England on the pope's instructions as travelling-companion to Theodore and Hadrian, he had been out of the country for at least five years and possibly longer. The point is significant since Benedict would not then have been in any way concerned with the synod of Whitby at which Wilfrid, his companion to Lyons on the first journey, played such an important part.

The travellers left Rome on 27 May 668 and although both Hadrian and Benedict Biscop had some familiarity with the route, the journey to Canterbury took twelve months and was not without some misadventures. Theodore himself was then aged 66 and found his strength taxed by the difficulties of travel. The first part of the journey was made by sea to Marseilles, and thence to Arles where the travellers were detained by the archbishop to await the leave of Ebroin, mayor of the palace, to continue their journey. Perhaps they had hoped to reach England by the autumn, but the enforced delay at Arles resulted in their being overtaken by a hard winter in northern France and they were driven to find refuge where they could. Theodore would have been able to put the winter months to good advantage since his host was Agilbert, Bishop of Paris, that same Agilbert who had formerly served as bishop among the West Saxons and who, some four years before Theodore's arrival, had assisted in the consecration of Wilfrid as bishop in a ceremony at Compiègne. Hadrian stayed first at Sens and later at Meaux, but, a little strangely, nothing is recorded of the whereabouts of Benedict during these winter months or indeed at any stage of the journey. Meanwhile an officer of government was sent by King Egbert of Kent to meet the travellers and, with Ebroin's leave, he escorted Theodore to the coast at Étaples, but Theodore, weakened by illness, had to remain there for some time before he was strong enough to complete the journey. Hadrian was at first detained on suspicion of complicity in some political plot, but he was later set free and travelled on to Canterbury.

This account of Theodore's journey, which is derived from Bede's *History*,[9] presumably rests on Canterbury sources, but if we compare it, particularly as it concerns the fortunes of Benedict Biscop, with the account of the same journey given by Bede in the *Historia Abbatum*, we are left with the impression of some slight conflict between the Canterbury tradition and the Jarrow tradition which would rest ultimately on the personal recollections of Benedict Biscop himself. In the *History* Bede says nothing about the presence of Benedict Biscop in Rome when Wigheard arrived or about his returning to England on the orders of the pope as guide to Theodore. Whether or not he omitted these details because he thought them of insufficient importance for inclusion in a general work, he does make the point with some force that Hadrian insisted on accompanying Theodore partly because he had himself twice previously visited Gaul and was therefore the more familiar with the route. Bede does not say how long Hadrian was detained in northern Gaul after Theodore had gone ahead to England, but he does state that immediately on Hadrian's arrival (*statim ut ad illum venit*) Theodore gave him the monastery of St Peter, identifiable beyond any doubt with the monastery now known as St Augustine's by Bede's reference to it as the place where the archbishops of Canterbury were customarily buried. When we look at the *Historia Abbatum* we find Bede saying that Benedict returned to England as guide to Theodore, saying nothing about any delay in the arrival of Hadrian and stating unambiguously that Benedict took charge of the monastery later ruled by Hadrian and that Benedict continued to rule it for two years. Medieval Canterbury tradition, represented by Thomas of Elmham, asserted that Benedict Biscop was never abbot of St Augustine's, but it seems doubtful if such a conclusion can fairly be drawn from Bede's evidence. The conflict could be reconciled either by supposing that Hadrian was delayed in France for as long as two years, which seems unlikely, or that Benedict himself, perhaps offended at having to give place at Canterbury to Hadrian, slightly exaggerated his own claims.

It was not long before Benedict Biscop left Canterbury for his fourth visit to Rome, and, if we follow the *Historia Abbatum*, we can place this journey in the years 671–2. Benedict's previous journies had been undertaken primarily to improve his own knowledge of the Christian faith and of the organisation of the church in southern lands at a time when Christianity among the English greatly needed the help and inspiration of the older churches,[10] but on this occasion, perhaps already resolved by his experiences at Lérins to found a new monastery, he seems to have gone primarily for books. Not only did he acquire a large number of books in Italy itself, either by purchase or by the gift of friends, but he also, as he travelled down the Rhône valley, commissioned other friends to make purchases for him and these he collected at Vienne on his way back to England. He was now aged about 45 and on reaching England again, it was not his intention either to go back to Canterbury – and one wonders if this was because his relations with Hadrian had been strained – or to return to Northumbria, but to go rather to Wessex where he may have expected to receive land for a monastery from the king, Cenwalh, by whom he had been befriended on earlier occasions.[11] And again we may wonder if his attention had been directed towards Wessex by Agilbert, the bishop of Paris, but his purpose was defeated by Cenwalh's death at this time. In the previous year Osuiu, king of Northumbria, at whose court Benedict had served as a young man, but who had later forbidden Alchfrith to accompany Benedict to Rome, had died and been succeeded by Ecgfrith in February 671. Perhaps it was news of this change which prompted Benedict to go back to his native Northumbria which, so far as we know, he had not visited for some twenty years. Wilfrid, from whom he had parted company at Lyons *c.* 653, was now back in Northumbria, with episcopal orders, and busily engaged on the repair of the church at York as well as the building of his two new churches at Ripon and Hexham. He had weathered the storm caused by Theodore's determination to increase the number of Northumbrian bishoprics and was enjoying one of the few periods of peace in his stormy life.

The outcome of Benedict's visit to King Ecgfrith, to whom he recounted his experiences since leaving Northumbria and to whom he showed the books and relics brought back from his most recent journey, was a gift of land for the endowment of a monastery on the north bank of the river Wear not far from its mouth. The gift, of 70 households according to one source, and of 50 households, but later increased, according to another,[12] had previously been part of the king's estates, not land which had previously been taken away from others, as Bede was at pains to emphasise, no doubt with an eye on the different practices of later times.[13] Some of the endowments of Wilfrid's new church at Ripon which was dedicated at about this same time, were given 'with the agreement and over the signatures of the bishops and all the chief men',[14] and it may well be that Benedict, accustomed to the ways of Gaul and Italy, secured some written confirmation of the gift, but unfortunately there are no surviving documents relating to any of the estates of either Wearmouth or Jarrow at any time before the Norman Conquest. We may presume that the monastery at Wearmouth was built on the land given by King Ecgfrith and that the estate lay along the north bank of the river, but we cannot equate the amount of land given – *terra septuaginta familiarum* – with modern acres.

Benedict Biscop, now mature in years, rich in experience gained by his travels and devoted to the monastic ideals which he had learnt at Lérins, turned with vigour to his new venture, despite ill-health. He began by securing the help of a fellow-Northumbrian nobleman, Ceolfrith, who like Benedict himself, had abandoned secular life and become a monk in early manhood. Born *c.* 642 Ceolfrith was to die on his way to Rome in his 75th year after being abbot of Bede's monastery for 35 years and it was he, perhaps even more than Benedict Biscop himself, who became the dominant influence in Bede's life. He went first to a monastery at Gilling, in the North Riding of Yorkshire, whose second abbot was his own brother, Cynefrith. The house had been founded by King Osuiu in expiation of a crime, and its first abbot, Trumhere, though of English birth, received his education and his ecclesiastical orders from the Irish, later becoming bishop among the Mercians. When Ceolfrith reached Gilling *c.* 660 his brother had already left, going like many other Englishmen at this time to continue his studies in Ireland, and the monastery was being governed by Tunberht who later became bishop of Hexham. Perhaps because of the circumstances of its foundation Gilling seems not to have prospered and it has left no mark in later history. Ceolfrith's arrival was followed soon afterwards by the great outbreak of plague and the monastery seems then to have been abandoned. The abbot, with Ceolfrith and many of the monks, went at Wilfrid's invitation to Ripon.[15]

Wilfrid had acquired Ripon after the group of monks, including Eata and Cuthbert of Melrose, to whom it had originally been given, had left, choosing to continue in the Scottish ways learnt at Melrose rather than conform to Roman ways as a condition of remaining at Ripon. The chronology of these events is uncertain, though it is clear beyond doubt that the dispute which led to Eata's withdrawal occurred some years before the synod of Whitby, and it is probable that Wilfrid got possession of Ripon *c.* 660, with Ceolfrith and his fellow monks moving from Gilling to Ripon three or four years later. During the next ten years or so while Ceolfrith was a monk at Ripon he would be closely concerned with the physical transformation of the monastery from the primitive aspect which it is likely to have had during Eata's days to the more enduring and grandiose form which Wilfrid imposed upon it. He would witness the early stages in the building, and possibly the completion, of the new stone church. It is likely that he would see the rich vestments acquired for the altar, as well as the copy of the Gospels written in letters of gold. He would learn about the use of choirs from the teaching of Ædde and Æona, the two Kentish singing-masters brought to Ripon by Wilfrid, and it is possible that he may also have acquired some knowledge of the Rule of St Benedict.

Ceolfrith was ordained priest at Ripon by Wilfrid when he was aged about 27, and soon afterwards he travelled southwards to gain wider knowledge of the practices of monastic life. He went first to Kent where he is likely to have met Theodore and Benedict Biscop lately arrived from Rome. Indeed if Benedict remained at St Augustine's monastery in Canterbury for the years 669–71, it is certain that he and Ceolfrith would meet there, and it is a fair conjecture that from such a meeting may have arisen Benedict's subsequent request for Ceolfrith's help in the foundation of Wearmouth. From Kent Ceolfrith went to East Anglia to visit Botulph, abbot of the monastery at Iken, overlooking the estuary of the Alde some three or four miles inland from the coast, within a few miles of Rendlesham, an estate of the East Anglian kings at this date, and within a few miles also of the royal mausoleum at Sutton Hoo where the ship with its renowned treasure had not been long buried. Nothing further is known of Botulph from early sources, save that he enjoyed a widespread reputation for learning and for the quality of his spiritual life.[16]

From East Anglia Ceolfrith returned to Ripon. Although he had not had the wider experience won by Benedict and Wilfrid from their Gaulish and Italian travels, his biographer could later claim, perhaps with no more than pardonable exaggeration, that at that time no man could be found of greater learning in the ecclesiastical or monastic rule. How it was that Benedict succeeded in persuading Ceolfrith to leave Ripon we do not know, though we may guess that the ways of Wilfrid seemed unattractive to a man who, despite his priestly orders, his learning and his noble birth, yet enjoyed holding the office of monastic baker, sifting the flour, cleaning the oven and baking the bread. For all Wilfrid's achievements, and they were considerable, he seems not to have been interested in scholarship. Save for Hexham, and that thanks to the work of Acca, none of Wilfrid's foundations became centres of scholarship, and it may have been this factor that attracted Ceolfrith to join himself with Benedict Biscop whose scholarly interests were already apparent. From Benedict's point of view the help of Ceolfrith was doubly valuable in that not only was he instructed in monastic discipline, but was also in priest's orders and so could perform the service of the altar.

REFERENCES

1   *EVW c.* iii, also *Frithegodi Breviloquium*, ed. A. Campbell (Zurich 1950), *c.* iii. See also H. Ström, *Old English Personal Names in Bede's History* (Lund 1939), 65.

2   K. Hughes, 'The Changing Theory and Practice of Irish Pilgrimage,' *Journ. Eccles. Hist.* XI (1960), 143–51.

3   *HAbb c.* 1.

4   *EVW c.* iii.

5   *HE* III, 20; V, 19; *EVW c.* iii.

6   *Acts* XV, 36–9.

7   *HAbb c.* 2.

8   *HAbb c.* 3 and *Bed. Hom.* I, 13, *lines* 107–13. Florence of Worcester gives 665 for the second journey and the *ASC* northern recension 667 for Wigheard's arrival, but these are probably no more than inferences from Bede's account.

9   *HE* IV, 1.

10 *Bed. Hom.* I, 13, *lines* 101–7.

11 *HAbb c.* 4.

12 Cf. *HAbb c.* 4 with *AVCeol c.* 7.

13 *Bed. Hom.* I, 13, *lines* 113–16.

14 *EVW c.* xvii.

15 *AVCeol cc.* 1–3.

16 *AVCeol c.* 4. I accept the identification of *Icanho* with Iken proposed by F. S. Stevenson, *Proc. Suffolk Inst. of Arch. and Nat. Hist.* xviii (1922), 29–52. For relations between Botulph's monastery and Much Wenlock in the west midlands see H. P. R. Finberg, *The Early Charters of the West Midlands* (Leicester 1961), 207–8.

living, sleeping, eating and cooking, are likely to have been of timber, the customary building material among the Anglo-Saxons at this age, but Benedict was determined that from the first the church should be after the fashion of buildings such as he had seen on his travels in Gaul and Italy. The church at Wearmouth, Bede wrote, was to be a stone building constructed *iuxta Romanorum ... morem*, a phrase which should be interpreted as referring to the materials used rather than to the style of the building itself. Elsewhere Bede refers to the desire of Nechtan, king of the Picts, to build a church *iuxta morem Romanorum ... de lapide*, to the church at Whithorn which was called *Candida Casa* because it was built of stone which was not usual among the Britons – *insolito Brettonibus more* – and to the church at Lindisfarne which was not built of stone but of hewn oak with a thatched roof *more Scottorum*.[3] Although supplies of building stone would be available on a number of abandoned Roman sites at no great distance, local skills were inadequate for the kind of church Benedict wished to have and he therefore crossed the sea to Gaul to secure from a friend, Abbot Torhthelm, both master-builders (*architecti*) and stone-masons (*cementarii*). We do not know the whereabouts of Torhthelm's monastery, but it is a matter of some note that a man with an English name should have been abbot of a monastery in Gaul at this date.

While Benedict was away in Gaul difficulties arose at Wearmouth. Ceolfrith, confronted with the jealousies and bitter persecutions of some of the high-born members of the community who would not submit to monastic discipline, found his responsibilities greater than he could carry and he decided to return to the more peaceful life at Ripon. Bede says nothing of these troubles of which we learn only from the *Life of Ceolfrith*, but both sources in telling of the death of Benedict some fifteen years later hint at one possible cause. In his address from his deathbed Benedict spoke of a brother from whom he had long been estranged, one who, though his brother in the flesh, 'walks not in the way of truth', and rather than have this brother succeed him in the office of abbot he would prefer the whole monastery to be reduced to a waste place.[4] Ceolfrith's position may well have been made difficult in Benedict's absence, especially if there were others seeking to make profit for themselves out of the king's benefaction. On his return from Gaul Benedict went to Ripon and was able to persuade Ceolfrith to go back to Wearmouth with him.

According to the *Life of Ceolfrith* Benedict went to Gaul in the year after the foundation of the monastery – *secundo fundati monasterii anno*. Bede, with slight variation, states that he went when an interval of not more than one year had elapsed since the foundation of the monastery – *nec plusquam unius anni spatio post fundatum monasterium interiecto*.[5] Since Bede does not say that less than one year had elapsed, the phrase should be taken to mean that one year had elapsed, but not two. Accordingly, if 673 is accepted as the date of foundation, both sources point to 674 as the date of Benedict's journey, in which case the building of the church cannot have begun at the earliest before the summer or autumn of 674 and more probably in 675. The work proceeded so rapidly that within less than a year from the laying of the foundations the roof was on and mass was being said within the building, even though there was still work to be done. Benedict's next need was for glass-makers of whom, according to Bede, there were none in Britain at that time. Wilfrid had used glass for the windows of the church at York whose restoration had been completed three or four years earlier, but this fact does not necessarily invalidate Bede's statement about the lack of glass-makers in Britain, since Wilfrid, like Benedict, may have got his glass or his glass-makers from Gaul. Almost a hundred years later the abbot of Wearmouth and Jarrow was asking the archbishop of Mainz if he could send him someone who could make glass vessels, because his own people were not skilled in the art. Benedict on this occasion, perhaps remembering what had happened on his previous visit to Gaul, did not go himself, but sent messengers to bring the glass-makers back. They were needed, Bede writes, *ad cancellandas aecclesiae porticumque et caenaculorum eius fenestras. Cancellare*, 'to lattice', implies the use of small leaded pieces of glass. *Caenaculum* could mean either 'refectory' or 'upper storey', but if it had meant the former one would not have expected the use of the plural. Moroever, since surviving architectural remains have suggested the possibility of an upper floor above the nave of the church, and since this passage seems to refer to the church in particular rather than to the monastic buildings in general, it should probably be translated 'for latticing the windows of the church and its chapels and upper storeys'.

The glass-makers not only completed the work which they had come to do, but they also gave the English instruction in their craft which, as Bede remarks, was well suited for the manufacture of lamps for the enclosed places in the church as well as of glass vessels of many different uses. Other items needed for the church, but not obtainable at home, such as sacred vessels for the service of the altar and vestments, were also procured by Benedict from abroad. When it was completed the church was dedicated to St Peter, but the exact date of dedication is not known since there is no surviving counterpart at Wearmouth to the inscription which records the dedication of the church at Jarrow to St Paul. The year of dedication is likely to have been 675 or 676.

When the building of the church had been completed and the life of the monastery organised according to rule, Benedict set out once more to Rome, this being his fifth visit and the fourth time that he had made the journey directly from England. Taking with him Ceolfrith who was anxious to learn more in Rome than he had been able to do in Britain about the duties of the priesthood, he left the monastery in charge of a priest and kinsman, Eosterwine, who later became abbot. We do not know when the travellers set out, but we do know that when they reached Rome the papacy was occupied by Agatho who was elected only in the summer of 678, and we know also that they were back in England by 679 or early in 680. Although there were no doubt some pilgrims who travelled in twos and threes, or perhaps even as solitaries, it would surely be a mistake to envisage two high-born men such as Benedict and Ceolfrith travelling in this fashion. Even though their company may not have grown to the number of the 80 who went with Ceolfrith in

716, there were great dangers to be faced, other than the mere physical hardships involved, in a journey of more than 2,000 miles on foot, on horseback and by sea. To meet these dangers and to protect the treasures which the travellers intended to bring back with them a group of armed retainers would certainly be needed.

Nothing has been recorded about the course of the journey itself, either outward or homeward, but the travellers reached Rome safely and were honourably received there by Pope Agatho. In retrospect this particular journey of Benedict's seemed of sufficient importance to Bede to be given some prominence in the *Ecclesiastical History*, as well as in the *History of the Abbots*,[6] and if we recall his survey of the state of the church in Northumbria written in 734[7] we can understand why he regarded the letter of privilege given by Agatho as being by no means the least important part of the large quantities of spiritual merchandise brought back with them by the travellers. The letter itself has not survived and apart from a general statement that it was designed to secure the safety and freedom of the monastery from all external interference in perpetuity, we know only that it contained specific reference to the freedom of the monastery to elect its abbot on grounds of personal merit rather than of hereditary qualification. Bede was at pains to emphasise that the privilege had been secured 'with the permission, agreement, desire and encouragement' of King Ecgfrith and he records that after it had been brought back to England it was publicly confirmed by the king and bishops assembled in synod. Perhaps Bede had in mind the quarrel of Wilfrid and Ecgfrith and the accompanying rejection of papal authority embodied in documents brought from Rome by Wilfrid. Wilfrid's own case shows clearly enough why an abbot might wish to seek papal protection against interference either by civil authority or by the bishop of the diocese, and shows also how ineffective such protection might be with Rome so far away. But Wearmouth and Jarrow were royal foundations by origin and their history, so far as it is known, tells only of good relations with successive Northumbrian kings.

[169]

When the travellers returned to England they had in their company John, *archicantor* of the church of St Peter in Rome and abbot of the Roman monastery of St Martin *post S. Petrum*.[8] Abbot John was sent to England with a twofold commission from Pope Agatho – to teach the monks at Wearmouth the method of singing which was practised at St Peter's itself and to make diligent enquiry into the state of the faith in England. For the latter purpose he brought with him a copy of the decrees of the Lateran Council of 649 which he presented to a synod of the English church summoned to Hatfield by Archbishop Theodore. A copy of the proceedings of the synod which had found the faith free from all taint of heresy, was given to Abbot John to take back with him to Rome. He himself died on the way but the testimony was taken on by others. Bede's historical sense rightly led him to give prominence to this aspect of Abbot John's mission in the *Ecclesiastical History*,[9] whereas in the sources more particularly concerned with Wearmouth we learn only of the other aspect of his mission.

The first singing-master in Northumbria known to us by name was James the Deacon, a member of the mission of Paulinus who remained in his church at York after Paulinus himself had withdrawn to Kent on the death of Edwin. When peace had been restored after the accession of Oswald, James, then living mostly in a village near Catterick, taught many of the faithful to sing 'according to the fashion of the Romans or of the men of Kent'. James survived – *senex et plenus dierum* – until Bede's own time, that is at least until 672. Excepting the instruction given by James the Deacon, singing in the churches of the English was confined to Kent until the times of Archbishop Theodore when it began to spread more widely. Putta who was appointed to the see of Rochester was a skilled singer in the Roman manner which he had learnt from some members of the Gregorian mission. Wilfrid brought the singing-masters Ædde and Æona from Kent to Ripon and with their help he introduced the 'use of a double choir singing in harmony with reciprocal responsions and antiphons'. In later years when the singing at Hexham had fallen from its previous excellence Acca, himself a skilful singer, turned again to Kent for a teacher, though by his name, Maban, he was not English.[10]

When Abbot John reached Wearmouth he taught the singers the ceremonial manner of singing, as he himself practised it in St Peter's at Rome, and also how to read aloud. In addition, he had committed to writing everything that was needed for the celebration of days of festival throughout the complete cycle of the church year. Much of what he had had put into writing at this time was still preserved in the library forty or more years later when Bede was writing the *History of the Abbots*, and had been copied by many people from elsewhere. He also taught singers who came to him for instruction from almost all the other monasteries of Northumbria.[11] The *Life of Ceolfrith* describes John as teaching singing *et uiua uoce simul et litteris*, but we should not infer either from this passage or from Bede's reference to written works that scores with musical notation were being used at this date. The singers would learn the tunes *uiua uoce* from their teacher and only the words to be sung or chanted would be in writing. John's activities were not confined to the teaching of singing, for he also gave instruction in another skill which had an important part to play in regular monastic observance, the art of reading aloud, an art difficult enough to practice at any time in a ceremonial context and all the more so when the matter to be read was in an unfamiliar language and perhaps not always fully understood by those who did the reading.

It seems unlikely that within a bare two or three years of the building of the church at Wearmouth there would already be scribes capable of copying not only the decrees of the Lateran Council of 649 which Abbot John had brought from Rome, but also all the material which he had given them for all the church festivals of the year. Perhaps we ought rather to envisage Abbot John being accompanied by his own scribes who would be able to write their own account of the state of the faith in the English church. None of these early documents has survived but it may have been through the agency of Abbot John that the Mediterranean uncial hand, later developed to such a high degree of excellence by the scribes of Wearmouth and Jarrow, was first introduced. When we reflect upon the consequences for Bede's monastery, whether they were to be experienced in the choir, at the lectern or in the scriptorium, and upon the consequences for other monasteries whose monks had themselves gone to Wearmouth to learn, it becomes difficult to exaggerate the importance of Abbot John's visit.

The travellers also brought back with them a supply of sacred relics, some for Wearmouth itself and some for other English churches, a large number of books and a collection of pictures. The sources do not specify any particular relics, nor do they name any individual books, but the pictures have been described in some detail. The *Life of Ceolfrith* refers only to Benedict's wish to secure in Rome 'a representation of the stories of the Scriptures worthy of reverence',[12] without stating what he did in fact bring back. Bede on the other hand, who had a lifelong familiarity with the paintings themselves, described their content in detail. He uses the two words *picturae* and *imagines*, but in such a way as to show that by *imagines* he meant the representations of divine or human beings displayed on the *picturae*. In other words the *imagines* were part of the *picturae* and not distinct objects. The pictures were to be used for the adornment of St Peter's church at Wearmouth. Along its south wall were placed scenes from the Gospels, while scenes from the Revelation of St John were displayed along the north wall. Bede's account which, so far as the north and south walls are concerned, is quite free from ambiguity, implies that the scenes displayed were of some elaboration involving groups of figures, and thus it is difficult to avoid the conclusion that by *picturae* Bede meant two-dimensional pictures or paintings such as we still understand by those terms. We should probably envisage a series of separate paintings displayed at intervals along the north and south walls. Since no fragment of any of these works has survived, we can only guess at the manner of their execution, but we may think of the Madonna and Child in Sta. Francesca Romana in Rome which was painted in a wax medium on linen glued to a wooden panel and is held to be of seventh-century date, if not earlier.[13]

There remains one other painting or series of paintings which presents some difficulty: *imaginem uidelicet beatae Dei genetricis semperque uirginis Mariae, simul et duodecim apostolorum, quibus mediam eiusdem aecclesiae testudinem, ducto a pariete ad parietem tabulato praecingeret.*[14] Bede here used the singular *imaginem*, in contrast with the *imagines* of the north and south walls, thus seeming to imply that the Virgin and the twelve Apostles were all depicted on one painting. On the other hand, the relative plural *quibus* suggests the possibility that there was one painting of the Virgin and other paintings of the Apostles. The second difficulty is of the way in which this painting or series of paintings was displayed. The passage quoted above may be translated: 'namely a representation of the blessed mother of God and ever-virgin Mary, and likewise of the twelve Apostles, with which he might gird the central vault of the church itself after wooden boarding had been laid from wall to wall.' But the difficulty is to know exactly what Bede meant by *tabulatum*. Did he mean that the upper vault forming the roof over the nave of the church was shut off by the insertion of a flat wooden ceiling to which the paintings were then attached so as to give something of the same effect as a painted ceiling? Or did he mean, as seems more likely, that some form of wooden staging resembling a rood screen was built across the church from wall to wall with the painting or paintings displayed upon it vertically? Whatever may have been the exact arrangement, the result, Bede remarks, was that all those who entered the church, even though they were unable to read, beheld the countenance of Christ and his saints in whichever direction they looked. And though they were looking only at pictures, they would be prompted to reflect upon the Incarnation of the Lord, and with the perils of the last judgement before them they might examine their own hearts the more closely. Bede's attitude towards paintings in churches corresponds closely with the view expressed a hundred years earlier by Gregory the Great in letters written to Serenus, bishop of Marseilles. Gregory had heard that Serenus had ordered some images (*imagines*) in churches to be destroyed and thrown out. While praising his zeal in seeking to prevent the

17

The Foundation of Jarrow

The zeal displayed by Benedict Biscop and the evident success of his monastery at Wearmouth encouraged King Ecgfrith to endow a second foundation, and for this purpose he gave Benedict a site some few miles away from Wearmouth on a low eminence at the confluence of the Don with the Tyne where extensive mudflats, commemorated in the place-name Jarrow, offered a sheltered haven for shipping. Bede himself never used any other name save Jarrow, but other sources refer to the place as *portus Egfridi regis* and to Ecgfrith's monastery as *æt Donemuthan*.[1] The new foundation was colonised by a group of monks who moved from Wearmouth with Ceolfrith as their abbot. The *Life of Ceolfrith* says that the migrants numbered 22, but only 10 of them were tonsured monks. Bede gives the number of monks as 17 and it is very probable that, as a boy of 9 or 10, he was among the company which moved to the new foundation. Developments at Jarrow followed much the same pattern as had been set at Wearmouth. Ecgfrith's endowment was given 'eight years after they had begun the aforesaid monastery', i.e. Wearmouth.[2] First the necessary monastic buildings were erected and 'after one year' Ceolfrith and his companions moved. 'In the third year from the foundation of the monastery' the building of the church began and work proceeded so fast that it was dedicated in the second year after that in which it had been begun.[3] Unfortunately no early source relates these chronological data to the year of the Incarnation, and still less to any particular month within a year. Despite their relative detail they leave some slight ambiguities. We do not know whether to reckon the date of Ecgfrith's second gift as eight years from 674 when work at Wearmouth 'began' or from

673 when it was formally founded, nor do we know whether our authorities in referring to a 'year' mean a calendar year, a regnal year or even a monastic year. Fortunately we do know beyond all reasonable doubt the date of the dedication of the new church at Jarrow. It is recorded on the contemporary dedication inscription from which we learn that the ceremony took place on 23 April in the 15th year of King Ecgfrith and the fourth of Abbot Ceolfrith.[4] Again there is no correlation in the inscription with the year of the Incarnation, since the era *annus domini* had not yet come into common use, but the 15th regnal year of King Ecgfrith began in February 685, and we may therefore date the dedication of the church to St Paul on 23 April 685, a date which was in fact a Sunday, the normal day for the dedication of a new church. On the whole it seems likely that the new monastery was founded at some time within the calendar year 681.

As the body cannot be torn away from the head through which it breathes, neither can the head be heedless of the body without which it cannot live – this was the analogy used by Bede to describe the relationship of the two monasteries to each other.[5] Yet during the first few years of their joint existence the two houses were independent of one another ecclesiastically as well as geographically, with Benedict Biscop abbot of St Peter's at Wearmouth and Ceolfrith abbot of St Paul's at Jarrow. Moreover, Benedict appointed Eosterwine, a kinsman in priest's orders, as abbot at Wearmouth, so that for several years from 681 there were no less than three abbots at the two monasteries. The ground on which this irregular arrangement was defended was that Benedict Biscop, because of his wisdom and wide experience was frequently required to attend upon the king at court and therefore had not time enough to handle the affairs of his monastery. In addition he was making preparations for another journey to Rome. Bede, probably using the *Liber Pontificalis* as his source, defended the arrangement by referring to the tradition that St Peter himself had appointed two pontiffs to govern the church at Rome. This situation continued for five years until the death of Eosterwine in March 686. Benedict

Biscop was away in Rome at the time and in his absence the monks of Wearmouth, with Ceolfrith's approval, elected Sigfrid as abbot, but by 688 both Benedict Biscop, now returned from Rome, and Sigfrid, were sick men. On 12 May 688 Ceolfrith was appointed sole abbot over both houses. Sigfrid died on 22 August 688 and Benedict Biscop himself on 12 January 689.[6] Thereafter, so far as we can trace their history, Wearmouth and Jarrow continued under the rule of a single abbot. Bede, writing of himself at the end of his *History*, described himself as 'priest of the monastery of the blessed apostles Peter and Paul which is at Wearmouth and at Jarrow'.

Eosterwine was born in 650 and, like his older kinsman Benedict Biscop, had served as a fighting man at the North-umbrian court before abandoning his secular life at the age of 24 to become one of the original community at Wearmouth. He was ordained to the priesthood in 679 and appointed abbot in 682, holding the office for four years until his death in 686 at the age of 36.[7] Bede's account of the abbacy of Eosterwine whom he portrays as a cheerful gentle man of great physical strength, readier to warn than to punish transgressors, helps to remind us that however great may have been the scholarly distinction of some, much of the daily life of most of the monks would necessarily be passed in supplying the material needs of the community. Although he was abbot, Eosterwine delighted in using his strength on the tasks of threshing and winnowing the corn, milking the ewes and cows, working in the bakehouse and in the kitchen. If monastic business took him outside the precincts of the monastery and he came upon some of the brothers at work, he would take his turn at guiding the plough, wielding the smith's hammer or any other task that needed to be done. We can also win at least a brief glimpse of the monastic buildings from Bede's account of the way in which, even after he had been made abbot, Eosterwine would eat in common with the other brethren, and of how, even during his last illness, when he knew that he was dying, he still slept in the common dormitory, save for the last five days of his life when he moved into a room apart.

Eosterwine died on the night of 6 March 686, one of the victims of a widespread outbreak of plague which caused the death of many monks both at Wearmouth and at Jarrow. This disaster, befalling within less than a year of the dedication of the church at Jarrow might well have brought about the extinction of the new community. Of those who could read or preach or recite the antiphons or responsions, all were carried off by the sickness save Ceolfrith himself and one young lad who had been taught by Ceolfrith and who was still alive and in priest's orders when the *Life of Ceolfrith* was being written. The writer of the *Life* recalled how this same lad, now grown to manhood, used to tell of his master's deeds either in writing or by word of mouth to all who wanted to know.[8] Between them, these two, the abbot and the boy, contrived to carry on with the daily service until others could be trained to help them in their task. It has long been supposed that the lad who figures in this incident which is recorded only in the *Life of Ceolfrith* and not by Bede in the *History of the Abbots*, was in fact Bede himself. If he was born *c.* 672 he would be aged about 14 when the two monasteries were smitten with the plague. He himself never says whether he spent his life at Wearmouth or at Jarrow, but the tradition of his particular association with Jarrow, resting presumably on his own statement that he was educated first at the hands of Benedict Biscop and later of Ceolfrith whom we know to have been at Jarrow, is old enough to deserve respect. The aptness of the chronological evidence, the reference to the boy who had become a priest engaged in the writing or telling of history, and the fact that he himself does not record the incident, all these are consistent with the belief that the boy who figures in the story of the plague was indeed the young Bede.

Meanwhile Benedict Biscop had gone on his sixth and last visit to Rome. King Ecgfrith who was killed in battle on 21 May 685, was still alive when he set out, and Eosterwine who died in March 686 was dead when he got back. Some five or six years had passed since his previous visit to Rome and he was now a man approaching 60. Nothing has been recorded about the journey itself but he returned from it, as from his previous visit, heavily laden with gifts for the two foundations, including another large supply of books and also a number of pictures. We know nothing in detail about the books, but once again Bede has left an account of the pictures in which he refers both to the subject matter of some of them, and also to the way in which they were arranged. One group, portraying the story of Christ, was used by Benedict 'to garland in full circle the whole church of the blessed mother of God which he had built in the older monastery'.[9] This is the first reference to a church at Wearmouth dedicated to the Virgin Mary. It was not unusual for there to be two, or even more than two, churches within a single monastery, and it must be inferred from this passage that a second church, dedicated to St Mary, had been built at Wearmouth before Benedict set out for Rome, and that some of the pictures which he had brought back from this visit were to be displayed along its walls in much the same way as those brought back from Rome on the fifth visit were displayed in the church of St Peter. The other pictures were for St Paul's church at Jarrow. They were designed to demonstrate, by means of type and anti-type, certain correspondences between the Old and the New Testaments. Bede illustrates how this was done by describing two of the pairs of pictures. One pair showed Isaac carrying the wood with which he was to be sacrificed and immediately next to it a picture of the Lord carrying the Cross upon which He too was to be sacrificed. In a second pair Moses raising the serpent in the desert was displayed beside the Son of Man raised aloft upon the Cross. In addition, Benedict brought back with him two silken cloaks of incomparable workmanship which he later gave to King Aldfrith and his councillors in exchange for the land of three households on the south bank of the Wear near its mouth.

On his return from Rome Benedict learnt that King Ecgfrith had lately been killed in battle against the Picts, at Dunnichen Moss in Angus, and that he had been succeeded by Aldfrith, described by Bede as Ecgfrith's bastard brother.[10] Aldfrith, son of Osuiu and of an unknown mother, won for himself a remarkable reputation for learning among men who themselves rank as the greatest scholars of the Anglo-Saxon period. Knowing the tendencies of Eddius to exaggeration, we might be inclined to discount something of his phrase *rex sapientissimus* were it not that Aldhelm dedicated to Aldfrith his work on metres, that Irish tradition remembered him as a scholar of renown, that Bede described him as *uir undecumque doctissimus* and *uir in scripturis doctissimus*, and that Alcuin wrote of him as *rex simul atque magister*.[11] Of his early life we know next to nothing save that some years of it were spent in 'self-imposed exile to gratify his love of wisdom' among the Irish, and specifically at Iona where he became the friend and pupil of its ninth abbot, Adomnan.[12] His stay among the Irish, to whom he became known as Fland Fína had been long enough for him to win a reputation as a writer in their own language.

It was of great significance for the further development of Wearmouth and Jarrow that for the next 20 years (685–705) the monks were to enjoy the protection and patronage of a scholarly king whose knowledge had not been acquired in Gaul or Italy but from the teaching of Scottish and Irish scholars. One of the most striking features in the early history of the twin monasteries is the closeness of their relationship with Rome, despite the distance and all the dangers of travel. The churches themselves, the singing and chanting, the first books for the libraries, the text of the Gospels, the uncial hand practised by the scribes – all these, so far as our evidence goes – came either directly from Italy or intermediately through Gaul. Even after the death of Benedict Biscop the closeness of the Roman relationship was maintained by delegations sent to Rome in 701 and 716, but after Aldfrith's accession in 685 there are some signs of a growing and fruitful contact with centres of Celtic Christianity.

King Ecgfrith's death in battle against the Picts was regarded as a punishment for the sins he had committed in refusing to listen to those who had tried to dissuade him not only from attacking the Picts in 685, but also from sending an army against the Irish in 684. Despite the fact that it was Ecgfrith who had given their first endowments to both Wearmouth and

Jarrow, Bede severely condemned his action in attacking the Irish, that 'unoffending people, always most friendly to the English nation'.[13] Aldfrith himself had been in Iona before becoming king and after his accession, Adomnan, ninth abbot of Iona and the biographer of Columba, paid two visits to Northumbria, probably during the years 686–8. He had been sent to Aldfrith as an ambassador from the Irish to re-establish the friendly relations between the Irish and the Northumbrians which had been damaged by Ecgfrith's attack in 684, and he was able to take back to Ireland 60 Irishmen who had been taken prisoner in the campaign. We know that during one or other, and possibly both, of his Northumbrian visits, Adomnan went to Wearmouth and Jarrow where he met Ceolfrith and discussed with him the differing English and Irish monastic practices. We may think it very probable that Bede, then aged about 17, would meet the visiting abbot from Iona and that the discussions which took place during his visit would arouse Bede's interest in the complexities of the Easter problem. After staying in the monastery for some while and examining the manner of life practised there, Adomnan returned to Iona and tried to persuade the monks to accept the observance of the catholic Easter. He was not successful but in Ireland itself he did succeed in persuading many of those who were not subject to Iona to make the change. At this date most of the southern Irish had long since accepted the catholic Easter, but it was not until 716 that Iona also came into conformity.[14]

During the years 686–9 there were other changes which had a more immediate effect upon Wearmouth and Jarrow. When it became apparent that neither Sigfrid nor Benedict Biscop had long to live, Ceolfrith was appointed sole abbot of both houses, on 12 May 688, with a deathbed injunction from Benedict that thereafter the two houses should always remain under the control of a single abbot who was not to be chosen on grounds of consanguinity, but solely because of his fitness for the task. Benedict Biscop was buried at Wearmouth *in porticu sancti Petri ad orientem altaris*.[15] Late in life Bede honoured his first teacher and abbot by composing for him a homily to be delivered on his

festal day, the only one of the fifty homilies Bede wrote to be
devoted to a contemporary individual rather than to the major
church festivals.[16] For Bede, Benedict Biscop was the man who,
in the words of St Matthew's Gospel, had forsaken all to follow
Christ, the man who would receive a hundredfold reward and
would inherit everlasting life. A tireless traveller, always seeking
the best, it had not been his way, as it had been of some, to
return from his journeys empty-handed and without profit.
Stone-masons, glass-makers, sacred relics, books, teachers of
singing and reading, paintings, letters of privilege, sacred vessels,
vestments for the altars – all these and more he had brought
back for his monastery. The list must surely impress us no less
than it impressed Bede. 'In these and suchlike ways', Bede
wrote, 'he strove to concern himself with so many matters, that
there was no need for us to labour any more in this fashion. He
journeyed so many times to places across the sea to the end that
we, being abundantly endowed with all kinds of saving knowledge, might be at rest within the cloisters of the monastery,
serving Christ in sure and certain freedom.'[17] Benedict Biscop
was not a man who won fame by working the hagiographer's
miracles, or sanctity by fighting demons in desert places, but a
man who, with a rich experience of the world and a clear vision
of a manner of life before him, devoted all his abundant energy
to overcoming every kind of practical obstacle which might
hinder the realisation of that vision. Born into a bleak and
largely pagan world, he bequeathed a legacy which enriched the
Christian civilisation of western Europe for centuries to come.

REFERENCES

1   Symeon of Durham, *Hist. Dun. Ecc. RS* I, 51. *ASC* 794 *D, E.*
2   *AVCeol c.* 11.
3   *HAbb* 7; *AVCeol* 12.
4   P. Hunter Blair, *An Introduction to Anglo-Saxon England* (Cambridge 1956), p. 156 and Pl. VI.
5   *HAbb c.* 7.
6   *AVCeol cc.* 15–18. *HAbb cc.* 10–13.

7   *HAbb c.* 8.

8   *AVCeol c.* 14.

9   *HAbb c.* 9. I take *maiore* in this passage to mean 'older' rather than 'larger'.

10   *BVC c.* XXIV.

11   *EVW c.* XLIV; *HE* IV, 26; V, 12. Alcuin, *De Sanct. Ebor.* ed. *RS 1*, 845.

12   *BVC* XXIV; *AVC* III, 6. See also *AdVC* p. 54.

13   *HE* IV, 26.

14   *AdVC* p. 94 and II, 46.

15   *AVCeol c.* 18.

16   *Bed. Hom.* I, 13.

17   *Ibid. lines* 185–9.

18

Abbacy of Ceolfrith

Reckoning from his appointment on 12 May 688, at about the age of 46, Ceolfrith, who had already ruled Jarrow for several years held office as sole abbot of the two foundations for just over 28 years. These years from 688 to 716, within which some of the earlier works of Bede were written, may well have been among the most fruitful and prosperous in their whole history. Under Ceolfrith's rule, with the support of a sympathetic king, new oratories were built, additions were made to the plate and vestments of the churches, the size of the library was doubled, fresh endowments of land were received, another mission was sent to Rome and the communities themselves expanded so greatly that when Ceolfrith laid down his office to go to Rome in 716 he left behind him in the two monasteries more than 600 monks with lands, 'that according to the customary reckoning of the English might support almost 150 households'.[1] The original endowments given by Ecgfrith amounted, if we take Bede's figure for Jarrow, to the land of 110 households. Shortly before his death Benedict Biscop was negotiating with King Aldfrith for the acquisition for Jarrow of an estate which was valued at 8 households and lay close to the river *Fresca*. The transaction was completed by Ceolfrith, and since both king and abbot were scholars who set a high price upon the materials of learning, we may guess that the price finally paid – a book – was not reached without much preliminary haggling. The book, described as a Codex Cosmographiorum, was one of those bought by Benedict in Rome. It is just possible, though in no way susceptible of proof, that this book, like the Codex Grandior, had formerly been in the library of Cassiodorus at Vivarium in southern Italy, and that it contained the works of the four cosmographers whom Cassiodorus had specially recommended for study by monks – Julius Honorius, Marcellinus, Dionysius Exiguus and Ptolemy.[2] The Cosmography of Julius Honorius was certainly known in the west in the eighth century. An uncial manuscript of the work which was probably written in Italy seems to have migrated to some centre under Anglo-Saxon influence by the eighth century when it received corrections written in an insular minuscule hand.[3]

King Aldfrith would be particularly anxious to secure the Wearmouth book on cosmography because he already had in his possession a book about the experiences of a traveller in the eastern Mediterranean. Among those who went on pilgrimage to the Holy Land in the seventh century there was a Gaulish bishop whose name was Arculf but whose see is not known. Journeying to the east c. 670 he visited not only Jerusalem, but also Damascus, Constantinople and Alexandria, as well as many islands. He was returning home by sea, presumably along the Atlantic coast of France when a violent storm drove his ship northwards up the west coast of Britain and eventually brought him after many mishaps to Iona where he was entertained by Adomnan. While he was Adomnan's guest Arculf gave him an account of his travels and Adomnan took down notes on wax tablets from which he later wrote a work which he called *De Locis Sanctis*. When he visited Northumbria Adomnan presented this work to King Aldfrith, no doubt as a present in return for the release of the Irish prisoners captured by his predecessor, and through the generosity of the king lesser persons, among whom we may number Bede, were able to read the book. A few years later, perhaps as early as c. 703, Bede himself wrote a short tract on the same theme, composed partly from his own work and partly from Adomnan's treatise. Bede's own work, also known as the *De Locis Sanctis*, concludes with a chapter describing how it had come into being through the storm which carried Arculf to Iona and also showing that he had written the work for some individual – *tibi legenda transmittimus*[4] – but as there is no dedication we do not know who the individual was, though it might well have been King Aldfrith himself since he did not die until the end of 705. In later years Bede quoted some extracts from his own *De Locis Sanctis* both in his *Commentary on Acts* and also in his *Ecclesiastical History*. As a historian Bede was very much alive to the value of Adomnan's work which derived from the experiences of a recent traveller and was therefore of great help to those who, like himself, lived far away from the Holy Places and could know no more about them than they could learn by reading.[5]

The whereabouts of the estate which King Aldfrith gave in exchange for the book on cosmography is not known since the river *Fresca* cannot now be identified, but it seems to have lain at some distance away since, after Aldfrith's death and during the reign of his successor Osred (705–11) it was exchanged for a much larger estate of 28 households which lay nearer the monastery *ad uillam Sambuce*, with an additional money payment to compensate for the greater value of the new purchase. *Sambuce* too remains unidentified. Another estate of 10 house-holds at *Daltun*, to be identified with Dalton-le-Dale, or less probably with Dawdon, in County Durham, came to Wear-mouth from Witmær who had originally received it from King Aldfrith and who had later joined the community at Wear-mouth. Witmær, though no more than a name to us, was of an earlier generation than Bede who knew him as a man 'learned in every kind of knowledge, both secular and divine'.[6] The original endowments together with the estates at *Sambuce* and Dalton-le-Dale amount to a total of 148 households. To this we should add the 3 given by King Aldfrith in exchange for the two cloaks, giving a total of about 150 households, as the *Life* expresses it, at the time of Ceolfrith's resignation.

Benedict Biscop had paid his sixth and last visit to Rome in the years 685–6 and, as Bede observed, the two foundations were evidently now so well furnished that there was the less need for further travelling. Nevertheless a group of monks were in Rome in the year 701,[7] though the little that we know about this visit derives from indirect allusion rather than from any detailed account of the journey itself. Sergius who was pope at this time (687–701) was closely concerned with the affairs of a

number of travellers from England. Apart from his involvement
in the quarrels of Wilfrid, he stood sponsor at the baptism of a
young West Saxon king, Cædwalla, who had abdicated after a
brief reign and who after being baptised in Rome, died there
very soon afterwards and was buried in St Peter's. Sergius also
received two visits from the Northumbrian missionary Willibrord and on the second occasion he consecrated him bishop to
the Frisians in the year 696.[8] We do not know when the monks
set out for Rome from Wearmouth and Jarrow, nor when they
returned, but only that they were in Rome in 701. Among their
number was Hwætbert who later became abbot in succession to
Ceolfrith in 716 and who was still holding the office more than
ten years after Bede's death. Hwætbert himself remained in
Rome for a considerable time, making use of the opportunity to
learn, copy out and bring back whatever he thought might be
useful, and no doubt it was while he was in Rome that he
acquired his skill in writing, singing, reading and teaching upon
which Bede later commented.[9] We know nothing in detail about
the fruits of this visit save that the monks brought back with
them a letter of privilege from Pope Sergius similar to that which
had been given to Benedict Biscop by Pope Agatho some years
before. After this document had been brought back to England
it was exhibited before a synod and confirmed by the signatures
of the bishops attending the synod and of King Aldfrith himself.
It was to Hwætbert that Bede dedicated both his commentary
on the Apocalypse and his scientific treatise *De Temporum
Ratione*. Through his zeal for piety he became known as Eusebius
and under that name he was the author of a collection of Latin
riddles.

The influence of Wearmouth and Jarrow which spread to
parts of the Irish church as a result of Adomnan's visits in the
years 686–8, was extended to the Pictish church in the early
years of the eighth century. Since there are no native Pictish
ecclesiastical records of this period we know nothing from the
Pictish point of view about the circumstances which prompted
the Pictish church to abandon its Celtic practices, learnt
initially from Iona, and to conform to Roman usage. According

to Bede, our sole authority, Nechtan, king of the Picts, sent a delegation to Wearmouth and Jarrow asking abbot Ceolfrith to send him a letter setting out the arguments which would enable him to confute those who wished to retain the old practices, both in the keeping of Easter and in the form of the tonsure. He also asked for mastermasons to be sent so that he could build a church in the Roman fashion, a church to be dedicated to St Peter. We do not know the exact date of this mission but it was about 710. In his *Ecclesiastical History* Bede, always ready to make the most of any opportunity to argue the cause of Rome, reproduced the full text of the long letter which was sent to Nechtan and in which the history of the Easter problem was explained.[10] By this date Bede had already written some of his earlier works, including the shorter of his two works on chronology, the *De Temporibus*, but even so there does not seem to be adequate ground for the widely-held view that Bede himself was the author of the letter. We need not doubt that this letter, with its references, certainly at several removes, to Plato's *Republic* as well as to the perils of Scylla and Charybdis, could have been written by Ceolfrith himself. Whoever the author, he remarked in the course of the letter that there were at that time many people in the churches throughout Britain who could very easily extend Easter tables as far into the future as they wished, even to the grand cycle of 532 years. Bede states that the letter was read to King Nechtan and a number of his more learned men and then translated into their own language. The king declared himself convinced by the arguments and proceeded to order the suppression of the old Easter tables based on the 84-year cycle and the distribution throughout his kingdom of the more accurate 19-year cycle which would have been the one in use throughout the English church after the synod of Whitby. A few years later, in 716, the church at Iona itself came into conformity, and there then remained only the church in Wales retaining the old ways.

The distinction achieved by Benedict Biscop's two foundations undoubtedly owed a great deal to their position as a meeting-place between Christian traditions of widely differing backgrounds. On the one hand there were close links with Rome and also with Gaul, both with the old Gallo-Roman centres of Christianity in Provençe and with the more recent monastic foundations of the north; and on the other hand there were equally close relations with Irish, Scottish and Pictish centres, where, particularly among the Irish, there was great devotion to scholarship and learning. The *Life of Ceolfrith* and the *History of the Abbots*, our main sources for the early history of the two monasteries, naturally concern themselves with major incidents – foundations, succession of abbots, furnishing of churches and libraries, relations with Rome, with the Columban church and with the Pictish church – but it would surely be a very great mistake to assume from the silence of these sources that Bede's monastery was not also in close and continuing contact with other Northumbrian monastic centres, three of them in particular – Whitby, Lindisfarne and Hexham. As we have seen, Whitby was the likely source of much of Bede's information about the traditions of the Gregorian mission. Whether or not Bede himself ever went to Lindisfarne – and he may well have done so – he was certainly well informed about its history and particularly about Cuthbert himself. We can hardly doubt that there would be frequent intercourse between Jarrow and Lindisfarne, an intercourse which would be likely to include the exchange of books. The bishopric of Hexham passed after the death of Wilfrid into the hands of Acca who had been to Rome in Wilfrid's company and to whom Bede dedicated many of his works in terms of great affection. Acca added to the work begun by Wilfrid by extending the church, adorning it with objects of gold, silver and precious stones, procuring relics for it and securing the services of a singing-master from Kent who remained at Hexham for twelve years teaching new ecclesiastical songs as well as achieving the better performance of the old which had lapsed somewhat by neglect. Acca, himself a singer of excellence, was also a scholar and Bede comments on the diligence with which he assembled a very splendid library containing a great many books.[11] The collecting of a library in the conditions of the early eighth century would have involved extensive travelling, such as has been recorded for Wearmouth and Jarrow, but of which we know nothing for Hexham. Unhappily no trace of any book from Acca's library has survived and we do not know whether any works of Biblical exegesis, hagiography or history were produced at Hexham, though it was at the prompting of Acca among others that Eddius wrote the *Life of Wilfrid*, probably at Ripon.

Bede's monastery, favoured by its geographical locality, was equally fortunate in its early abbots. Save for the short-lived Eosterwine and Sigfrid, it was governed from its foundation in 673 until at least 745 by only three men, Benedict Biscop, Ceolfrith and Hwætbert, all of whom were men of wide experience whose travels had taken them as far as Rome. Writing of the years shortly before 720, Bede remarked that in those times a great many of the English race were in the habit of going from Britain to Rome, nobles and men of common birth, women as well as men, officers of government as well as ordinary people.[12] When we recall how, in the previous century, English women had gone to be educated in the monasteries of northern Gaul and how men had travelled to Ireland in search of scholarship, we can see not only something of the fervour with which at least a small element of Anglo-Saxon society sought to make the transition from pagan barbarism to a literate Christian civilisation, but also how in England itself some of the monasteries, and particularly Bede's, after absorbing richly varied foreign influences, were in their turn able to win intellectual, and in some cases artistic, supremacy.

Many of those who went to Rome did so *pro amore Dei*, intending to return to their own countries after their visit, but others went in the hope that they might end their lives at the thresholds of the Apostles. In the early summer of 716 Abbot Ceolfrith who had already visited Rome once in company with Benedict Biscop, decided to return there for his last days. Save perhaps for the death of Bede himself, there is no incident in Anglo-Saxon history before the days of Alfred the Great which has been described in such vivid detail as the departure of Ceolfrith from his monastery.[13] Aged 74, a priest for 47 years

and an abbot for 35, he was prompted to his decision by increasing age and a sense of failing physical strength. Keeping
his own intentions to himself, he put in hand all the preparations
for the sending of an embassy to Rome. A ship was got ready,
suitable gifts were chosen and a list was compiled with the
names of those who were to go. It was only when the day of
departure itself approached that Ceolfrith revealed his own
intention to form one of the company of travellers. The monks of
Wearmouth who were the first to learn sought to dissuade him,
but he would relent only so far as to remain with them for the
remainder of that day – Tuesday 2 June 716 – and the following
night. The next day he went to Jarrow where he stayed over-
night, returning to Wearmouth as the Thursday dawned. After
mass had been sung in the churches of St Peter and St Mary at
Wearmouth, he summoned all the brethren to St Peter's church
and there, after kindling the incense himself and holding the
censor in his hand, he took up his position on the steps where he
had been accustomed to read to the congregation, and took his
farewells. Then he went to the oratory of St Lawrence in the
dormitory, and after the singing of an antiphon from Isaiah
and of the 66th Psalm, he again addressed the brethren, urging
them to live at peace with one another and with their brothers
of St Paul's at Jarrow, remembering that they were one
monastery to be ruled by one abbot. After the address and
further singing, the company made its way down to the river
bank and Ceolfrith entered a boat, sitting in the prow, with
deacons beside him, one holding a gold cross which Ceolfrith
himself had made, and the other lighted candles. The boat
crossed the river and when it reached the other side Ceolfrith,
himself overcome with grief, voiced a prayer for the company
remaining on the other bank. He then made obeisance to the
cross, mounted a horse and rode away, the day of his departure
being Thursday 4 June.

The monks of Wearmouth went back to their monastery to
consider the choosing of a successor. Before going Ceolfrith had
told them they were to celebrate his going by feasting rather
than by fasting and he had even delayed starting so that those

who were going with him might enjoy the midday meal. It was agreed among them that they would fast on the Friday until the ninth hour of the Saturday when they would break their fast before beginning to observe the vigils of Whit Sunday. On Whit Sunday itself several of the monks came to Wearmouth from Jarrow and by unanimous consent they chose Hwætbert as their new abbot. Like Bede, he had been in the monastery since childhood and if his ordination to the priesthood in 704 had been at the canonical age of 24, his birth would have fallen c. 680, making him Bede's junior by some 8 or 9 years and his age at his election to the abbacy about 36.

Immediately after he had been chosen abbot Hwætbert wrote a letter commending his predecessor to the care of the pope, now Gregory II (715–31) and then set off with a number of monks in pursuit of Ceolfrith. They found him in a monastery in a place called *Cornu Vallis* which has not been identified but which may possibly have been the monastery in which Willibrord's father lived near the mouth of the Humber. After reading the letter to Ceolfrith, Hwætbert gave it to him, with some presents to be taken to Rome, and then, after receiving Ceolfrith's advice on how to govern the monastery, he went back to Wearmouth where his election was confirmed by Acca, bishop of Hexham. Ceolfrith who had had to wait for a ship eventually sailed from the Humber on Saturday 4 July in a coasting vessel which made three calls on the way before reaching the coast of France on Wednesday 12 August, 69 days after leaving Wearmouth. He was well received in France by King Chilperic II who gave him letters of commendation for use throughout his kingdom and also commended him to Liutprand king of the Lombards. Meanwhile, Ceolfrith himself was beginning to suffer severely from the strain of the journey. One day of the sea voyage had been spent tossing in a storm and on land he had become so weak that he could no longer ride but had to be carried in a horse litter. The band of travellers which had grown to a company of no fewer than 80, eventually reached the city of Langres in the plain of Burgundy at 9 o'clock on the morning of 25 September and there, at 4 o'clock in the afternoon of the same day, Ceolfrith died, 113 days after leaving Wearmouth and with no more than half the journey completed. His body was carried to a monastery about a mile and a half to the south of the city and there it was buried in the church of the triune martyrs Speusippus, Eleusippus and Melieusippus, though Alcuin records that it was later brought back to Wearmouth. After the burial some of the monks returned to Wearmouth to tell what had happened, but others completed the journey to Rome, taking with them their gifts for the pope, among them a precious book which is still preserved in Italy and which we now know as the Codex Amiatinus.[14] When they too returned to Wearmouth they brought with them a letter from Pope Gregory to their new abbot expressing the hope that the grace which had once been given to Ceolfrith might now adorn his pupil and successor.

Bede, growing from childhood to middle age, had been intimately associated with Ceolfrith for almost forty years, and during the last months of his abbacy he had been engaged upon his *Commentary on Samuel* which he dedicated to Acca. He had already completed the first three books when Ceolfrith left and what the change meant to him personally we can best understand from the words with which he opened the fourth book of the commentary: 'After I had finished the third book of my commentary on the blessed Samuel I thought that when my delight in studying and writing had been renewed by resting for a while I would at length set my hand to the beginning of the fourth. But this rest of mine, if indeed unexpected anguish of mind can be called rest, has proved to be much longer than I had intended because of a new turn in our affairs, and particularly because of the departure of my most reverend abbot. After attending to the oversight of the monastery for a long time, he suddenly decided to go to Rome and in his old age to breathe his last breath amid places made sacred by the bodies of the blessed apostles and martyrs of Christ, bringing to the minds of those who had been entrusted to his care a sense of stunned confusion which was all the greater because his departure had been unexpected.'[15]

REFERENCES

1 *AVCeol c.* 33.
2 *CI* I, xxv.
3 *CLA* V, 550. *HAbb c.* 15.
4 Ed. P. Geyer, *CSEL, XXXIX,* 323.
5 *HE* V, 15.
6 *HAbb c.* 15.
7 *BdTR c.* XLVII, *lines* 56–65.
8 *HE* V, 7, 11.
9 *HAbb c.* 18.
10 *HE* V, 21.
11 *HE* V, 20.
12 *BdTR Chron.* ed. Mommsen, *MGH Auct. Ant.* XIII, 320.
13 *HAbb cc.* 16–23; *AVCeol cc.* 21–38.
14 See below, pp. 221–2.
15 *In I Sam.* ed. Hurst, p. 212, *lines* 1–12.

PART FOUR

Learning, Teaching and Writing

There is a closely similar passage in the slightly earlier *Life of Ceolfrith*,[3] and in his homily on Benedict Biscop Bede wrote:

He soon organised [the monastery] which he had received both within and without in a most excellent fashion according to regular discipline, not enjoining upon us rules of his own devising, but proposing for observance by himself and his companions the best-established rules of the ancient monasteries which he had learnt on his pilgrimage.[4]

These passages, although not independent of one another, leave no room for doubt that Benedict Biscop himself compiled the rule for observance at Wearmouth and Jarrow, even though this rule was original only in a very limited sense, since it was no more than a distillation of all that he had found best in his wide experience. Two other passages show that Benedict's rule was still being observed more than 25 years later. The occasion was Ceolfrith's leave-taking in 716 when he was setting out towards Rome on his final pilgrimage. The *Life of Ceolfrith* records that he then enjoined the brethren 'to keep the rule which he had taught'[5]: and in the *History of the Abbots* Bede wrote that Ceolfrith decided to lay down his office 'after a long course of monastic discipline which the wise father compiled for himself and likewise for his companions on the authority of the ancients'.[6] It is clear from the context that the *pater prouuidus* was Benedict Biscop. At this date, then, 716, after the monastery at Wearmouth had been in existence for 43 years and when Bede himself was aged about 45, the rule compiled by Benedict Biscop was still being observed at Wearmouth and Jarrow.

Nevertheless, there are references to the Rule of St Benedict of Nursia in the context of Wearmouth and Jarrow. Shortly before his death in 689 Benedict Biscop appointed Ceolfrith sole abbot of the two houses and commanded that the monastery, although situated in two places, should always remain under one abbot and be safe-guarded by the same protection of privilege, 'and in accordance with a clause in that same letter of privilege, which he had obtained from Pope Agatho, as well as with the rule of the holy father Benedict,' a new abbot must never be chosen on

the grounds of kinship.[7] Similarly, on the day of his final departure in June 716, Ceolfrith urged the brethren to appoint as
abbot one of their number 'according to the rule of the holy
father Benedict and the statutes of their privilege'.[8] These
passages seem not to leave any doubt that the Benedictine
procedure in the election of an abbot was known at Wearmouth
and Jarrow, nor that both Benedict Biscop (d. 689) and
Ceolfrith (d. 716) intended this procedure to be followed.
Nevertheless, they do not provide conclusive evidence that the
Benedictine Rule was being observed at Wearmouth and
Jarrow in respects other than that of abbatial election or even
that the complete Rule was known there as early as 688 or 716.
Since these two references to the Benedictine Rule only concern
abbatial election and since in both instances immediately
adjacent clauses refer to statutes about abbatial election in the
letters of papal privilege, it seems by no means unlikely that the
letters of privilege themselves contained clauses specifying that
the election of the abbot was to proceed according to the
Benedictine Rule. It is of course very probable that Benedict
Biscop would become familiar with the Benedictine Rule during
his travels and that it would hold a prominent place among the
various rules from which he made his own compilation. What
seems to be the earliest direct evidence for the presence of the
Benedictine Rule at Wearmouth and Jarrow is the reference
which Bede makes to its seventh chapter in the *Commentary on
Ezra and Nehemiah* which he wrote between 725 and 731.[9]

Although the influence of the Benedictine Rule may have
been considerable, especially as the eighth century advanced,
the composite or mixed rule such as was observed at Bede's
monastery was probably characteristic of much of Anglo-
Saxon monasticism during Bede's lifetime. Only in the case of
Wilfrid's foundations have we any evidence for the observance
of the Benedictine Rule to the exclusion of all else, and even
here the evidence rests upon the claims made by Eddius in
passages which tell nothing about where Wilfrid first became
acquainted with the Benedictine Rule and which are not
chronologically precise. Wearmouth and Jarrow being

'Roman' foundations from the first, were not troubled with the difficulties likely to arise at houses which were Columban in origin but conformed to 'Roman' practices after the synod of Whitby. We may presume that from its foundation in 635 until 664 the rule observed at Lindisfarne would be the Columban rule brought from Iona, and this may have been the case also at Melrose, as well as at Ripon where, in the days before Wilfrid acquired the site, the same rules of discipline were observed as at Melrose.[10] The departure of those monks who were unwilling to accept conformity with Rome is likely to have disrupted the life at Lindisfarne and to have led to a considerable weakening of regular monastic discipline, but the Lindisfarne author of the *Life of Cuthbert* claims that when Cuthbert went from Melrose to Lindisfarne 'he arranged our rule of life which we composed then for the first time and which we observe even to this day along with the rule of Benedict'.[11] The passage seems to imply that the rule observed at Lindisfarne after the synod of Whitby had been compiled by Cuthbert himself in collaboration with the other monks, but unfortunately its author, who was writing *c.*705, some twenty years after Cuthbert's death, does not make it clear whether what he calls the *Regula Benedicti* had been used by Cuthbert himself or had first come to Lindisfarne at a later date, nor is it in any case wholly certain that he was referring to the Rule of St Benedict of Nursia and not to the rule compiled by Benedict Biscop of Jarrow. Whatever may have been the exact situation at Lindisfarne, Cuthbert himself had considerable difficulty in persuading some of the monks to accept his new rule.[12] Since no copy of either the Lindisfarne rule of Cuthbert or the Jarrow rule of Benedict Biscop has survived, or indeed of any other rule composed specifically for an English monastery, it is perhaps the more remarkable that the oldest surviving copy of the Rule of St Benedict of Nursia in the whole of Europe should be contained in an English manuscript. Written in a very beautiful English uncial hand, with variant readings added by the scribe himself and so testifying to the current circulation in England of a second text of the Rule, the manuscript (now Oxford Bodleian MS Hatton 48) is believed to have been written *c.* 700 and is known to have been at Worcester in the eleventh century. Although its date is not undisputed and the place of its composition is as yet undetermined, it seems not to be a manuscript of Northumbrian origin and in view of the evidence of Eddius it would seem natural to associate it with the scenes of Wilfrid's monastic activities, perhaps in the midlands.[13]

The Rule of St Benedict, distinguishing between the coenobites who lived together in monasteries and the anchorites or hermits who lived alone, reflects, in correspondence with the similar division which we have seen marked by Isidore, a widely-held distinction within the monastic life as a whole between the active and the contemplative life. This distinction, developed from a mystical interpretation either of the lives of Martha and Mary or of Peter and John, was familiar to Bede who, like all others concerning themselves with the doctrine, regarded the contemplative as the superior way of life, though recognising that such a life was open only to the few. It was not until a man had submitted himself for many years to strict monastic discipline, to daily prayer and penance, that he might eventually learn so to set himself free from the affairs of the world that he could begin to contemplate celestial joys, so far at least as it was permitted for mortal men to do.[14] Instances of those who turned to the contemplative life of the hermit, familiar enough in the context of Irish Christianity, are not wanting from the world more directly known to Bede. To some extent the contemplative life could be lived amid the active life of the monastery, as was the way of Cuthbert while he was in the community at Lindisfarne, though, after some years there, he felt the urge to withdraw to the solitude of Farne, a place 'shut in on the landward side by very deep water and on the seaward side by the boundless ocean'.[15] In the sight of Bede, Cuthbert was not the unwashed eccentric solitary which the modern world might have held him to be, but a soldier of Christ armed with the helmet of salvation, the shield of faith and the sword of the spirit. Thus equipped, he overcame the usurping army of demons, made himself monarch of his land

and 'built a city fitted for his rule, and in it houses equally suited
to his city'. Cuthbert's 'city' on Farne – now the Inner Farne,
about 16 acres in total area, separated by 1½ miles of turbulent
water from the nearest mainland shore and about 7 miles by
water from Lindisfarne – was an almost circular area measuring
some 4 or 5 poles from wall to wall. The enclosing wall, which
was built of rough stone and turf, was higher on the outside than
a man standing upright, but was yet higher on the inside
because the living rock had been so cut away that a man
standing within could see nothing except the sky. Within this
enclosing wall Cuthbert made two buildings, of which the one
was an oratory and the other a habitation for ordinary purposes. Further away, at the landing-stage, there was a large
house where visiting brethren could rest.[16] In moving to his
'city' on Farne, Cuthbert was following the example of the
founder of the monastery at Lindisfarne, Aidan himself, who
used often to withdraw there for prayer and contemplation.
Aidan's little cell, whence he had once seen the flames rising
from the stronghold at Bamburgh during a Mercian attack,
was still to be seen in Bede's day.[17]

Cuthbert had two successors in his hermitage during Bede's
lifetime. The first was Æthilwald who entered upon the
contemplative life after many years of monastic discipline at
Ripon. He found that the oratory, crudely built of wooden
planks, was falling apart and he asked the monks when they
came to visit him to bring with them a calf skin which he could
attach to the boards and so keep out the storms from the corner
where he and his predecessor used most often to stand or kneel
at their devotions. After living in the hermitage for twelve
years, Æthilwald died there and was buried in Lindisfarne.[18]
Bishop Eadfrith of Lindisfarne, the same whom we shall find
associated with the Lindisfarne Gospels, restored the oratory
from its foundations for the benefit of Æthilwald's successor,
Felgild, who was still alive c. 721 when Bede wrote his *Life of
Cuthbert*, though he was then more than 70 years of age. Among
Cuthbert's friends had been a priest called Herbert who lived
as an anchorite on an island in Derwentwater and who was

visited there by Cuthbert himself,[19] and in the next generation there was Guthlac whose renown attracted the attentions of a biographer. Guthlac, born of royal stock in the midlands, won a reputation as a soldier before taking monastic vows at Repton, then a double house ruled by an abbess. There he was taught reading, the chant and the full observance of the monastic discipline, but after the relatively short period of two years in the monastery, he was prompted by his study of the lives of earlier hermits to undertake the contemplative life of the solitary. Leaving Repton with the consent of his elders, he made his way to 'a most dismal fen of immense size, which begins at the banks of the river Granta not far from the camp which is called Cambridge, and stretches from the south as far north as the sea'.[20] Learning from a local inhabitant of a remote island hidden in the depths of the fen, he made his way thither in a fisherman's boat, travelling 'through trackless bogs within the confines of the dismal marsh' till he reached Crowland. After visiting Repton to take his last farewells of his former companions, he returned to Crowland where, on this island surrounded by the fen, he found an earthen mound which had been dug open by some who had hoped to discover treasure there. Within the mound there was 'a sort of cistern' and in this he began to dwell, after building a hut over it.[21] His biographer, Felix, saw Guthlac in much the same way as Bede saw Cuthbert – a warrior, armed with the shield of faith, the breastplate of hope, the helmet of chastity, the bow of patience and the arrows of psalmody, 'he hurled himself against the torrid troops of Tartarus'. After living as a solitary for fifteen years Guthlac died in a corner of his oratory facing the altar, in the year 716.

Save as providing the source of stories about their prowess in battle against the old enemy, the solitary contemplatives, by the very nature of their withdrawal, made no contribution to the material civilisation of their world, in marked contrast to the active life led by the coenobites in their monasteries. The first aim of the active life, as Bede defined it,[22] was to devote oneself to righteous works, and especially to keep oneself unspotted from the world, restraining mind, hand, tongue and all the other members of the body from every kind of sinful pollution; and then to help one's neighbour to the best of one's ability, by giving food to the hungry, drink to the thirsty and clothing to the cold, by receiving the destitute and the wanderers into one's home, by visiting the sick and burying the dead, by snatching the helpless out of the power of the stronger, and the destitute and the poor from those who laid hold of them, by showing the truth to those who erred and by submitting oneself to the demands of brotherly love, and especially by striving for righteousness even unto death.

Whether we regard the *cohors militum* numbering more than 600 as embracing the entire population of the two foundations or merely the professed monks, we must in either case envisage the two monasteries themselves as covering a large area and as having substantial buildings which would in total make a prominent mark upon a countryside otherwise characterised by the remains of Roman towns and frontier works or by the modest villages and farms of its contemporary inhabitants. The most important building in any monastery would be the church, but it was not uncommon for an Anglo-Saxon monastery to have more than one church, and we know this to have been the case at Wearmouth, as well as at Wilfrid's Hexham and at the monastery of St Augustine at Canterbury. The church of St Peter at Wearmouth, as Bede knew it, has perished save for the west wall of the nave and a two-storeyed western entrance porch which has a complex architectural history and which now forms the lower stages of a tower raised upon it at a much later date in the Anglo-Saxon period. We do not know where the church of St Mary stood, but it was built before 716. The quality of the workmanship displayed by the earliest surviving remains of St Peter's suggests that the outcome of the work directed by the Gaulish master-builders is likely to have been a church of considerable elaboration and dignity. It is possible that the building of St Mary's church was prompted by the activities of Pope John VII (705-7) who, amid much work of restoration, built an oratory dedicated to St Mary within the church of St Peter in Rome. This oratory was renowned for its great beauty and especially for its mosaics which survived until the beginning of the seventeenth century. Bede knew about Pope John's building activities from the *Liber Pontificalis* and he referred to St Mary's oratory in the chronicle of the sixth age in the *De Temporum Ratione*. Although the oratory would not yet have been built when Hwætbert was in Rome in 701, it is quite possible that later visitors to Rome may have brought back news of it.[23]

At a very early stage in its history, if not from the very first, its stone fabric was embellished with sculptured figures, and enriched with baluster shafts and rounded arches turned in regularly-shaped voussoirs of which some are likely to have been taken from abandoned Roman sites. Its nave, narrow but so lofty as to suggest that it may have been divided into two storeys, is likely to have been flanked either by aisles or by partly-enclosed chapels which would give the general appearance of a basilican plan such as was taken by the church of St Paul at Jarrow. Its windows were probably small, but, to judge from the many fragments recovered by excavation on the site of some of the monastic buildings,[24] as well as from the written evidence, they would be glazed in leaded and coloured glass, and by the same token, the interior walls were probably covered with plaster which is likely to have been decorated. The western entrance-porch (*porticus ingressus*) was the original burial-place of Abbot Eosterwine, and there was another *porticus* to the east of the altar in which Benedict Biscop was buried. We know nothing about the original shape of the east end, but we may infer from the description of Abbot Ceolfrith's farewell address, given from the steps where he had been accustomed to read, and after praying at the altar, that the altar itself and perhaps the whole of the east end was raised above the level of the nave. There was also a *sacrarium*, defined by Isidore of Seville as a place in which holy things were put and preserved.[25] Since Abbot Sigfrid was originally buried outside the *sacrarium* to the south, presumably the *sacrarium* itself was an adjunct to the church on its southern side.

The accumulation, preservation and display of sacred relics

played a very important part in the religious observances of Bede's age, and with the passing of time such relics would come to include the bones of the early abbots. After the departure of Ceolfrith in 716, the remains of the two abbots Eosterwine and Sigfrid were removed from their original burial-places and put in a single shrine (*theca*), but with a central partition to keep the two apart, which was then placed near the remains of Benedict Biscop in the *porticus* to the east of the altar. Elsewhere Bede records[26] how the bones of the Northumbrian king Oswald who was killed in battle, were placed in the monastery at Bardney in Lincolnshire. After the bones had been enshrined and placed in the church, the king's standard of purple and gold was hung above the tomb, and the water in which the bones had been washed was poured away in a corner of the *sacrarium*, giving miraculous powers to the earth upon which it fell. Any attempt to visualise the church of St Peter as Bede saw it must take into account much that has vanished beyond the mere architectural structure – the Italian paintings on the walls, the reliquaries upon which much wealth and skill would be expended, the glazed lamps, the altar cloths and the vestments of the clergy. We know that there was a gold cross at Wearmouth and that in earlier days King Edwin had had a number of precious vessels, among which there were a large gold cross and a silver chalice, consecrated for service at the altar. Both of these were taken to Kent by Paulinus after the death of Edwin and were still preserved there in Bede's time.[27] We need not doubt that the candlesticks and the vessels used for the service of the altar at both Wearmouth and Jarrow would be made of precious metals, probably silver, and some of them may have been antique vessels secured in Gaul or Italy and then consecrated to Christian uses. In 621 the Gaulish bishop Desiderius bequeathed to his church at Auxerre a collection of silver dishes (*missoria*) on some of which were portrayed figures from pagan classical antiquity – Mercury and Apollo, Dionysius and Ariadne, wrestlers and fawns. One of the dishes was engraved with scenes from the story of Aeneas.[28] It may well be that some of the silver dishes which were found in the ship-burial at Sutton

Hoo and which include a large Byzantine salver, a group of smaller bowls ornamented with a cruciform pattern and a pair of spoons inscribed with the names of Saul and Paul, should be regarded as ecclesiastical plate looted from some Christian centre in south-eastern England at a time when the activities of missionaries tended to alternate with relapses to paganism.

The interior of the church of St Paul at Jarrow is likely to have been generally similar to that of St Peter at Wearmouth, but we can reconstruct the plan of St Paul's with rather greater certainty since much of the church which Bede knew survived until late in the 18th century when it was destroyed to make way for a new nave which was in its turn displaced by the present nave, built in 1866.[29] Doubtless the original church will have undergone a great deal of change and repair during the centuries, but from drawings and a plan made in the eighteenth century we can recognise a basilican church with a western porch, a nave and a series of chapels on either side of the nave but separated from it by an arcade of four arches. The resulting church would have been not unlike the existing church at Brixworth in Northamptonshire, but before it was reduced in size by the loss of its side chapels. The stone inscription recording the dedication of the church to St Paul is now preserved above the chancel arch, though this was certainly not its original position. The Jarrow Rood stone, with its reference to the vision seen by Constantine the Great before the battle of the Milvian Bridge,[30] is likely to date from an early period in the history of St Paul's church. Although the written records tell of only one church at Jarrow, there was a second church, perhaps hardly more than an oratory, which lay to the east of St Paul's and was later united to it by a porch. This eastern element, built largely of re-used Roman masonry and with the outline of original doors and windows still to be seen, remains in use today as the chancel.

The church, which is likely to have been the physical, as it was certainly the spiritual, centre of the monastery, was the place in which the monks spent a large part of their daily life in fulfilment of their paramount duty, the celebration of that great body of praise and prayer which constituted the Divine Office and which is called the *Opus Dei* in the Rule of St Benedict. Although Bede and other Northumbrian sources refer several times to different parts of the Office – matins, the rest which followed the midday meal, vespers, seasons of fasting or feasting and so forth – we have insufficient evidence to reconstruct the monastic *horarium* in detail. Nevertheless it is likely that the Office observed at Wearmouth and Jarrow would correspond broadly with the instructions which St Benedict gave for the performance of the *Opus Dei* and which he based upon the words of the Psalmist – 'Seven times a day do I praise thee' and 'At midnight I will rise to give thanks unto thee.'[31] Upon this authority St Benedict enjoined the observance of the night Office, Nocturns (known in later teminology as Matins), and of the seven day hours, Matins (later known as Lauds), Prime, Tierce, Sext, Nones, Vespers and Compline.[32] To this daily round of prayer there would of course be added a number of other devotional practices appropriate to the general seasons and the specific occasions of the ecclesiastical year. It is also probable that the *horarium* observed by Bede would follow the Benedictine division into a winter and a summer season changing at 1 November and at Easter.

Regarding idleness as the enemy of the soul, St Benedict prescribed that when monks were not engaged in prayer they should occupy themselves at certain fixed times either in manual labour or in the reading of sacred works.[33] It is to be presumed that when King Ecgfrith or some other benefactor gave an estate for the endowment of Wearmouth or Jarrow he would in effect be transferring the ownership of a number of farms or villages which were already fully in occupation and which would then render to the monastery an amount of produce similar to that which had gone to the previous owner. Even so, as we know from the account of the abbacy of Eosterwine, the monks did themselves engage in all the activities needed for their own maintenance – the growing and harvesting of grain, the milling and baking of flour, the raising of sheep and cattle, for milk, butter and cheese as well as for wool and hides. Calf-skin of the very best quality was needed for the preparation of the vellum used in the scriptorium. It has been reckoned that a manuscript of 240 leaves would require the skins of 100–120 animals.[34] The monks would also need to occupy themselves in the skills of the blacksmith, the carpenter and the stonemason to make their farm implements and to maintain and extend the many buildings which formed part of the monastery as a whole – the dormitory, the refectory, the library, the infirmary, the house for the novices, the guest-house, as well as the kitchens, store-houses and barns. With both Wearmouth and Jarrow situated by the side of tidal rivers, there would also be need of boats to serve as ferries and doubtless also for fishing.

REFERENCES

1   *AVCeol c.* 33.
2   *HAbb c.* 11.
3   *AVCeol c.* 6.
4   *Hom.* I, 13, *lines* 116–20.
5   *C.* 23.
6   *C.* 16.
7   *AVCeol c.* 16; cf. *HAbb c.* 11.
8   *AVCeol c.* 25; cf. *HAbb c.* 16.
9   *PL* 91, 892; cf. *BR* VII, 6.
10 *BVC c.* VII.
11 *AVC* III, 1.
12 *BVC c.* XVI.
13 N. R. Ker, *Catalogue of Manuscripts containing Anglo-Saxon* (Oxford 1957), no. 327; *The Rule of St Benedict*, ed. D. H. Farmer, Early English MSS in Facsimile, vol. XV (Copenhagen, 1968).
14 *Bed. Hom.* I, 9, *lines* 163–74.
15 *AVC* III, 1; *BVC c.* XVII.
16 *BVC c.* XVII.
17 *HE* III, 16.
18 *HE* V, 1; *BVC c.* XLVI.
19 *AVC* IV, 9; *BVC c.* XXVIII.
20 *Vita Guthlaci*, c. XXIV.
21 *Ibid.* c. XXVIII.

22 *Hom.* I, 9, *lines* 151–63.

23 *TASA* I, 432–46; and for St. Mary's oratory in Rome see *Lib. Pont.* 88, 1, ed. L. Duchesne (Paris 1886), 385, also *BdTR Chron. MGH Auct. Ant.* XIII, 317, and *Rev. Archéologique* 34 (1877), 145–62.

24 Dr Rosemary Cramp of Durham University is engaged in excavations which are likely to extend over several years.

25 J. F. Niermeyer, *Med. Lat. Lex. Min. s.v.*, p. 928.

26 *HE* III, 11.

27 *HE* II, 20.

28 P. Riché, *Education et Culture*, p. 252 and *n.* 222.

29 *TASA* I, 338–49.

30 *Archaeologia Aeliana*, 4th s. XXI (1943), 121–6.

31 *Psalm* 118 (119 in the *A.V.*), *vv.* 62 and 164.

32 *BR c.* XVI.

33 *Ibid. c.* XLVIII.

34 R. Powell, *The Library*, *Trans. Biblio. Soc.* 5th s. 20 (1965), 259–76.

The Bible in the West

The observance of the monastic rule, dominated by the daily performance of the *Opus Dei* and varied by periods of manual labour and the reading of sacred books, constituted the life lived by the monks of Wearmouth and Jarrow, as of a great many other foundations widely spread throughout the greater part of England in the seventh and eighth centuries. It was one of the functions of this life, perhaps more readily seen in retrospect than by contemporaries, to serve as the prime agent in creating an educated and literate element in that pagan society which had possessed the former British provinces of the Roman empire. The task which it had to face was not merely the teaching of the simplest elements of the Christian faith to a rustic population, but also the training and educating from an early age of those who would in time be able to teach others and to hold office as bishops, abbots or priests. It is the particular distinction of Wearmouth and Jarrow that from the first their founder, Benedict Biscop, set out to endow them as richly as he could with the means which would enable them to become centres of educational and intellectual studies. Had we been better informed about the history of the monastery of Whitby we might have been able to trace in greater detail not only the circumstances which led the English to venerate Gregory the Great, rather than Augustine, as the apostle and teacher of the English nation, but also the extent to which the monks of Wearmouth and Jarrow, and particularly Bede himself, came to be influenced by Gregory the Great's views on the need for a well-educated clergy. Gregory's vigorous condemnation of ignorant men who presumed to undertake the office of teacher, like physicians of the mind who strove to effect their cures without any knowledge of spiritual precepts, finds its place in the first chapter of the *Book of Pastoral Care*. This was the book, believed to have been first brought to England by Augustine himself, and certainly known at both Whitby and Jarrow, that was particularly commended by Bede in the letter which he wrote the year before his death to his former pupil Egbert who in 735 became the first archbishop of York. In Bede's sight, it was not merely bishops, priests, deacons and the rulers of monasteries who were as shepherds entrusted with the safe-keeping of flocks; so also were all those faithful people who kept vigilant watch over their own small homes. And each of those in charge of the daily instruction of one or two of the brethren within the monastery owed them the duty of a shepherd in fulfilment of the command to feed them with the riches of God's word.[1]

The Word of God, revealed to man through the books embodied in the Old and New Testaments, was the ultimate foundation upon which the whole of Bede's world was built. Although he wrote books on orthography and metre, on chronology and cosmology, on the lives of saints and abbots, and on the history of the Church in England, the greater part of his working life, from the time when he received priest's orders until he was almost 60 years of age, was devoted to studying the meaning of Holy Writ and its interpretation in the light of the writings of the Fathers. If the church was the spiritual heart of the monastery, the Bible was the ultimate source of spiritual knowledge. St Paul writing his Epistle to the Romans in *c.* A.D. 58 used the Greek language, and with the spread of Christianity westwards from Palestine towards Italy it was in Greek that the Scriptures first came to be known, but although the bishops of Rome continued to use Greek for some time, it was inevitable, with the further spread of Christianity to areas less closely associated with the use of the Greek language, that the need for a Latin version would become steadily greater.

There is no ground for thinking that a complete Latin version of the whole Bible was brought into being by a single translator or by a group of translators working together, and we ought rather to envisage a gradual accumulation resulting from the translation of individual parts of the Bible to meet particular needs as they arose. Indeed it was not until 397 that the Council of Carthage established a list of canonical books which came to be universally recognised in the west. Modern Biblical scholars use the term 'Old-Latin Bible' for the western Latin translation which was known to the Fathers as *vetus editio* or *antiqua interpretatio*. There is no single surviving codex which contains the whole of the Old-Latin Bible, and it would in any case be wrong to envisage the existence of a single established Old-Latin version of the whole Bible in the sense of the modern Authorised or Revised Versions of the English Bible. Pandects, or complete copies of the whole Bible, were exceedingly rare in the early centuries of Christianity and even by Bede's time they were certainly not common. We should rather think of the Old-Latin Bible as comprising a number of separate books in different translations in use mainly in Italy and Africa, and as contrasting with the new Latin version, partly revision and partly fresh translation from Greek or Hebrew, which was made by Jerome near the end of the fourth century and which we know as the Vulgate.

It was the inadequacy and variety of existing Latin translations that led Pope Damasus (366–84) to give his encouragement to Jerome in making a revised version of the whole Bible. Jerome, a distinguished scholar who had studied Latin and Greek in Rome, had travelled west to Gaul as well as East to Antioch, before living for some years as a hermit in the Syrian desert, where he learnt Hebrew. Beginning his work in 382 Jerome quickly completed his new version of the four Gospels, and to it there was later added a dedicatory letter addressed to Pope Damasus in explanation of the circumstances in which the work had been undertaken. This letter, beginning with the words *Novum opus facere me cogis ex ueteri*, continued to be associated with Jerome's version of the Gospels and we find it, sometimes with richly-illuminated initials, as the preface to copies of the Gospels which were circulating in both the English and the Irish church during Bede's lifetime. Jerome's version of

the four Gospels came rapidly into general use in the western
church, but there is some doubt about the extent to which he
was concerned with the revision of the later books of the New
Testament. For his first revision of the Old Testament Jerome
was able to secure from the library in Caesarea the original copy
of the great work produced by Origen in the earlier part of the
third century and commonly known as the *Hexapla*. This was a
version of the Old Testament which contained the Hebrew text
written both in Hebrew and in Greek characters, and also the
Greek text of the Septuagint and three different Greek translations made by other scholars – all six versions being set out in
parallel columns. The most enduring part of Jerome's work
upon the *Hexapla* was his new version of that part of the Bible
which, next to the four Gospels, was most widely used – the
Psalter. This version, known as the Gallican Psalter (*Psalterium
Gallicanum*) because of its great popularity in Gaul, eventually
came to be recognised throughout the western church, save in
Rome itself. Until as late as the 16th century the church in
Rome used the Roman Psalter (*Psalterium Romanum*) which was
a version based directly upon the Septuagint and has often been
thought to have been the work of Jerome as well, though this is
disputed. It remains uncertain how much of the rest of the Old
Testament Jerome revised from the *Hexapla*, before he turned to
a new undertaking – a complete revision of the Old Testament
based directly upon the Hebrew text. This great work, the
Vulgate, which occupied him for some fifteen years and was
completed in 405, naturally included a new version of the
Psalter, known as the Hebrew Psalter, but it never displaced
the Gallican Psalter.[2]

Recalling the warning given by Cassiodorus lest presump-
tuous scribes should enfeeble God's Word by adopting the more
familiar idioms of current speech, we can easily see that a new
translation of the Bible was bound to meet with the hostility of
those who then, even as now, regarded the text with which they
were familiar as the revealed Word of God in a very literal
sense. Nevertheless, Jerome's work, and particularly his version
of the Gospels, did come to be recognised for the very great

achievement which it was. It came into use particularly in the western church and in the fifth century it found favour with such Gaulish churchmen as Prosper of Aquitaine and Avitus of Vienne. Gregory the Great, writing a dedicatory letter to Leander of Seville as preface to his *Commentary on Job*, expressed his preference for the new translation, but remarked that as occasion arose he would use the witness sometimes of the old version and sometimes of the new, and at about the same date Leander's brother, Isidore, could write of Jerome's translation as being generally used in the churches everywhere.[3] Yet the Old-Latin version of the Gospels was still being copied in the sixth or seventh centuries, as we may see from the Codex Valerianus which is believed to have been written at that time in northern Italy or possibly in Illyrium. This copy of the Gospels, written in good uncials, may have been associated with Freising in Bavaria where some of the books of the Old Testament were being copied in the Old-Latin version as late as the eighth or ninth centuries.[4] Yet, even with the further widespread acceptance of Jerome's Vulgate in the western church, it would be wrong to envisage the Bible of Bede's age as comprising two distinct and instantly recognisable versions, the Old-Latin version and the new version of Jerome. It was seldom that the complete Bible was copied in its entirety and, with the multiplication of copies of individual books made by scribes of varying skill and accuracy from exemplars of differing date and origin, anything like uniformity could never have been achieved. What was at base an Old-Latin text might be corrected against Jerome's translation and equally his own new version might be corrupted in varying degree by Old-Latin readings.

There can be no doubt that copies of the Gospels, as well as of other parts of both the Old and the New Testaments, were circulating in Britain during the time of the Roman occupation, or that they continued to circulate in those western parts of the country which did not pass into English occupation, but we have no surviving fragment of any book, Biblical or otherwise, which is known to have been used in Britain during the Roman

H   [215]

occupation. Queen Bertha's Frankish chaplain, Liudhard, would certainly have had a copy of the Gospels, as well as service-books, for use in the church of St Martin at Canterbury in the services which were being held there before the arrival of Augustine. Even without the direct testimony of Bede that Gregory sent Augustine *codices plurimos*,[5] we would have been bound to presume the accumulation of a number of books at Canterbury, and also some at Rochester, in the decade following 597. These would be Italian books, likely to have been written in the uncial script commonly in use in the Mediterranean countries in this age, and during the seventh century such Italian books in England would increase both in their total number and in the area of their distribution, first by the extension of the Roman mission to Northumbria and later by the activities of Benedict Biscop as he accumulated books for the Wearmouth and Jarrow libraries. We may also think it certain that books would be brought to England by Theodore and Hadrian, by Wilfrid, and by some of the many anonymous Englishmen who made pilgrimages to Rome in the seventh century.

There still survives, in varying degree of completeness, a small number of these Mediterranean books which were being used in England in the seventh century and which may have served as models for copies written subsequently in English scriptoria. One of these, a copy of the four Gospels written according to Jerome's text and held by palaeographers to have been written in Italy in the sixth century, used formerly to belong to St Augustine's monastery at Canterbury. Knowing this, and knowing also that it bears upon it alterations to the original text which prove that it was certainly in England by Bede's lifetime at the latest, we surely need not hesitate to accept the Canterbury tradition that it had once belonged to Augustine himself.[6] This book, now in Cambridge and commonly known as the *Gospels of St Augustine*, is textually related to another copy of the Gospels believed to have been written in Italy in the seventh century and known to have been in England by the eighth. Now preserved in Oxford, this Gospel Book bears a marginal addition on one of its pages written in an Anglo-Saxon hand and referring to St Chad. Perhaps it was at one time connected with Lichfield, but if so we do not know how or when it got there, nor do we know anything about how it reached England in the first place. There were close, if somewhat unhappy, relations between Lichfield and Canterbury in the eighth century and it is easy to envisage circumstances in which an Italian book belonging to the library at Canterbury might have got to Lichfield.[7] A third copy of the Gospels, written in an Italian uncial hand of the sixth century and now commonly known as the Burchard Gospels, has particularly interesting associations with Bede's monastery. Again we know nothing of the way in which it reached England or of its journey to its present home in Würzburg, though we may guess that it was among the books which went from England to the continent in the train of English missionaries in the eighth century. The particular interest of this book is that, having apparently become defective, it was restored by the addition of some twelve folios to replace the lost parts. The handwriting of these additional folios is characteristic of the Wearmouth/Jarrow scriptorium during Bede's lifetime.[8]

Other manuscripts, though not themselves of Italian origin, nevertheless give interesting evidence of Italian, and particularly South Italian, influence upon the texts of the Gospels associated directly or indirectly with Northumbria. It was common practice for at least the more elaborate of the Gospels to contain such subsidiary material as the Letter to Pope Damasus, his Prologue to the Gospels, the Eusebian Canon tables and tables for feast days for lessons associated with each of the four Gospels. All these are found, for example, in the Lindisfarne Gospels. It has long been recognised that the table of feast days in the Lindisfarne Gospels includes certain festivals which are associated with the neighbourhood of Naples, in particular the nativity of St Januarius who was martyred in the Diocletianic persecutions and came to be honoured as the patron saint of Naples. The same list of Neapolitan feasts is also found in another, probably Northumbrian, copy of the Gospels which is

textually akin to the Lindisfarne Gospels.[9] A similar association
is disclosed by a scribal note on the famous Echternach Gospels,
now in Paris, which are held to have been written either in
Northumbria itself or in Echternach, the Anglo-Saxon monast-
tery founded by the Northumbrian missionary Willibald.[10] The
note (f. 222v) records that the text has been collated with a
manuscript from the library of Eugippius which was itself
believed to have belonged to Jerome. We are not to interpret
this note as referring to the Echternach Gospels themselves, but
rather as having been copied from the exemplar which the
Echternach scribe was using. Eugippius (d. 535) was abbot of
Lucullanum near Naples, and the scribal note on the Echternach Gospels is good evidence that somewhere in their ancestry
there lies a Neapolitan Gospel Book of at least early sixth-
century date. These and other indications allow us to recognise
an Italo-Northumbrian version of Jerome's Gospels in contrast
with an 'Irish' text which we also find circulating in Northumbria, though it would be wrong to make too rigid a distinction. Another eighth-century manuscript of the Gospels
believed to have been written in Northumbria, and now in
Durham, presents the first three Gospels in a text of the Irish
type, whereas the fourth Gospel is of the Italian type found in
the Lindisfarne Gospels and the Codex Amiatinus.[11]

At a very early date, believed to be *c.* A.D. 150, the Assyrian
Gnostic writer Tatian compiled a single continuous narrative of
the life of Christ from the four separate Gospels. This work,
known as the Diatessaron or Harmony of the Gospels, came to
enjoy a wide circulation in the Syrian-speaking churches. A
sixth-century Latin Diatessaron survives in an Italian manuscript of very particular interest.[12] Written in Italy, and perhaps
at Capua, for Victor, bishop of Capua 541–54, this manuscript
was read, corrected and annotated by Victor himself who added
his signature in two places and dated his entries 546 and 547.
The manuscript bears upon it marginal additions and corrections
made in an insular uncial hand dated to the eighth century, as
well as in an Anglo-Saxon minuscule of the type used at Fulda in
the ninth century. There can be no doubt that the book had

come into Anglo-Saxon hands by the eighth century, and it is possible that by that date it had already reached its present home, Fulda, the monastery founded by the West Saxon missionary Boniface. It may be that this notable book was among other Italian works brought to England in the seventh or eighth centuries and taken thence to Germany by Anglo-Saxon missionaries. On the other hand it may have travelled directly to Fulda from Italy.

Although copies of the Gospels comprise far the greater part of all the manuscripts which had English associations during the age of Bede, other works are found among the books imported from the Mediterranean. The library of Durham Cathedral contains a fragment of Maccabees written in an Italian uncial hand of the sixth century,[13] and at Würzburg there is preserved the oldest surviving uncial manuscript which is known to have been in England at an early stage in its history. This manuscript, of Jerome's *Commentary on Ecclesiastes*,[14] written in an Italian uncial hand of the fifth century, bears upon its flyleaf (f. 1) an Anglo-Saxon inscription of the eighth century recording that the book belonged to Abbess Cuthswith – *Cuthsuuithae boec thaerae abbatissan*. An authentic charter issued in 693 records a grant of land by Oshere, king of the Hwicce, to a certain Abbess Cuthswith for the building of a monastery in a place which cannot be exactly located but which lay in the west midlands, probably in Warwickshire.[15] We cannot be certain that the two are identical, but the records do not tell of any other abbess of the same name at the appropriate date. A fifth-century Italian copy of a work originally written by Jerome, coming into the possession of an English abbess by *c.* 700, and subsequently finding its way to Würzburg, where it may already have been by the tenth century, is a striking instance of the way in which manuscripts travelled in this age, as also of the general flow of intellectual currents from the eastern Mediterranean to Italy, to England and then on to a Germany still emerging from paganism. Moreover the book warns us against supposing that intellectual activities were being pursued only in those monasteries whose history is known to us, and the happy chance that led to the addition of a one-time owner's name tells us that there were women as well as men engaging in Biblical studies in the age of Bede.

REFERENCES

1 *Bed. Hom.* I, 7, *lines* 104–11.

2 See H. W. Robinson, *Ancient and English Versions of the Bible* (Oxford 1940), 110–15, also M. L. W. Laistner, *Thought and Letters in Western Europe* (London 1957), 68–9.

3 *De Ecc. Off.* I, xii, 8, *PL* LXXXIII, 748.

4 *CLA* IX, 1249 and 1254.

5 *HE* I, 29.

6 *CLA* II, 126.

7 *CLA* II, 230, and *LEU, Pl.* IV. The reference to *ceadda* is on the lower margin of *f.* 149v.

8 *CLA* IX, 1423ab, and *LEU, Pl.* III, but D. H. Wright, *Traditio* XVII (1961), 441–56, argues that the restoration work was done at a Northumbrian foundation on the continent. For a catalogue of surviving Gospel Books see P. McGurk, *Latin Gospel Books from A.D. 400 to A.D. 800, Les Publications de Scriptorium,* vol V (1961). The author lists 138 manuscripts, and about half of this total are associated directly or indirectly with the British Isles.

9 *CLA* II, 213.

10 *CLA* V, 578.

11 *CLA* II, 148ab.

12 *CLA* VIII, 1196.

13 *CLA* II, 153, *LEU, Pl.* IIb.

14 *CLA* IX, 1430a, *LEU, Pl.* Ia. N. Ker, *Catalogue,* No. 401.

15 Birch, *Cart. Sax.* Nos. 85, 122.

21

The Northumbrian Bible

The presentation of the complete Latin Bible raised editorial problems as well as problems of translation, and it was to this aspect of Biblical studies that Cassiodorus devoted much time at Vivarium in southern Italy. We have already noted his description of the three Bibles to be found in the library there – one in nine separate volumes, a second contained in a single volume of smaller writing, and a third, also in a single volume but a larger book written in clearer writing.[1] We have also seen that this last Bible, now known as the Codex Grandior, was used by Bede. It was presumably the sight of a complete copy of the whole Bible in a single volume which prompted Abbot Ceolfrith to a similar undertaking. His anonymous biographer records how he splendidly enlarged the collection of books which either he himself or Benedict Biscop had brought from Rome and how 'amongst other things he caused three pandects to be transcribed, two of which he placed in the churches of his two monasteries, so that all who wished to read any chapter of either Testament might easily find what they wanted, whilst, as to the third, he decided when he was about to go to Rome, to offer it as a gift to St Peter, prince of the apostles.'[2] Bede, describing the same undertaking, writes that Ceolfrith 'added three pandects of the new translation to the one of the old translation which he had brought from Rome. On going back to Rome in his old age he took one of them with him as a present among other gifts, and he left the other two, one to each of his monasteries.'[3] A later passage in the anonymous life of Ceolfrith records how after his death and burial at Langres in Burgundy in 716, some of his companions continued the journey to Rome to deliver the gifts which he had been taking. 'Among these gifts there was the pandect, as we have said, translated from the Hebrew and Greek sources according to the interpretation of the blessed priest Jerome.' At the beginning of this pandect there stood some verses whose text is given in full by the author of the anonymous *Life* and which conveyed pledges of devoted affection for St Peter from 'Ceolfrith, abbot from the farthest limits of the English' – *Ceolfridus Anglorum extremis de finibus abbas.*

We may note the distinction which Bede makes between the *uetusta translatio*, that is the Old-Latin version, of which Ceolfrith had brought a copy back from Rome, and the *noua translatio*, the translation by Jerome which formed the basis of the three new pandects which Ceolfrith caused to be made. So far as we know the only occasion when Ceolfrith visited Rome was when he accompanied Benedict Biscop on the journey of 678–9, and it was presumably then that he acquired a copy of the Old-Latin Bible. This Bible acquired by Ceolfrith was evidently not the Codex Grandior of Cassiodorus since the latter contained the Old Testament in the form revised by Jerome from the *Hexapla*. It is evident that Bede had seen and used the Codex Grandior, but it does not follow that it belonged to the Jarrow library, since it would not have been difficult for Bede to have borrowed it if it had been, for example, at Lindisfarne. Although we know that the three pandects had been completed before 716 when Abbot Ceolfrith set off for Rome with one of them, we cannot say exactly when they were made, save that they were not begun until after Ceolfrith became sole abbot of the two monasteries in 688. Bede's words seem to imply that the pandect which Ceolfrith took with him on his journey had already been completed some years before he set out for Rome in his old age, and we might be wiser to think of such an ambitious undertaking as belonging to Ceolfrith's middle years rather than to his old age.

The two pandects which were put in the churches at Wearmouth and Jarrow have perished with the exception of a few leaves of which some were used as wrappers for account books of the reign of Edward the Sixth and another was found in a bookshop at no great distance from Jarrow.[4] The survival of these few leaves suggests that the two pandects themselves may well have remained complete, though not necessarily in their original homes, until the time of the Reformation. The book which was taken on to Rome after Ceolfrith's death at Langres in 716 found its way to the abbey of Monte Amiata whence it was removed to Florence in 1782, and there it is still preserved in its entirety in the Laurentian library. This book, universally known as the Codex Amiatinus, comprises more than 1000 leaves, each of them measuring more than 20 inches high by more than 13 inches across. Written in a number of sections by several scribes in an uncial script of remarkable elegance and beauty it must surely rank among the most important manuscripts surviving from the early middle ages of western Europe, not only for its great palaeographical interest and for its testimony to the civilisation of the age which produced it, but also because it is the earliest surviving complete Latin Bible.[5]

The Latin verses which the author of Ceolfrith's *Life* described as standing at the head of the book still remain, though their superficial content does not now correspond exactly with their original content. Towards the end of the ninth century, when the book had been in Italy for almost two hundred years, Peter the Lombard, abbot of the monastery of Monte Amiata, erased Ceolfrith's name from the dedicatory inscription and inserted his own in its place, so that instead of *Ceolfridus Anglorum* the reader now sees the name *Petrus Langobardorum*. It was an Italian scholar who, towards the end of the nineteenth century, first revealed the machinations of Peter the Lombard by showing that his name had been inserted into the space left by the erasure of Abbot Ceolfrith's name. In its general external form the Codex Amiatinus, and presumably the sister pandects as well, appears to have been modelled closely upon the Codex Grandior of Cassiodorus, not merely in the arrangement of its text, but also in the use of some illustrations. A well-known picture on one of the earlier folios of the book shows a seated scribe who is identified by a Latin distich in the upper margin of the page as Ezra making good the damage done to the sacred books of Scripture by the sword of the enemy. Whatever the

historical truth may have been, Jewish tradition represents Ezra
as the great priest and scribe who was responsible for settling
the canon of Jewish Scripture by his work as a restorer, cor-
rector and editor of the texts. There is an obvious parallel
between the work traditionally achieved by Ezra in the fifth and
fourth centuries B.C. and the work done by Cassiodorus at
Vivarium about a thousand years later. Most scholars are
agreed in thinking that the scribe who is seated and engaged in
writing in a book which he holds open on his knee, though
nominally identified with Ezra, is in fact intended to represent
Cassiodorus himself. In the background there stands an open
cupboard (*armarium*) on whose shelves are laid nine volumes,
surely representing the Vivarium Bible which Cassiodorus
describes as being assembled by him in nine separate volumes.
Among the implements lying on the floor there is one much
smaller book, to be identified with the pandect 'written in a
rather smaller hand in 53 gatherings of six folios each in order
that the compactness of the writing might shorten the inordinate
length of the copious text'.[6] And finally we may take the work
upon which the scribe is engaged as the Codex Grandior itself.
It seems likely that this picture should be regarded as a copy
made in Jarrow or Wearmouth of what was originally the
frontispiece of the Codex Grandior from Vivarium.

Although in its general format the Codex Amiatinus seems to
have been based on the Codex Grandior as its model, this was
not the case with the text of the Bible which it contains and
which is derived from a variety of different exemplars. The
Gospels present a good text of the Vulgate, closely related to the
text found in the Lindisfarne Gospels, as well as in other Northumbrian manuscripts, and having characteristics which suggest
that it was based on an exemplar from southern Italy in the
neighbourhood of Naples. There are likely to have been Italian
manuscripts available for many of the other books of the Bible
as well, but the Psalms seem to be based on a rather poor Irish
text. The work which Ceolfrith put in hand in the making of
the three great pandects was not merely the mechanical copying
of a number of separate manuscripts so as to make three single

and identical copies of the whole Bible each in one volume.
More than that, it was the completion of a revised and edited
version of the whole Bible based on the best available manuscripts. Ceolfrith himself is likely to have directed the whole of
this undertaking, as Cassiodorus had directed a similar undertaking at Vivarium, and we may regard the sole surviving
pandect as the outcome of long and laborious textual and
editorial work undertaken at Wearmouth and Jarrow in the
closing years of the seventh century, a necessary preliminary to
the great work of Biblical commentary to which Bede devoted
the greater part of his studies in the early decades of the eighth.

When Ceolfrith took the pandect with him as he set off for
Rome, in the hope of spending his last days there, he surely did
not take it only as an example of work which was being done in
an English scriptorium, but rather as the most valuable gift
which he could offer to the church of St Peter in Rome, and as
representing in his sight the greatest achievement of the monastery whose abbot he had been for so many years – nothing less
than a new edition of the Bible which, as the picture of the
scribe plainly tells, could claim to rank with the earlier achievements of Cassiodorus and Ezra. The next major revision of the
Latin Bible, made at the beginning of the ninth century, was
also the work of a Northumbrian scholar. It was undertaken at
the request of Charlemagne by Alcuin who had been born in
Northumbria and received his education in the school at York
which first achieved distinction under the direction of Bede's
pupil, Egbert, and which seems to have rivalled, and perhaps
superseded, Wearmouth and Jarrow after the death of Bede, as
the chief centre of intellectual studies in England during the
second half of the eighth century.

We may think it unlikely that there were many, if indeed any,
other centres of Biblical studies which, like Vivarium in the days
of Cassiodorus and Wearmouth and Jarrow in the days of Bede,
possessed no less than three complete copies of the whole Bible.
There remain five volumes and parts of a sixth of the Old
Testament written at Corbie at the order of Abbot Maurdramn
who was in office 772–81 and they may represent the surviving

parts of a complete Bible.[7] Corbie itself, in Picardy, was originally founded, as was Chelles, by Balthild, the English queen of Clovis II. Dating from the later eighth or early ninth century there survive the Le Puy Bible, thought to have been written for Theodulf, bishop of Orléans (d. 821) and also a Bible from the scriptorium at Tours and now preserved at St Gall.[8] But if the complete Bible was rare, copies of the Gospels were undoubtedly very numerous. There still survive, in conditions varying from the complete to the mere scrap re-used for the binding of a later work, some 30–35 manuscripts of the Gospels which are believed to have been written in England alone in the seventh or eighth centuries. Statistical precision is not possible since we cannot always distinguish with certainty between a manuscript written in England and another written abroad by an English scribe. Three of these Gospel manuscripts have been attributed to the Wearmouth/Jarrow scriptorium,[9] one is from Lindisfarne and some fifteen others are thought to be Northumbrian in general. Of the others, two seem to have associations with the west midlands near the Welsh border,[10] and three with southern England, perhaps Canterbury.[11]

Although we may suppose that the copies of the Gospels which were in daily use in the many monasteries and churches of Bede's age were for the most part plain and unadorned texts, there were other copies for whose enrichment scribes and artists gave the utmost of their very considerable skills. Not only was honour thus done to the sacred text itself, but the ignorant and the illiterate were the more impressed by the splendid appearance of the Word of God. Wilfrid's motive in securing for his church at Ripon a copy of the Gospels all written in letters of gold on purple parchment was doubtless the same as prompted the missionary Boniface to write from Germany to Eadburga, abbess in Thanet, asking her to have made for him a copy of the Epistles of St Peter written in letters of gold so that reverence for the Scriptures might be visibly impressed upon the worldly minded people to whom he was preaching.[12]

The Italian Gospel Book which is believed to have belonged

to St Augustine of Canterbury was originally enriched with a series of miniatures, although only two of these now survive, one of them containing a series of twelve small scenes representing incidents in the life of Christ from the entry into Jerusalem to the carrying of the Cross to Golgotha by Simon of Cyrene, and the other portraying St Luke seated upon a chair within an alcove, with the head and forequarters of a winged calf, carrying a book between his forepaws, above him.[13] Although the Crucifixion is represented in one early Northumbrian Gospel Book,[14] it never became part of the English tradition in Bede's time to show scenes from the life of Christ such as are found in St Augustine's Italian book. But the portrayal of the evangelists became a regular feature, each of the four being normally shown at the beginning of his Gospel, and each accompanied either on the same or on the adjacent leaf by the appropriate evangelistic symbol whose origins lay ultimately in the description in the Book of Revelation of the four beasts who sat about the throne: 'And the first beast was like a lion, and the second beast like a calf, and the third beast had a face as a man, and the fourth beast was like a flying eagle.'[15] In England in the seventh century these symbols, sometimes shown complete and sometimes only as half of the creature, are found associated respectively with Mark, Luke, Matthew and John. Bede interpreted the four symbols as representing Christ, the man and the calf standing for the humility of His incarnation and sacrifice, the lion and the eagle for the courage and sublimity of His resurrection and ascension into Heaven.[16]

One of the most striking manifestations of the Hiberno-Saxon civilisation of the world of Bede is now to be found in the series of richly decorated Gospel Books associated with Ireland, England and centres of missionary activity abroad. The difficulty of establishing the date and place at which these books were produced has led to continuing discussion which in most cases can hardly result in more than approximate answers. Saving the sixth-century Gospels used by St Augustine at Canterbury, the earliest of these illuminated copies of the Gospels which we can place in an historical context is the book

which Wilfrid gave to his new church at Ripon in the 670s.
Though it does not now survive this book consisted of an
illuminated copy of the Gospels written in letters of gold on
parchment dyed purple, and the words in which Eddius
describes it[17] imply that it was newly-made at Wilfrid's orders,
and not an old book obtained from some other church or library. Gospels written on purple parchment are found in four
manuscripts dating from the late fifth or early sixth centuries.
All are now preserved in Italy – at Brescia, Naples, Sarezzano
and Trent – and all are believed to have been written in Italy,
probably in the north.[18] Three of the four contain the pre-
Jerome version of the Gospels, and in all four the text is written
in letters of silver, with gold used only occasionally, as in the
Nomina Sacra, the openings of the Gospels and so forth. There is
no evidence for the presentation of the Gospels in this way
outside Italy before the date of Wilfrid's Ripon Gospels, and
perhaps we ought to think of Wilfrid's order being completed in
some north Italian scriptorium. One English manuscript of the
eighth century contains four purple leaves and makes some use
of gold and silver.[19] From the late eighth or the early ninth
centuries there are two 'purple' Gospel Books of which both are
thought to have been written in close association with Charlemagne's court. One of the two, now at Abbeville, is written in
gold, and the other, now in Vienna, is written mostly in gold
but with some silver.[20] This last, which was kept at Aachen
until 1798, was the book on which German kings and emperors
used to take their Coronation oath. It is very likely that Alcuin,
who was closely concerned with the revision of the Bible at
Charlemagne's school, himself saw the Ripon Gospels and it
may well have been his influence which prompted the writing
of these sumptuous books in Charlemagne's time.

It is possible that the Book of Durrow, now in Dublin, which
contains a Vulgate text, but not the Italo-Northumbrian type,
may be earlier than the Ripon Gospels, and there is a good case
for believing that it was written and illuminated in a scriptorium
of Irish rather than English background, possibly at Durrow
itself, though there were certainly Irish monasteries outside

Ireland where such a work could have been produced in the seventh century.[21] The book itself, with some of its abstract designs showing a remarkably close resemblance to patterns found on English jewellery from the ship-burial at Sutton Hoo, is at once a reminder that Irish missionaries had worked in East Anglia and a warning against the dangers of thinking that the civilisation of this age was characterised by modern notions of 'Irish' or 'English' nationalism. Among later illuminated Gospels certainly produced in Ireland are the Book of Mac Regol,[22] now in Oxford, which is held to have been written and illuminated by Mac Regol, Abbot of Birr of Offaly, who died in 822 and the Book of Kells in Dublin, which is attributed to the eighth or ninth centuries.[23] The Gospels now at Lichfield, and sometimes known as the St Chad Gospels, are thought to belong to the age of Bede but, although the book is known to have been in Wales by the ninth century or earlier, its place of origin is uncertain.[24] The Codex Aureus which contains the Gospels written in an English uncial hand of the eighth century and is now preserved in Stockholm, was presented to Christ Church, Canterbury, after having been recovered from a band of Viking raiders into whose hands it had fallen in the ninth century, and it may have been at Canterbury that the book was originally written.[25] Other illuminated copies of the Gospels either found their way abroad with Irish or English missionaries, or else were produced in the scriptoria of continental houses founded by them. Among these are the Irish St Gall Gospels and two English books of the seventh or eighth centuries, known as the Echternach Gospels, now in Paris, and the Maihingen Gospels, now at Schloss Harburg in Germany.[26]

There is no surviving Gospel Book of this richly illuminated type, whether complete or fragmentary which can be attributed with certainty to the Wearmouth/Jarrow scriptorium, but the Codex Amiatinus, and other Jarrow manuscripts, offer sufficient evidence that there were scribes and artists in Bede's monastery who were capable of producing work of the highest quality, comparable with that to be found in the book which many would regard as the noblest of all the surviving manuscripts from the age of Bede – the Lindisfarne Gospels.[27] When we reflect how little has survived from a library which is likely to have numbered hundreds of volumes it would be unwise to assume that nothing similar was to be found at Wearmouth or Jarrow. In the tenth century a priest of the church of St Cuthbert wrote an interlinear English gloss to the Latin text of the Lindisfarne Gospels, as a help to those who in that later age had little Latin, and at the end of the Gospel of St John he added, also in English, a short account of the origin of the book itself. 'Eadfrith, bishop of the Lindisfarne church, originally wrote this book, for God and St Cuthbert and, jointly, for all the saints whose relics are in the island. And Ethiluald, bishop of the Lindisfarne islanders, impressed it on the outside and covered it – as well he knew how to do.' Aldred added that an anchorite called Billfrith adorned it on the outside with gold and silver and precious stones. The two bishops named in this account held office, the first 698–721 and the second 721–40, and we need have no hesitation in accepting the authenticity of their association with the book itself. Aldred's word 'wrote' (*awrat*) can be interpreted in several different ways, but it is currently claimed by those who have made the most detailed study of the book that it was produced in a relatively short period, perhaps two years, of sustained work by a single man who himself not only wrote the text, but also produced the illuminations, and that that man was Bishop Eadfrith himself. This must remain a matter of opinion, but we can certainly believe that the book was produced at Lindisfarne, that Bishop Eadfrith was concerned in its production and that it was completed shortly before or shortly after 700.

The Lindisfarne Gospels offer an almost unlimited number of topics for discussion. The book is the only one in the whole series of Hiberno-Saxon illuminated Gospels which can be closely located both in place and in date. Artistic analysis of its richly varied illumination reveals much that is Celtic and something that is English, while its portraiture of the evangelists takes us back to a south Italian Gospel Book which in its turn had received some Greek influences. Such portraits were of course based on standard models and were only original in a limited sense. We ought not to forget that there were portraits of the Apostles hanging in Bede's churches. The text, written in an outstandingly beautiful half-uncial script, represents an excellent version of Jerome's Vulgate, resembling that of the Codex Amiatinus, but not derived directly from it. The book contains liturgical indications showing honour to certain saints associated with southern Italy and particularly with the neighbourhood of Naples. Reflecting on these and many other aspects of this manuscript, we can see the Lindisfarne Gospels as being in some sense a distillation of the history of the Christian church among the English from the days of Augustine's arrival in Canterbury until the death of Cuthbert on Farne in 687. Yet Bede's contemporaries would not have regarded the book in this light. It was a book written expressly for 'God and St Cuthbert' and for all the saints whose relics were kept and honoured in the island of Lindisfarne, and in this light we ought to see it as one aspect of a phenomenon which played a part of great importance in the western church of its age – the cult of the saint.

Cuthbert died in his hermitage on Farne in 687 and almost from the very moment of his death we can trace the beginnings of a cult which made St Cuthbert perhaps the most renowned of all English saints. In the later Middle Ages, as the patron beneath whose banner the northern English defended his patrimony against the Scots, he outstripped in fame the other two English saints who had been his chief rivals in the twelfth century – St Edmund of Bury and St Audrey of Ely. Cuthbert's body was taken from his hermitage to Lindisfarne and there, the head wrapped in a cloth and the unconsecrated host placed upon the breast, it was dressed in priest's robes, its feet were shod and the whole enveloped in a waxed shroud. Thus prepared, the body was placed in a stone coffin in the church of St Peter on the right side of the altar. Eleven years later on the anniversary of his death, 20 March 698, it was decided that the coffin should be opened and when this was done it was found that the body had been preserved uncorrupt – like the body of St Audrey at Ely which was similarly disinterred, and the garments in which it had been clothed were as new. The remains were then buried afresh, but instead of being put back in their original sarcophagus, they were placed in a light chest above the ground where they could be venerated, and within a very short period the fame of Cuthbert's incorruptible body with its miraculous powers began to spread across England and also over the sea to the continent.[28]

The later history of the relics – the flight from Lindisfarne in 875 before the danger of Viking attacks, the seven years of wandering, the settlement first at Chester-le-Street and then at Durham, the translation of the remains in 1104, the destruction of the shrine in 1542, the re-opening of the coffin in 1827 and the treatment of the surviving relics themselves in the 1950s — all these mark later stages in the history of the cult.[29] The continuing veneration of the saint throughout the middle ages has resulted in the survival of much, in addition to the Lindisfarne Book itself, that must have been seen by the monks of Wearmouth and Jarrow, if not also by Bede himself. We still have the small gold pectoral cross, with a garnet at its centre, which Cuthbert wore during his lifetime and which was buried with his body in 687. We also have the wooden reliquary-coffin in which the body was placed on the occasion of the first translation of the remains in 698. Made of oak boards, it is uniquely interesting not only because of its direct association with the saint, but also because, although now comprising many small fragments of wood, it is the only large carved wooden object which has substantially survived from the whole of the Anglo-Saxon period. The lid bears the figure of Christ, together with the four creatures representing the four Evangelists whose names are cut, each near to the appropriate symbol, in either the Latin or the runic alphabet. The twelve Apostles are carved along one side and five archangels along the other. At one end were the two archangels, Michael and Gabriel, and at the other the Virgin and Child. We know that there were other objects within the coffin, including a small piece of oak decorated with embossed silver and used as an altar, and a bone comb, so plain and unadorned that it seems unlikely to have been placed among the relics unless it had belonged to the saint himself. Nothing has survived of Cuthbert's own vestments, and it seems likely that the fragments of figured silks of Byzantine or Persian origin found in the coffin represent the gifts of later pilgrims to the shrine, as do the stole and maniple skilfully embroidered in gold threads by the ladies of the West Saxon court in the early years of the tenth century.

The translation and enshrining of the relics and the composition of the great illuminated Book of the Gospels were accompanied, or soon followed, by the writing of a *Life* of the saint himself by one of the monks of Lindisfarne whose name is not known to us. On these foundations the cult grew rapidly, furthered by a considerable contribution from Wearmouth and Jarrow. The coffin reliquary had been originally fitted with a wooden lid resting upon three transverse bars and offering a secure place on which small gifts for the shrine could be placed without disturbing the saint himself. When the relics were again translated in 1104 there was found lying on this inner lid a book which is now identified with a copy of the Gospel of St John commonly known as the Stonyhurst Gospel.[30] Still preserving its original binding, it was written by a master scribe whose skill and scholarly care has left us a text which is as accurate as it is beautiful. It is in form a real miniature, with the writing on each page covering an area less than a sixth part of a single page of the Codex Amiatinus. This book was written, not at Lindisfarne, but at either Wearmouth or Jarrow during Bede's lifetime. We hear nothing about its association with St Cuthbert earlier than 1104, and it can only be matter for conjecture whether the book was used by Cuthbert himself during his lifetime, in which case we must suppose it to have been written before 687, or whether it was a gift in later years from Abbot Ceolfrith.

The Latin Bible, with Jerome's version of the Gospels and the Roman Psalter, were the foundations of Christianity in England in the seventh and eighth centuries. Bede certainly recognised the importance of Hebrew for a proper understanding of the Bible, but the claim formerly made that he himself knew the language rested on a mistaken interpretation of his phrase *iuxta*

Hebraicam veritatem and his references to certain Hebrew words in a passage in his school-book *De Schematibus et Tropis*. Both in this passage, and also in passages in the *De Temporum Ratione*, where, for example, he writes of following *hebraicam magis veritatem quam lxx translatorum editionem*,[31] the distinction which he was making was between Jerome's translation from the Hebrew original and the *antiqua translatio* made from the Greek of the Septuagint. Any gleanings of Hebrew that Bede may have gathered reached him through Jerome rather than directly from any Hebrew source. On the other hand it is possible that the Greek Septuagint itself was sometimes used by Bede, and it is certain not only that he used a Greek version of *Acts*, but also that at least in later life, he knew enough Greek to be able to make effective comparisons between the Greek and Latin versions before him. We still possess the Greek copy of *Acts* which Bede himself is believed to have used when writing his *Retractions on Acts* in his later years. Now in Oxford, the book is thought to have been originally written somewhere in Sardinia in the sixth century. After Bede had used it, it found its way in the eighth century to Hornbach in the diocese of Metz, and thence to the cathedral of Würzburg, whose first bishop was an English follower of the great West Saxon missionary, Boniface.[32] Whether or not there were Greek versions of other Biblical books in the library at Jarrow, the use of any part of the Bible in Greek would have been limited to a very small number of scholars in England, including perhaps that Tobias, bishop of Rochester who had learnt Greek at the Canterbury school during the archbishopric of Theodore and is said to have been as fluent in Latin and Greek as in his own tongue. Theodore himself, a Greek by birth as well as by education, seems certain to have brought parts at least of the Greek Bible to Canterbury.[33]

Latin, however, remained the language of scholarship and Biblical studies throughout Bede's lifetime and beyond. The part played by English, over and above its function as the medium of everyday speech, is not easy to determine. It was certainly used, as we have seen, to convey the content of Biblical stories in poetic form to those who had no Latin, but, save for the brief *Hymn to Creation* composed by Caedmon, no Anglo-Saxon poetry, whether religious or otherwise, survives in any manuscript as old as the time of Bede. Yet Bede realised that if the elementary teachings of Christianity were to be made more widely known, they would need to be presented to the English in their own language. Although when homilies were committed to writing Latin was the language used, we may surely suppose that preaching to ordinary people was in English. Apart from the illiterate mass of the people who certainly knew no Latin, Bede was well aware that there were clerics and monks who were likewise ignorant of Latin. Such people were to be encouraged to repeat at least the Lord's Prayer and the Creed in their own language, and to this end Bede himself had often given translations of both to those who had no Latin.[34] Bede's last work, completed only on his deathbed, was an English translation of part of the Gospel according to St John.[35] None of this translation now survives, but it was, so far as we know, the first attempt to present any part of the Bible itself in English.

REFERENCES

1   See above p. 128.
2   *AVCeol c.* 20.
3   *HAbb c.* 15.
4   *CLA* II, 177; *LEU*, Pl. X.
5   *CLA* III, 299; *LEU*, Pl. VIII. Much has been written about this MS, but I refer only to B. Fischer, 'Codex Amiatinus und Cassiodor', *Biblische Zeitschrift, n.f.* 6 (1962), 57–79, where references to earlier works will be found. Palaeographers are now agreed upon the English origin of this MS, against earlier claims for an Italian origin.
6   *CI* I, xii, 3.
7   *CLA* VI, 707.
8   *CLA* VI, 768; VII, 904.
9   *CLA* II, 150, 260; X, 1587.
10 *CLA* II, 157, 159.
11 *CLA* II, 214; X, 1567; XI, 1642.

12 *Bonifatii Epistulæ*, ed. R. Rau (Darmstadt 1968), No. 35, pp. 114-15.

13 F. Wormald, *The Miniatures in the Gospels of St. Augustine* (Cambridge 1954), Pls. I, II.

14 *CLA* II, 149. For a detailed discussion of its iconography see O.-K. Werckmeister, *Irisch-northumbrische Buchmalerei* (Berlin 1967), 53–97.

15 *Rev.* 4, 7.

16 *In I Sam.* p. 159, lines 946–50.

17 *EVW c.* XVII.

18 *CLA* III, 281, 399; IV, 436ab (fragments only), and 437 (with one leaf in London and one in Dublin).

19 The so-called Canterbury Gospels, *CLA* II, 214.

20 *CLA* VI, 704; X, 1469.

21 For facsimile edition see *Evangeliorum Quattuor Codex Durmachensis* (Olten-Lausanne-Fribourg 1960). For date and place of origin, see K. Hughes, *The Church in Early Irish Society*, 100–1.

22 *CLA* II, 231.

23 *CLA* II, 274. For the art of these and other Irish manuscripts see F. Henry, *Irish Art* (rev. ed. London 1965), esp. pp. 159–202.

24 *CLA* II, 159.

25 *CLA* XI, 1642, and Ker, *Catalogue*, No. 385.

26 *CLA* VII, 901; V, 578; VIII, 1215.

27 For facsimile edition see *Evangeliorum Quattuor Codex Lindisfarnensis* (Olten-Lausanne-Fribourg, 1956–60).

28 *AVC* IV, 13–14; *BVC* XL, XLII.

29 For a detailed study of the relics see *The Relics of Saint Cuthbert*, ed. C. F. Battiscombe (Oxford 1956).

30 *CLA* II, 260.

31 *BdTR* p. 175, *lines* 11–12; cf. also p. 307, *par.* 3, *line* 5, and p. 308, *par.* 3, *lines* 11–12. See E. F. Sutcliffe, 'The Venerable Bede's Knowledge of Hebrew', *Biblica*, 16 (1953), 300–6.

32 *CLA* II, 251.

33 A manuscript of the Gospels now at Durham, and written in the Irish tradition, has the *Pater Noster* written on *f.* 3v in the Greek language, but in the Latin alphabet, see *CLA* II, 147. For the doxology inscribed in Greek on the Fahan Mura slab from Donegal, see F. Henry, *Irish Art*, *125–7*.

34 *Ep. Egb.* 5.

35 *Ep. Cuthb. de Obitu Bedae*, ed. Dobbie, 122–3.

22

Education and the Grammarians

Bede, as we have seen, was by his own testimony seven years old
when he was entrusted for his education to the care of Benedict
Biscop at Wearmouth which had been founded in 673, only a
year or so after his birth. He was about seventeen when Benedict
Biscop died in 689, and by that date he had already been in the
care of Abbot Ceolfrith at Jarrow for some years. Since we know
that Benedict had been frequently called away from the
monastery to attend to the king's business, we may suspect that
it was Ceolfrith who was mainly responsible for Bede's education. Beyond his early skill as a singer, witnessed by the
incident of the plague at Jarrow in 686, we know nothing
directly about these early years of Bede's life before his ordination as deacon in his nineteenth year, c. 691. Nevertheless,
against the background of education and scholarship in western
Europe as a whole, we can infer something about the means
which enabled him later in his life to indulge his delight in
learning, teaching or writing. Bede's parents were not to know
that the age of seven was of significance within the educational
system of the Roman empire, where it marked the transition
from the child (*infans*) to the boy (*puer*) who at the age of
fourteen became a young man (*adolescens*) but when Bede
himself came later to read Gregory's *Commentary on Job*, he
would find the same threefold division between infancy, when
the infant, though living innocently, does not know how to give
expression to his innocence, the age of boyhood when the boy is
able to put into words what he wants to say, and the age of
adolescence which marks the beginning of labour.[1]

Before the collapse of the western Empire, the earliest education outside the home was acquired through the grammar
schools which concerned themselves with the basic elements of
literacy, as well as with more advanced subjects such as the
exposition of texts and grammatical analysis. At a later stage
pupils could pass to the schools of the rhetors where, over a
period of four to six years, they were taught those oratorical
skills which would enable them to play their part in a society
whose governors exercised their authority far more by the
spoken than by the written word. Those who professed Christianity, whether they intended to live as laymen in the secular
world, or to enter the church professionally as monks or clerics,
acquired their education, like other educated people, through
the grammar schools. Distinct and specifically Christian
schools did not exist. The extent to which the old system
deriving from classical antiquity was able to survive in the west
into the fifth century or later depended upon how greatly
western imperial society as a whole had been disrupted by the
barbarian invasions and the growth of the new western kingdoms. Despite the Vandal invasions, it was still possible for
classical studies to be pursued in North Africa until the capture
of Carthage by the Arabs in 698.[2] The Goths who entered Spain
did so as highly Romanised people and the province which they
occupied, in part, could find room for pagan classical literature
beside the Christian authors. Isidore's culture still looked
backwards beyond the early Christian writers to pagan classical
antiquity. In Gaul too there were places, particularly in Provençe and the Rhône valley, and perhaps also in Aquitaine,
where public teaching in the classical fashion may have continued into the later part of the fifth century, but disruption was
much more severe in the north. However much Gregory of
Tours may have been troubled by a sense of the inadequacy of
his education and scholarship, it was he, rather than Isidore,
who was breaking away from the forms of classical antiquity
into a primitive freshness.[3] We need not doubt that in Britain
during the Roman occupation there were schools at least in the
larger cities, even though the numbers receiving education in

them may not have been very large. Latin became the language of government, law and administration, as well as of large-scale commerce. Moreover it was the only language used for writing, save for an occasional inscription written in Greek. To the extent that it came to be spoken among the wealthier and more cultured elements of Romano-British society, it seems to have been characterised by stilted, archaic forms redolent of the schoolroom, rather than by the changing Vulgar Latin of other parts of the western Empire, particularly Gaul.[4] Though knowledge of Latin survived in western Britain, it is certain that no trace of any Romano-British schools survived in those easterly parts of the island which passed into Anglo-Saxon hands.

The decay of the old schools of the classical type was accompanied by the gradual growth of new, specifically Christian schools which might be associated with a bishop's household, with a parish priest or with a monastery, but there was an age of overlap during which some of those who later acquired renown as scholars of the church had received their first education in the secular schools. Caesarius who held the archbishopric of Arles 502–42, had living in his household a number of clerks who not only attended the Divine Office in the church, but also received instruction, in part from the reading aloud of the Scriptures at mealtimes[5] and in part from discussions in which Caesarius himself sought to provoke his pupils to enlarge their knowledge by asking more questions, 'for it is not always the cows which run to the calves, but sometimes the calves which hasten to the cows so that they may satisfy their hunger from the teats of their mothers'.[6] This kind of education, unlike that which had been given in the antique schools, was not designed to equip its recipients to play their part in the secular world, but to increase their knowledge of the Bible. Caesarius would not allow anyone in his church to be ordained deacon before the age of thirty, and however much older he might be, he was still not to become a deacon before he had read four times through all the books of the Old as well as the New Testament.[7] Whether or not in consequence of the example set by Caesarius of Arles, the Spanish bishops, meeting in the Council of Toledo in 527, determined that children intended by their parents for the ecclesiastical estate should live in the bishop's household and be educated, under the general oversight of the bishop, by a master appointed for that purpose. When they reached the age of eighteen they were to be allowed to choose between marriage and advancement to higher orders. In Provençe at about the same date an attempt was made to use the services of priests in a similar way. The Council of Vaison, held in 529, enjoined that, following the custom which was observed in Italy, priests should take young unmarried lectors into their houses and give them instruction in the Psalter, in sacred texts and in the Divine Law. If any of them later wished to marry, they were not to be forbidden to do so.[8]

In addition to the schools associated with the households of bishops or priests, it is clear that children went in considerable numbers and at a young age to be educated by monks or nuns in monasteries. When Caesarius of Arles drew up a rule for a community of nuns early in the sixth century, he envisaged that young girls would be received by the nuns though in general they were not to be accepted before the age of six or seven when they could begin both to learn and to obey[9] and we have already seen that in Spain Fructuosus contemplated the possibility that entire families with their children might enter monasteries.[10] The Benedictine Rule itself makes several references to children in monasteries, enjoining the graduation of disciplinary punishments according to age, so that, for example, those who could not understand the full meaning of excommunication might rather be punished by fasting or stripes, and commenting on the need for all members of the community to keep a close and watchful oversight of all the children who had not yet reached their fifteenth year.[11]

Unlike Italy, Spain and France, sixth-century England enjoyed neither an active city life nor an organised episcopacy, and in these circumstances we can safely assume that it was the monastic rather than the episcopal or priestly schools which played the chief part in the education of children in the age of Bede. Against the English background we can distinguish between children who were sent to a monastery at about the age of seven to be educated, but without any assumption that they would necessarily become professed monks or nuns, and other children who were dedicated by their parents to the service of God from an early age and who were not expected to return to the secular world. The Benedictine Rule laid down the procedure to be followed when parents, whether noble or poor, wished to devote to the monastic life a son who was too young to be able to make his own petition for admission.[12] In extreme cases children might be dedicated to the monastic life in their earliest infancy, and such a case, in the world of Bede, was that of the princess Ælflæd whose mother was the first Northumbrian to be baptised and who was dedicated to perpetual virginity by her father, King Osuiu, when she was scarcely a year old. This dedication in infancy was recalled in the epitaph by which after her death she was commemorated in her monastery at Whitby.[13] Bede writes merely of being entrusted by his kinsmen to Abbot Benedict for his education, without explicit reference to any intention to commit him to the monastic life. Hwætberht who succeeded Ceolfrith as abbot, had himself, like Bede first entered the monastery in childhood, and we may fairly assume that there would be a number of children between the ages of seven and fourteen at Wearmouth and Jarrow, as well as at most other Anglo-Saxon monastic communities of any size. Some of them would remain as monks and some of them would return to secular life. Wilfrid was about fourteen when he left service at the court to attend upon a nobleman who had withdrawn to Lindisfarne after being afflicted with some paralytic sickness, but he first received the monastic tonsure in Gaul when he was in his early twenties.[14]

Life in a monastery would provide a measure of security and continuity which is likely to have been rare in Bede's England as a whole. Comparison of its austere and strictly regulated ways should not be with the permissive attitude of modern society towards children, but with the brutality often associated with the ways of classical antiquity. Everyone who lived in a monastery learnt from the Gospel that he would not enter the kingdom of Heaven unless he received it as a little child. When Bede came to comment on this passage from St Mark's Gospel (x, 15) he borrowed Jerome's definition of a boy as one who 'does not persist in anger, is not mindful of injury, is not charmed by the sight of a beautiful woman and does not think other than he speaks'.[15] The definition may have been widely current in the west since it was used by Isidore, and also, with very slight variation, by Columban.[16] Bede adds, in further comment on the same passage, that the word of God was to be received in obedience without any hesitation, even as a young boy who is learning does not contradict his teachers or advance arguments in opposition to them, but faithfully receives what he is taught. As a pupil Bede would certainly be taught to obey, and as a teacher himself would expect obedience from his pupils. But his writings show no trace of any harshness towards children and when, in his *Commentary on Proverbs*, he remarks, 'we have known many boys endowed with wisdom', he may have been thinking not only of the young Jeremiah, but also of some whom he had known and taught himself.[17]

Familiarity with the concept of the seven liberal arts deriving from classical antiquity and emerging as the medieval trivium, comprising grammar, rhetoric and dialectic, and the more advanced quadrivium, embracing arithmetic, geometry, astronomy and music, can easily lead to exaggerated notions of the range of subjects which could be taught in an Anglo-Saxon monastic school. Bede's older contemporary Aldhelm, studying at Canterbury at about the time of Bede's birth, wrote to a bishop of Winchester complaining at the lack of time for the many subjects which he was trying to learn, including Roman law, literature, not only in prose, but also in verse with its many different metres, as well as music, arithmetic and all the mysteries of the stars in the heavens.[18] But Aldhelm was unique in his age for the ingenuity of his learning, and the Canterbury school, directed by two outstanding Mediterranean scholars, Archbishop Theodore and Abbot Hadrian, was so far as we know a short-lived phenomenon. Yet it may be that we underestimate the continuing importance of Canterbury as a centre of scholarship because of the lack of any early Canterbury historian and of surviving books of Theodore's age, whether imported or written in Canterbury itself. An eleventh-century manuscript written by an Italian scribe contains a body of material concerned with Biblical exegesis which is believed to derive, intermediately through Germany, from the teaching of Theodore himself. It is characterised in particular by its numerous citations from Greek theologians whose works were evidently expounded in the Canterbury school.[19] We ought also to remember that the first undoubtedly genuine Anglo-Saxon charters date from the time of Theodore.

Aldhelm himself has left a striking picture of Theodore confronted by his pupils, many Irishmen among them, 'like an angry boar surrounded by a pack of grinning Molossian hounds', but we ought to balance this picture with another which Bede painted of his own bishop, John of Hexham, at whose hands he was ordained first deacon and then priest. Bishop John who received his first education at Whitby, had also gone to Canterbury to learn from Archbishop Theodore, and in later years when he was attending a sick nun, he remembered how the archbishop had taught him that it was dangerous to undertake blood-letting when the moon was full and the tide high. Bishop John was able to cure of his affliction a dumb boy who lived near Hexham, and after loosening his tongue, he began to teach him the alphabet: ' "Say *A*". The boy said it. "Say *B*". The boy said this too. And when, in answer to the bishop, the boy replied with the names of all the letters, the bishop went on to put to him syllables and words to speak. And when the boy answered him appropriately in all points, he ordered him to speak longer sentences and so he did.'[20] Bede's description of this incident in the life of his bishop seems to take us very close to the schoolroom in which Bede himself and the other boys first learnt their letters.

Grammar, the full and detailed understanding of words and their various functions, was the foundation of literacy no less for those whose reading was to be sought in the Bible and the works of the Fathers, than for those who in other times and places enjoyed the pagan works of classical antiquity, and grammatical studies would unquestionably occupy a major place in an English monastic school of Bede's day, as also in the schools of Spain, Italy or Provence. Yet when Bede made his first approach to Latin he did so as to a wholly foreign language, unlike his contemporaries in the schools of the more southerly countries where Latin still remained the living spoken tongue, and, perhaps it was this distinction which led not only Bede himself, when he came to be the teacher, but also other English scholars, to compile their own grammatical treatises. In Bede's childhood, both in England itself and in the former western Empire as a whole, the most important and influential of the Roman imperial grammarians was Aelius Donatus who, living in the fourth century, numbered Jerome among the pupils for whom he had compiled his two *Artes Grammaticae*.[21] The first of the two, the *Ars Minor*, was a brief elementary treatise dealing with the eight parts of speech which he defined as noun, pronoun, verb, adverb, participle, conjunction, preposition, interjection. The work is cast throughout in a series of brief questions and equally concise answers, for example: 'How many genders of nouns are there? Four. What are they? Masculine, as *hic magister*, feminine as *haec musa*, neuter as *hoc scamnum*, and common, as *hic et haec sacerdos*', and, 'How many persons of pronouns are there? Three. What are they? First, *ego*. Second, *tu*. Third, *ille*', and so forth through declensions, cases and conjugations. Such, whether from the work of Donatus himself or from some other grammarian, would be the daily fare of the young boy at a monastic school. Although the stylus and wax tablet were certainly used in monasteries, we can assume that Donatus used the question and answer form because most elementary teaching in his day was done through the spoken rather than the written word, and that this continued to be the case. After mastering the basic elements, the pupil might have passed on to the topics discussed by Donatus in the *Ars Maior*, a work which not only dealt in greater detail with the parts of speech, but also handled such topics as syllables, feet, stress, barbarisms, solecisms and figures of speech.

[244]

Within the field of grammatical studies the work of Donatus won a high degree of authority which it continued to enjoy throughout the Anglo-Saxon period, so much so that in the twelfth century his name was used as a common noun signifying *grammar*, and it was possible to write of a Greek grammar as a *Donatus Graece* and an English grammar as a *Donatus Anglice*.[22] Yet there were a great many other grammarians who either wrote commentaries on the work of the master or else compiled their own grammatical treatises. The evidence either of direct citation or of surviving manuscripts associated with Anglo-Saxon centres in England or on the Continent yields the names of a surprisingly large number of these Latin grammarians of the late Imperial age. For example, in one of his schoolbooks, the *De Arte Metrica*,[23] Bede makes five references to Donatus, as well as others to the works of Sergius, Pompeius, Mallius Theodorus, Maximus Victorinus and Audacius. Of these other grammarians, both Sergius and Pompeius wrote commentaries on the work of Donatus and there still survive eighth-century copies of their writings which, though now preserved in Carinthia in Austria, are in Anglo-Saxon hands and probably came originally from some northern English scriptorium.[24] They seem to have been associated with another commentary on Donatus compiled by an anonymous Irishman, but written in the hand of an English scribe.[25] The transmission of the work of Pompeius, *Commentum in Artem Donati*, to the Continent, presumably in the wake of Anglo-Saxon missionaries, marks the end of a journey which seems to have brought it from North Africa, where it was originally written in the fifth century, across Spain to England. The work of Pompeius was a major source of Isidore's grammatical studies at Seville in the sixth century and in the middle of the seventh century it was extensively used by the Spanish grammarian, Archbishop Julian of Toledo, who wrote his own Grammar shortly before his death in 690. Julian's work the *Ars Grammatica*, evidently reached England within a short time of its composition and was taken thence to the Continent where there still survives a fragment of it written in an eighth-century Anglo-Saxon minuscule hand perhaps at some such

Anglo-Saxon Continental centre as Fulda.[26] All the surviving manuscripts of this work derive from an insular archetype.[27] The arrival in England of the grammatical works of Pompeius and of Julian of Toledo are among the many strands of evidence pointing to the closeness of the connexions with Spain in the seventh and eighth centuries. The works of several other grammarians of the late Imperial age are also found in a number of manuscripts which, though now housed in Continental libraries, betray English connexions through the handwriting of their scribes. They include the works of Diomedes, Charisius, Consentius and Priscianus.[28] Whether these particular manuscripts were written in England or at an English continental centre, we need not doubt that the grammatical treatises of their authors were known in England in Bede's time and that their transmission to the Continent was through the activities of English missionaries.

The works of these and other late imperial grammarians, with Donatus at their head, were at once the foundation upon which rested the teaching of Latin in English monastic schools in the seventh and eighth centuries, and the source books used by those English teachers who in their turn came to compile their own grammars. Among these latter were Tatwine, archbishop of Canterbury (731–4) and Boniface (680–754) the great West Saxon missionary who received his early education in Exeter and who, during the course of his long mission to the heathen Germans founded the abbey of Fulda (c. 742). Tatwine was probably a Mercian by birth, for Bede knew that before he became archbishop of Canterbury he had been a priest in a monastery at Breedon in Leicestershire. His *Ars Grammatica* followed the model of the *Ars Minor* of Donatus, dealing successively with the eight parts of speech and borrowing its illustrations from classical sources, at several removes from the originals, through the works of the earlier grammarians, though he did draw some examples from the Psalms. He compiled his grammar before going to Canterbury as archbishop in 731 and it seems to have been used not only in England, but also at English continental centres. Fragments of an eighth-century

[246]

manuscript of the work, written in an Anglo-Saxon hand, are now preserved partly at Carlsruhe and partly in the library of St Paul in Carinthia. This copy of Tatwine's work was probably written in the same English continental scriptorium which also produced copies of the grammatical works of Charisius, Diomedes and Consentius, as well as a copy of another English work of a different nature, the *De Laudibus Virginitate* of Aldhelm. These grammatical works, including Tatwine's, may have been formed into a single corpus of grammarians such as would have been of great value to those English missionaries who in the eighth century were introducing their recent converts to Biblical studies in much the same way as Bede and his contemporaries had been introduced to them in England in the seventh century.[29] Wider continental distribution of Tatwine's grammar is suggested by references to it in the early monastic catalogues of St Riquier in Picardy and of Lorsch near Mainz. No St Riquier copy survives but a ninth-century Lorsch copy is now preserved in the Vatican where it is found together with some of the works of the earlier grammarians – Donatus, Asper and Dynamius – as well as those of the Spaniard Julian of Toledo and the English Boniface.[30]

We do not know whether Boniface wrote his *Ars Grammatica* before or after he left England, but, like Tatwine, he depended upon the earlier grammarians, though not without some attempt at originality. The oldest manuscript of Boniface's *Ars Grammatica*, now in Paris, belongs to the eighth or ninth century, and is thought to have been written in northern France at some centre under Anglo-Saxon influence.[31] The interest of these Latin grammars of English origin is less in their content than in their mere existence which testifies both to the pursuit of Latin educational studies in Mercian and West Saxon centres not otherwise known for their intellectual activities and also to the part played by English grammarians in transmitting the late imperial grammatical traditions to the Continent. Tatwine's monastery at Breedon in Leicestershire has long been renowned for the notable collection of sculptured stones embedded in the fabric of the present church,[32] and Tatwine's grammar is a witness to the capacity of a monastery of whose history little is known, to provide an education which could lead one of its members to the archbishopric.

Whether we look to the writings of St Augustine of Hippo or of Cassiodorus or, nearer home, to the letters of Aldhelm, we find abundant evidence of the importance which Christian writers attached to the study of grammar as unlocking the door through which the pupil gained access to the Word of God. Bede himself was certainly no exception and as a teacher at Jarrow he may well have compiled his own manual for use in the schoolroom, though he himself does not tell of any such work. The list of his writings which he appended to the *Ecclesiastical History* names three books which are generally regarded as school books: 'A book on Orthography, arranged in alphabetical order: likewise a book on the Metrical Art, and added to it another little book concerning Figures of Speech or Tropes.' The first of these works, *De Orthographia*,[33] contains no evidence of the date at which it was written, but to judge from its subject matter as well as from the simple immaturity of its form, it may well be the first book which Bede wrote, and in that case we may attribute it to *c.* 700 when he was still in deacon's orders. The work consists of several hundred words arranged under the letters of the alphabet, though not in strict alphabetical order within each letter. Each word is the subject of a comment, usually brief but sometimes running to several lines. Its purpose is best illustrated by some examples. Under *acer* we find that the superlative is to be written *acerrimus* and not *acerissimus*. *Apud* is to be written with a *d*, but *caput* with a *t*. *Fremor* is the noise made by men, *fremitus* that made by beasts. *Luceo* and *lugeo* both have *luxi* in the perfect tense. Among the longer comments is that on *ab* and *ex* which evidently troubled the schoolboys of Bede's day no less than those of later ages – 'when someone says he is coming *a theatro*, he does not mean that he is coming out of the theatre itself, but away from the place which is nearest to the theatre. When he says he is coming *ex theatro* he means he is coming out of the theatre itself.' The work also contains a considerable number of the Greek equivalents of Latin words, enough to make one wonder if there were some to whom Bede was teaching Greek. In this work *De Orthographia* Bede was following a well-established pattern, and he took some of his examples from such earlier writers as Julius Modestus and Aelius Melissus who had themselves compiled treatises on the same subject. It is perhaps an indication of the early date of this work that most of his examples come, indirectly, from classical sources, including Virgil, Cicero, Livy and Ovid, but already Bede had begun the process of Christianising his examples in a way which he carried out much more completely in his other school books. It is of particular interest to find that, in addition to some dozen Biblical quotations, there are no fewer than ten citations from the works of Gregory the Great.

Bede's little work *De Orthographia* would have been useful to those who had learnt the basic elements of Latin grammar, such as they would have found in the *Ars Minor* of Donatus, and had advanced to the stage of writing Latin compositions. His other two school books, *De Arte Metrica* and *De Schematibus et Tropis*[34] were intended for more advanced pupils who had reached a standard broadly comparable with the beginnings of a modern sixth-form course in Latin. The titles of the two works are largely self-explanatory; the former consisting of instruction in the writing of Latin verse, with an introduction to different metres, and the latter of an exposition of the different figures with which speech might be clothed and adorned. Bede's own reference to these two books suggests that he regarded the second almost as though it were an appendix to the first, and we are probably justified in thinking that the two were written at much the same time. At the end of the work on metre there is a short personal passage in which Bede addresses his 'most beloved son and fellow-deacon Cuthbert'. He offers Cuthbert the results of his labours in searching through the works of ancient writers so that, just as he had tried to instruct him in Holy Scripture and in the statutes of the church, he might now teach him the art of metre 'which is not unknown in sacred books'.

The passage leaves the impression that Bede was dedicating the work to one who had been, and perhaps still was, a favourite pupil who had lately received deacon's orders. Although 25 was the canonical age for ordination to the diaconate, we do not know how strictly this age was enforced in eighth-century England. As we have seen, Bede himself became a deacon in his nineteenth year and others who showed good promise may have been ordained at an equally early age. Bede did not become a priest till his thirtieth year, c. 702, and we can easily envisage a gap of ten years or more between himself and the young Cuthbert which would allow for the relationship of master and pupil, and which would also allow Bede to call himself a 'fellow deacon' of Cuthbert's if this passage, and therefore the book as a whole, was written c. 701.[35]

As in his little work on orthography, so also in the work on metre, we can see Bede moving away from the pagan classical world by the introduction of illustrative examples drawn from the work of such Christian writers as Sedulius and Arator, even going to the extreme of showing that it was possible to write a hexameter composed entirely of Biblical names: *Sarra, Rebecca, Rachel, Ester, Iudith, Anna, Noemi*. But the work *De Schematibus* is particularly instructive on this head. To judge from the terms discussed, from the order in which they are presented and also from the wording of the definitions Bede based his book on the two consecutive chapters of Isidore of Seville's *Etymologiae* entitled *De Schematibus* and *De Tropis*,[36] but despite the correspondence of form there is a fundamental difference of substance. Whereas Isidore continued to draw the greater part of his illustrative examples through the grammarians from classical sources, Bede, in an opening paragraph in which he seems to be addressing the same former pupil and fellow-deacon Cuthbert, expressly claims the superiority of Holy Scripture over all other writings on the ground of its authority which was Divine, of its utility, in that it showed the way to eternal life, and of its antiquity. The result was the total Christianisation of his work *De Schematibus* in which all the illustrative examples are taken from the Bible with the exception of one which comes from the Christian poet Sedulius.

REFERENCES

1 *Greg. Mor.* XI, 46.
2 Riché, *Education et Culture*, 78.
3 J. Fontaine, *Isidore de Séville*, II, 886.
4 K. Jackson, *Language and History in Early Britain*, 76–112.
5 *V. Caes.* I, 62, ed. D. G. Morin, *S. Caes. Ep. Arelat. Op. Omn.* II (Maretioli 1942), 322.
6 *V. Caes.* I, 52, Morin, II, 317–18.
7 *V. Caes.* I, 56, Morin, II, 320.
8 *Concilium Vasense* 1, ed. C. de Clerq, *Concilia Galliae*, CCSL CXLVIII A, 78.
9 *Caes. Reg. Mon. c.* 7, Morin II, 104.
10 Above p. 136.
11 *BR cc.* XXX and LXX, 4.
12 *C.* LIX.
13 *HE* III, 24, and *Archaeologia* LXXXIX, pp. 41–2.
14 *EVW cc.* II and VI.
15 *In Marc.* III, x, 15, ed. Hurst, *CCSL* CXX, p. 559, *lines* 685–7.
16 *De Vet. et Nov. Test. Quaest.* XL, *PL*, LXXXIII, 207, and *Ep. MGH* III, 163, 29.
17 *PL* XCI, 1004.
18 *Aldhelmi Op.*, ed. R. Ehwald, *MGH Auct. Ant.* XV, 475 ff.
19 B. Bischoff, *Sacris Erudiri*, VI (1954), 190–5. I am indebted to Professor Whitelock for this reference.
20 *HE* V, 2.
21 Ed. H. Keil, *Grammatici Latini*, IV (Leipzig 1880), 353–402.
22 J. D. A. Ogilvy, *Books Known to the English, 597–1066* (Cambridge, Mass., 1967), 132.
23 Ed. H. Keil, *op. cit.*, VII, 227–60.
24 *CLA* X, 1451, 1453.
25 *CLA* X, 1452.
26 *CLA* VIII, 1210.
27 See C. H. Beeson, 'The Ars Grammatica of Julian of Toledo', *Studi e Testi*, 37 (1924), 50–70.
28 *CLA* VIII, 1125, 1227 (though perhaps Irish), 1126; VII, 1009; VIII, 1133.
29 *CLA* VIII, 1124–5, 1127, and X** 1127.

30 M. Roger, *L'enseignement des lettres classiques d'Ausone à Alcuin* (Paris 1905), 332–3.

31 *CLA* V, 672.

32 *Archaeologia* LXXVII (1928), 219–40.

33 Ed. Keil, *Gram. Lat.* VII, 261–94.

34 *Ibid.* VII, 227–60, and K. Halm, *Rhetores Latini Minores* (Leipzig 1863), 607–18.

35 M. L. Laistner, *A Hand-List of Bede Manuscripts* (Ithaca 1943), 131–2.

36 Isidore, *Etym.* I, 36–7.

23
Reading and Psalmody

We do not know whether Bede held any of the minor orders before his ordination to the diaconate, nor indeed do we hear anything directly about these minor orders in the context of Wearmouth and Jarrow, but from Spain we have Isidore of Seville's list of the six orders below that of deacon, with his definition of their several functions, beginning with the door-keeper (*ostiarius*) and passing thence to acolyte, exorcist, cantor (whom Isidore calls *psalmista*) lector and subdeacon.[1] We can hardly doubt that, whether formally or not, Bede would in his early days have performed the functions of both lector and cantor. It must be remembered that the reading of sacred books, the end to which the study of grammar in the monastic schools was devoted, involved the reading aloud to the community of the Bible and some of the works of the Fathers at certain times of the day which would be prescribed in the monastic rule. The lectors, in Isidore's view, are more than mere readers. They are those who announce or preach the Word of God[2] and for this reason they needed to be well-trained to perform their task properly. Isidore's remark that their knowledge of grammatical structure had to be sufficient to enable them to know when the sense of a group of words was complete, and when it carried over into an adjacent group of words, helps us to appreciate the real difficulty of reading aloud in a foreign language, often no doubt by the poor light of the candle, from a book which was written by hand and which might well have had no punctuation. Moreover, as he instances, there were places in Scripture where the use of a wrong stress or intonation could completely reverse the meaning of a particular passage and inexperienced readers often made mistakes of this kind. The voice of the lector must be clear and virile, avoiding extremes of humility and exaltation and not sounding like the voice of a woman. It was the duty of the lector to appeal to the ears and heart, rather than to the eye, and he must take care lest those who heard him became spectators rather than listeners. Those who were still quite young might, because of the purity of their voices, be admitted to the order of lector and there are several instances of distinguished churchmen whose ecclesiastical careers began in this way. Indeed the incident of the plague at Jarrow *c.* 686 seems to portray the young Bede, then aged about fourteen, as one who was already able to fulfil the duties of both lector and cantor.

The difficulties facing the young *lector* are vividly illustrated in a scene from the boyhood of Gregory who later became abbot of Utrecht and, after the death of Boniface, head of the Frisian church. Boniface was visiting a nunnery near Trèves and Gregory, then a boy of about fourteen, was given a book and asked to read. After he had finished the reading Boniface praised him but asked him if he understood what he was reading. Gregory then began to read from the book as before but Boniface, saying that this was not what he wanted, asked him to give an explanation of the passage in his own language, but this the unhappy boy could not do.[3]

Psalmody and the study of the Psalter played a dominant part in the monastic life of western Europe from its earliest days. Because of the importance of psalmody in the liturgical observances of the canonical hours, it became the first task of every novice to make himself familiar with the Psalms and even to learn the whole of the Psalter by heart. This he could well do, aided by the rhythms of the chant and the singing of the choir, even before he had acquired enough Latin to enable him to understand the meaning of the words themselves. For Caesarius, archbishop of Arles, the Psalms were indeed the weapons of the servants of God and one who was able to wield these weapons need have no fear of his adversaries.[4] When the hermit Guthlac fancied himself attacked in his fenland dwelling, with his buildings set on fire and himself thrown into the air on the points of his enemies' spears, he recited the first verse of the 67th Psalm: 'Let God arise, let his enemies be scattered,' and in a twinkling 'all the host of demons vanished like smoke from his presence'.[5] We find Cuthbert singing as he kept vigil at night along the seashore below Æbbe's monastery at Coldingham, in a shepherd's hut where he had taken shelter for the night, and as he walked round the island of Lindisfarne. Columba was transcribing a psalter on the last day of his life.[6] Ceolfrith, Bede's own teacher, had been in the habit of reciting the entire Psalter twice every day, and when he finally left Wearmouth on the journey which ended in his death at Langres, he chanted the whole Psalter from beginning to end three times every day.[7] The learning of the Psalter would certainly be one of the tasks undertaken by the pupils of a monastic school, and it is not likely that Bede, with his strong interest in singing, would have been behind the young Wilfrid who learnt the whole Psalter when he was at Lindisfarne at about the age of fourteen.[8]

Eddius tells us that when Wilfrid first read the Psalter he did so 'in Jerome's revision', but that when he went to Canterbury, where he spent a year before crossing to Gaul in company with Benedict Biscop, he learnt the Psalms by heart 'from the fifth edition, after the Roman use'.[9] Whether or not *quintam* is here a corruption of *antiquam*, the distinction is in any case between the two versions known as the Gallican Psalter and the Roman Psalter. We find a version of the Gallican Psalter in the Cathach of St Columba which is held to have been written late in the sixth or early in the seventh century.[10] This was presumably the version taken to Lindisfarne by Aidan when he and his companions settled there in 635 and it would still be in use at Lindisfarne when Wilfrid went there some twelve years before the synod of Whitby. Although the Gallican Psalter is likely to have spread from Lindisfarne to other parts of England where the Irish missionaries founded churches whose affiliations were with Iona rather than with Rome, it was the Roman Psalter which became the dominant version used in the Anglo-Saxon church as a whole until as late as the eleventh century. August-

ine would certainly have brought the Roman Psalter with him
to Canterbury and it would have reached Northumbria through
Paulinus whose companion, James the Deacon, continued to
teach psalmody in the Roman fashion in Northumbria even
down until the time of Bede's birth. The singing organised by
Wilfrid both at Ripon and at Hexham was likewise based on
the Roman ways practised in Kent. Roman contact was
renewed with the arrival at Wearmouth of Abbot John who,
himself the *archicantor* of St Peter's in Rome, firmly established
Roman psalmody not only at Wearmouth, but also in other
monasteries whose singers came to learn from him.[11]

Just as two Northumbrian manuscripts, the Lindisfarne
Gospels and the Codex Amiatinus, now supply the best witnesses to Jerome's version of the Gospels, so also it is a Canterbury manuscript which, with a group of related texts of English
origin, now offers the best and oldest witness to the Roman
Psalter. This manuscript, the Vespasian Psalter, now in the
British Museum, is believed to have been written in St Augustine's monastery at Canterbury in the first half of the eighth
century, probably during the later years of Bede's own lifetime,
and it is in no way unlikely that it derived its text directly or
indirectly from a copy of the Roman Psalter brought to Canterbury by St Augustine himself.[12] In addition to the Vespasian
Psalter, there are three other surviving copies of the Roman
version which come from English foundations and which are
written in English script – the Salaberga Psalter, now in Berlin,
which is held to have been written in Northumbria, but later
belonged to the monastery of St John at Laon, founded by
Salaberga who died in 665; the Morgan Psalter, now in New
York, thought to be of English, and probably southern English,
origin; and the Stuttgart Psalter which has been attributed to
an English continental centre and which belonged to Echternach in the ninth century.[13] There are also fragments of several
other copies of the Roman Psalter whose hands reveal English
associations. One of these is written in the capitular uncial
which is characteristic of the Wearmouth-Jarrow scriptorium
and it may date from Bede's own lifetime.[14] The quantity and

quality of the manuscript evidence leaves us in no doubt about the part played by English scribes in spreading the Roman Psalter not only throughout England but also to the Continent, and more particularly to those continental houses with English associations. There is no evidence that the Psalms were ever sung in English in Bede's age, but a continuous interlinear English gloss was added to the Vespasian Psalter, probably by a Mercian scribe working at Canterbury in the ninth century. We have no information about the musical instruments used to accompany the monastic singing of Bede's day. There was a harp of the kind called *rottae* in the monastery shortly after Bede's death, but nobody knew how to play it. A harp figures in Bede's account of Caedmon and the remains of one were found in the Sutton Hoo ship-burial. So far as we know there was no system of musical notation in use anywhere in western Europe in this age. As Isidore remarked: 'Unless the sounds are retained in man's memory they perish because they cannot be written down.'[15]

REFERENCES

1 *De Ecc. Off.* II, viii-xv, *PL* 83, 788–94.

2 *Ibid.* II, xi.

3 *Liudgeri Vit. Greg. Abb. Traiect.* c. 2, ed. O. Holder-Egger, *MGH*, *SS* XV, pt. i, p. 68. I am indebted to Professor Whitelock for drawing my attention to this passage.

4 *Sermones.* No. CCXXXVIII, ed. Morin, *CCSL* CIV, 950.

5 *Felix Vita Guth.* c. XXXIV. Psalm 68 in the Authorised Version.

6 *AVC* II, 3; *BVC cc.* V and XVI; *AdVC* III, 23.

7 *AVCeol c.* 33.

8 *EVW c.* II.

9 *Ibid. c.* III.

10 *CLA* II, 266.

11 See above pp. 170–2.

12 Facsimile edition with introduction by D. H. Wright, *Early English Manuscripts in Facsimile*, Vol. 14 (Copenhagen 1967).

13 *CLA* VIII, 1048; XI, 1661; IX, 1353.

away number in all things and all things perish. Take away computation from the world and everything is wrapped in blind ignorance.'[4] In practical terms, some knowledge of number was needed for a life which depended on the regular observance of the monastic horarium, and for the proper carving and setting of the monastic sundials or mass-clocks, such as are found built into the wall of the church at Escomb or carved on one face of the Bewcastle Cross.[5] Beyond the hours of the day lay the days of the week and the months of the year, with their associated days of festival or seasons of fasting. The calculation of the church calendar required a degree of skill and a knowledge of number which we, turning to the pocket-diary or the wrist-watch telling both time and date, cannot easily appreciate.[6] But beyond the practical application of number to daily life there was a widely-held belief in its efficacy as a means of spiritual progress, often expressed through the elaboration of ideas about the symbolism of number in Biblical contexts.

The interest of the western church in number was prompted and maintained by the need to determine afresh every year the date on which Christians were to celebrate their most important festival – Easter Day. While fixed dates had been adopted for some of the church festivals, for example the Nativity of Christ and of John the Baptist which were related respectively to the winter and summer solstices, Easter, evolving out of the Jewish Passover, was from the first, a moveable feast which depended on the lunar year and consequently could not recur annually on the same day of the Julian calendar which was based on the solar year. The need to reconcile these two different years led to problems which were argued, often with great heat, throughout the western church for many centuries.[7] In retrospect these arguments which were symptomatic of deeper divisions between different branches of the church, and notably between the 'Roman' and 'Celtic' groups in England, may seem tedious, but the determination in advance of the date upon which Easter was to be celebrated required the construction of complicated tables involving such matters as indictions, epacts, concurrents, intercalations, lunar cycles and so forth. Out of the controversies there arose a considerable body of computistical literature, in which the Irish were concerned no less than the English, and which stimulated a widespread interest in problems of chronology in general. As we have seen, it was Wearmouth and Jarrow, under the abbacy of Ceolfrith, Bede's teacher, which played the leading part in persuading the 'Celtic' groups to conform to 'Roman' practices after the decision taken at the synod of Whitby, a task which was still uncompleted at the time of Bede's death. Bede himself, through his passionate devotion to Roman ways, was deeply concerned in the Easter problem and out of this concern he developed a knowledge which gave him a great mastery of chronological problems.

Preceding the grammatical works in Bede's list of his own writings, we find three books grouped together, one on the Nature of Things, one on Times and one larger book on Times. These three works, commonly known by the Latin titles as the *De Natura Rerum*, the *De Temporibus* and the *De Temporum Ratione*, were written by Bede as manuals for use in the schoolrooms of Wearmouth and Jarrow, but the very large number of surviving manuscripts – not less than 125 of the first, 65 of the second and 135 of the third[8] – witnesses the widespread popularity which these works came to enjoy in medieval Europe. The *De Temporibus* was written in 703 at about the time when Bede was ordained to the priesthood. It seems very probable, though there is no direct evidence, that the *De Natura Rerum* was also written at about the same time. The *De Temporum Ratione* was written in 725, and in its *Preface* Bede explained that he had been persuaded to write at greater length by his pupils who had complained that the two earlier books had proved to be too condensed, especially the *De Temporibus*. He dedicated this longer work to his abbot, Hwætberht.[9] These three books comprise the total of Bede's scientific writings and even if their content may seem remote from both Greek and modern scientific knowledge, nevertheless they show a measure of attainment which is by no means negligible and was certainly far in advance of its own age, particularly in matters concerning the sun, moon, planets and stars. The universe was for Bede a place created by God in the manner described in the Book of Genesis, and it was therefore a place of order whose phenomena, whether observed in the skies or experienced on the earth, were all capable of rational explanation and not merely the outcome of caprice. He supposed it to be comprised of the four elements – earth, air, fire and water – and he believed that the global earth lay at the centre of this universe with the heavens revolving round it. In his commentary on Genesis he advanced the view that there were seven heavens surrounding the earth – air, ether, Olympus, fiery space, firmament, heaven of angels and heaven of Trinity.[10] He supposed the earth itself to be divided into five zones, two of extreme cold in the north and south, one of extreme heat in the middle and two intermediate temperate zones. Both of these latter were habitable, but only the more northerly of the two was in fact inhabited.[11] He believed that the stars, which received their light from the sun, were composed of different kinds of matter and that comets were portents of change, whether through death, pestilence, war or wind. Thunder was caused by winds escaping from clouds, in which they had been imprisoned and lightning was caused by the striking together of clouds, just as a spark is produced when two stones are struck together 'for the colliding of all kinds of matter produces fire'. The phenomena which produced the thunder and the lightning occurred simultaneously, but the lightning was seen by the eye more quickly than the thunder could reach the ears. Earthquakes were due to the violent rushing of winds through caves and the eruption of Etna was due to water leaking into the earth from the Mediterranean.[12]

The later of Bede's two books on Times, the *De Temporum Ratione*, though dealing with essentially the same topics, was expanded to more than twelve times the length of the earlier treatise. Those who used the later work would have found in its first chapter a detailed exposition of the art of finger-counting from one upwards to one million. After mastering this art, and before passing on to tables of the Greek and Roman numerals, they would be encouraged by learning to apply their knowledge

of finger-counting so that they could say secretly to one of their
friends, 'Be careful!' (*Caute age*).[13] Bede then proceeded to
discuss the divisions of time beginning with the smallest unit and
ending with the largest, but he devoted the greater part of the
work to a detailed exposition of a variety of problems concerning
the lunar and solar years. He taught that there were three kinds
of time determined respectively by nature, by custom or by
authority, the first was exemplified by the solar year of 365¼
days, the second by the reckoning of 30 days to the month,
since this belonged neither to the solar nor to the lunar year,
and the third by human authority when an olympiad was
reckoned at 4 years or by divine authority when the Sabbath
was accounted the seventh day.[14] Quoting the saying from the
Gospel according to St John, 'Are there not twelve hours in the
day?' (11,9) he defined an hour as the twelfth part of a day and
proceeded to discuss an ambiguity unfamiliar to a world which
does not depend for the reckoning of time on the primitive
mass-clock; if every day of the year was reckoned to contain
twelve hours, the hour of a summer day would be a much longer
period than the hour of a winter day, but if all the hours were to
be of equal length, there would need to be fewer of them in
winter than in summer.[15] He devoted a long and involved
chapter to discussion of the day itself, remarking how the
Hebrews had reckoned from dawn to dawn, the Egyptians from
sunset to sunset and the Romans from midnight to midnight,
and then showing how for Christians the order of darkness and
light possessed a mystical significance. From the first beginning of
time night had followed day according to the order of creation,
but through the Resurrection of Christ who rose from the dead
in the night and showed himself to his disciples in the day, the
whole order of time had been changed. When man had fallen
through sin from the light of paradise, it was fitting that the
night should follow the day, but when through faith in the
Resurrection he had been led back from the shadow of death to
the light of life, then indeed did the day follow the night.[16]

Darkness and light, because of their mystical significance,
were themes which seem to have possessed a particular fascin-

ation for Bede. We have already noticed one passage in which he gives a vivid description of distant lights shining through the darkness,[17] and there is another, perhaps even more striking, in which he seeks to explain by the analogy of a church illuminated at night, why the moon though in fact lower than the sun, might seem to be the higher of the two. You are to suppose that you go by night into some very large building, such as a church which is lit by a great number of lights burning in honour of the martyr whose festal day is being observed. Among these many lights, you see, suspended by chains from the ceiling, two very large lamps of fine workmanship, and of these two the one which is the nearer to you as you enter the church is also the one which is closest to the floor. So great is the size of the building and so great the height of the distant lamps that as you look through the darkness you see the rays cast by the flames, rather than the vessels which contain the flames. As you begin to walk forwards, raising your eyes to these lamps and looking through them to the wall or celing beyond, the nearer and the lower of the two will seem to be the higher, and the closer you approach to it, the higher it will seem to be, until, after you have made a more careful examination, you discover exactly how they are placed.[18]

Bede's scientific writings, although sometimes illuminated by his own observations, as in this analogy of the lamps hanging in a church, his comments about the tides or his remarks on the names by which the pagan English formerly called the months of the year[19], drew largely upon beliefs handed down through the works of earlier writers. As a scholar he himself was familiar with parts at least of Pliny's *Natural History*, some of which survives at Leyden in an eighth-century manuscript believed to have been copied in a northern English scriptorium from an ancient exemplar,[20] but it would be as a pupil in the monastic school that he would make his first acquaintance with the subjects about which he wrote later in his scientific treatises. We have already seen that the works of some of the cosmographers were known in Northumbria not later than 686 through the volume which Benedict Biscop brought back from one of his visits to Rome and later gave to King Aldfrith in exchange for an estate. Although Bede names Isidore of Seville only three times, 'in each case only to controvert him',[21] Isidore's writings won a rapid and widespread popularity in Britain in the seventh century and were extensively used by Bede himself. Some of Isidore's works were being used by Irish authors at least ten years before Bede's birth, and Aldhelm shows acquaintance with his *De Natura Rerum* in a letter which he wrote to Aldfrith, king of Northumbria, between 685 and 705. Whether the *De Natura Rerum* reached England from Ireland, perhaps through Malmesbury where Aldhelm was the pupil of an Irish scholar, or more directly from Spain across Gaul, there can be no doubt of the great popularity of the work in both Ireland and England in the seventh century, nor of the leading part played by English scribes in transmitting this and other works of Isidore to Germany in the eighth.[22]

Bede followed Isidore in dividing time into moments, hours, days, months, years, centuries and ages, and, like Isidore, he added to each of his works on Times a chronicle setting out the duration of the different ages of the world. For Bede, as for Isidore, St Augustine of Hippo and many other Christian writers, the temporal world was conceived as having a duration of Six Ages. Five of the Six Ages were already passed, their divisions being marked by Creation, the Flood, Abraham, David, the Captivity of Judah and the birth of Christ. Chronographers reached differing conclusions about the year in which the first age began, but most of them reached a figure between 5,000 and 5,500 years before the Advent. When Bede stated plainly at the end of his *De Temporibus* that how much of the Sixth Age remained was known only to God, he was doing neither more nor less than Isidore and Augustine who both asserted that this was a matter which could not be known to man. Nevertheless, some of those familiar with the calculations of the chronographers were also familiar with the words spoken by St Peter: 'But, beloved, be not ignorant of this one thing, that one day is with the Lord as a thousand years, and a thousand years as one day',[23] and it might be difficult to avoid supposing, and often fearing, that if the first Five Ages had lasted approximately a thousand years each, the Sixth and the last Age might be expected to do much the same. Moreover, if the first Five Ages had exceeded their allotted span by some three or four hundred years, might they not have done so by encroaching upon the Sixth? When Gregory the Great, writing to King Æthelbert of Kent in 601,[24] referred to the many disturbances of nature which foretold the approaching end of the world, he did not do so because he thought that such a threat might urge the English to become better Christians, but because he was influenced by the millennial beliefs of his age. The fear of world destruction is not a distinctively modern phenomenon.

Bede's interest in the doctine of the Six Ages, itself a commonplace of the time, was doubtless stimulated by his chronological studies, and we find repeated references to it throughout his writings. Yet out of this very interest, Bede became, to his horror, the object of a charge of heresy. Although he accepted the doctrine of the Six Ages, he was not content to follow the calculations of earlier writers about the number of years to be allotted to each of the Five Ages already passed. Isidore's figures were those derived from Jerome's translation of the Chronicle of Eusebius and they rested ultimately upon the Greek version of the Septuagint, but Bede himself approached the problem against the background of the years of Biblical study undertaken at Wearmouth and Jarrow during the abbacy of Ceolfrith and culminating in the production of the three pandects. Bede preferred to make his calculations from what he regarded as the most authoritative source – what he called the *Hebraica veritas*, that is to say Jerome's own translation from the Hebrew which we know as the Vulgate. Using this source, and making some use also of Josephus where the chronology of the Old Testament was obscure, he worked out his own figures without reference to the long-established chronology of tradition. His calculations greatly shortened the duration of the first two ages, and slightly shortened that of the fourth, with the final result that instead of a period of upwards of 5,000 years from the Creation to the birth of Christ, Bede concluded that the interval had been one of 3952 years. The charge of heresy arose from the magnitude of

Bede's variation from the figure accepted by Eusebius, Jerome, Isidore and others, with the consequence that Bede's date for the Incarnation, though marking the beginning of his own Sixth Age, fell in the Fifth Age as reckoned by the traditional chronology, and so it was said that he had denied that the Lord came in the flesh in the Sixth Age of the world. Bede had exposed himself to this charge, though all unwittingly, because his own standards of scholarship persuaded him that it was better to go back to primary sources, in this case the Latin translation of the Hebrew Bible, rather than to accept without questioning figures derived at third or fourth hand.

How deeply Bede felt the charge, and how angered by the ignorance of his accusors, is revealed in a letter which he wrote to Plegwine, a monk of Hexham who is otherwise unknown.[25] The letter was written in 708 five years after he had completed the *De Temporibus* in which he first published his new chronology. We learn from the letter that the charge had been made at a feast where some of those present, the worse for drink, had shouted accusations against Bede, calling him a heretic, and that Wilfrid, then holding the bishopric of Hexham, had been present at the occasion, but had said nothing in Bede's defence. It was Plegwine, the Hexham monk, who brought the news of the charge to Bede, and within a day or two Bede composed his answer in terms which suggest that he was not a man who would gladly suffer the folly or ignorance of those who had had the opportunity of learning better. He vigorously denied the charge and in the course of his defence he expressed his annoyance at those who asked him how many of the last thousand years yet remained and warned his readers against accepting the belief, such as he had found in a book which he had once read, that the time of the Last Judgement could be foretold by man. He also asked that the letter should be read in the presence of Bishop Wilfrid so that he might learn how undeserved had been the attack which he himself had witnessed.

A work which concluded with a survey of the five completed Ages of the world might logically be expected to contain a chronicle of the sixth and still unfinished Age. Such a chronicle forms the final chapter of the *De Temporibus*, though it comprises little more than a list of the emperors with their regnal years and its only reference to Britain is to the conversion of the Saxons, an event which is assigned, erroneously, to the reign of Phocas.[26] In his later work the *De Temporum Ratione*, Bede not only greatly enlarged the chronicle of the Sixth Age, drawing his information from a wide variety of sources, but he also added chapters dealing with the remainder of the Sixth Age yet to come and with the Seventh and Eighth Ages. The Seventh Age, also unfinished, was the age of all the souls of the blessed from the death of Abel until the final resurrection at the Last Judgement, and it was therefore contemporary with all the other Six Ages. The Eighth Age, the age of eternal happiness or eternal damnation, would begin after the end of the present world. The enlarged chronicle of the Sixth Age, which came to enjoy great popularity and was frequently copied as an independent work, contains several references to events in the history of the English in Britain, but by this date (725) Bede, now well past middle age, was already gathering information for his own *Ecclesiastical History of the English Nation*.

Bede dated the sequence of events in his two chronicles of the Sixth Age by reference to the *annus mundi*, the same era as that used by Eusebius, Jerome and Isidore, but he corrected the dates according to his own view of the year of Creation. In the *Ecclesiastical History* he abandoned the *annus mundi* and used instead the *annus domini*, thereby setting a fashion which has become the universal practice of western Christian civilisation. The use of the *annus domini* arose from the need to have some means of identifying the individual years within the cyclical Easter tables, whether comprising an 84-year cycle, a 19-year cycle or the grand Paschal Cycle of 532 years after which the data began to repeat themselves. Such artificial eras as the 4-year Olympiad or the 15-year Indiction were unsatisfactory because they were not cumulative and in any case they were too short. Equally unsatisfactory from the Christian point of view were eras resting on an imperial basis, although the Alexandrian church for a time used an era calculated from the reign of

Diocletian. The introduction of the Christian era was due to two men who played leading parts in the computistical problems of their age, Victorius of Aquitaine, of whom we know little save that he was a contemporary of Pope Leo the Great (440–61) and Dionysius Exiguus, a Scythian monk who was living in Rome in the first half of the sixth century. Victorius, arguing from the function of the Easter table itself, used the *annus Passionis*, reckoning that the Crucifixion had taken place in what we now call A.D. 29, but Dionysius, perhaps influenced by the development of the doctrine of the Six Ages of the world, argued that the era used should be reckoned from the beginning of the Sixth and still-current Age, that is from the birth of Christ. In this way, as a means of identifying individual years within a recurring cycle the *annus domini* came into being. The *annus passionis* was being used in Rome in 701 when it was believed that Christ had lived in the flesh for a little more than 33 years. This belief was signified by the inscribed labels which were placed upon candles at Easter time. The Jarrow monks, including Hwætbert, who were in Rome in the *Annus Domini* 701 told Bede when they got home how they had seen candles dedicated to St Mary bearing the inscription, 'From the Passion of Our Lord Jesus Christ there are 688 years'.[27]

Bede's *Ecclesiastical History* is the first major historical work in which the chronology is based throughout on the *annus domini*, and we have now become so used to this convention that we find it difficult to appreciate the magnitude of Bede's achievement in equating so many events with an individual *annus domini*. He had to take account in his various chronological calculations of several different eras of the world with different starting points, of Imperial regnal years from both the eastern and the western empire, of consular years, of Indictions which might begin variously on 1 September, 25 September or 25 January, of the calendar year which might begin on 1 January, in September or at Christmas, and also of the regnal years of half-a-dozen Anglo-Saxon kings reigning contemporaneously but succeeding to their several kingdoms at different dates in a year which had no uniform beginning even within England

9   There are modern editions of the *De Temporibus* and the *De Temporum Ratione*, omitting the two chronicles, for which see Mommsen's edition in *MGH, Auct. Ant.* XIII. For the *De Natura Rerum* we must still use either Migne in *PL* or Giles.

10 *PL* XLI, 192.

11 *De Nat. Rer. c.* ix.

12 *Ibid. cc.* xxviii, xxix, xlix.

13 *BdTR c.* I.

14 *Ibid. c.* II.

15 *Ibid. c.* III.

16 *Ibid. c.* V. Bede also enunciated this doctrine in his homily for the Vigils of Easter in a passage of great beauty, *Hom.* II, 7, *lines* 51–68.

17 See above, pp. 12–13.

18 *BdTR c.* XXVI. I cannot accept the view advanced by C. W. Jones, p. 127, that Anglo-Saxon churches were so small that Bede could not have written this passage from his own observation. Jones may have been thinking of the surviving oratory, now the chancel, at Jarrow, rather than St. Paul's church which does not survive, but which we know to have been a church of considerable dignity. Bishop Egbert's church at York, as well as Wilfrid's churches at Ripon and Hexham, may have been as large or larger.

19 *BdTR c.* XV.

20 *CLA* X, 1578.

21 Laistner in *Bede: Life, Times and Writings*, 256.

22 On the spread of Isidore's *De Natura Rerum* across Europe see J. Fontaine, *Isidore de Séville, Traité de la Nature*, esp. 38–81. Cf. K. Hughes, 'Irish Monks and Learning', *los monjes y los estudios* (1963), 6–11. See also below pp. 292–3.

23 *2 Peter* 3, 8.

24 See above, pp. 60–1.

25 Ed. C. W. Jones, *op. cit.* 307–15.

26 See above, p. 68.

27 *BdTR c.* XLVII.

28 *In I Sam.* p. 69, *lines* 50–4.

25

The Lives of Saints

'Chronology was one starting-point of Bede's historiography; hagiography, the literary expression of the cult of the saints, was the second.'[1] Arguments about the date of Easter or the age of the world were topics which exercised the minds of scholars, but which were of small consequence to an illiterate population scarcely removed from paganism. The *Life* of the saint, on the other hand, offered a medium through which a strong appeal could be addressed to the unlettered, an appeal whose strength was very greatly increased if the subject of the *Life* was a man who had lived locally and whose deeds were still fresh in living memory. It was Athanasius who set the pattern for western hagiography in his *Life of St Antony*, an Egyptian who was born in the third century into a wealthy Christian family, but who renounced all his worldly wealth in order to devote himself to a life of asceticism in the desert, and so came to be represented by his biographer as the ideal monk. The work quickly achieved great popularity and was known both to St Jerome and to St Augustine of Hippo. Written originally in Greek, it was translated into Latin by Evagrius. The Latin version was already known in Gaul before the end of the fourth century and in later years it was in the libraries of both Jarrow and Lindisfarne.

The popularity of the *Life of St Antony* was due partly to the great authority of Athanasius himself, the champion of orthodoxy against the Aryan heresy and the author of several works in support of the Christian faith as it had been proclaimed at the Council of Nicaea in 325. Athanasius portrayed Antony as one who, despite his withdrawal to the solitude of the desert, yet reverenced the law of the Church and was not ashamed to bow his head to bishops and priests. He represented him as arguing against the Greek philosophers, and particularly against the Neo-Platonism taught by Plotinus, showing that it was not syllogisms and sophistries that made converts to Hellenism from Christianity, but that the power of the Cross was always triumphant over magic and sorcery. Antony became, through the writing of Athanasius, the archetype of the Christian who rebelled against the wealth, culture and philosophical ideals of Mediterranean paganism, and it was because of this that he came to be regarded as the father of western monasticism.

This aspect of the *Life* would still have its appeal for a scholar, such as Bede, who knew something about the background of the age in which it had been written, but there would be others, less scholarly than Bede, who could read or listen to the *Life*, as they could still today, with great profit and enjoyment. Among the more engaging of its characters are the demons with whom Antony struggled in the desert. They came in many shapes, sometimes even as monks. They made a great din, pounding, leaping and laughing hideously. Sometimes they seemed able to foretell the future, but this was only because by travelling faster they were able to get ahead of the news. Occasionally they were caught out because the traveller whose arrival they had gone ahead to foretell turned back without their knowing. It is easy to dismiss the 'demons' as the ravings of a mind disordered by excessive fasting, if, that is, we forget that it is Athanasius and not Antony who is writing. But if we look more closely at the demons who often 'conform themselves to the attitude they find us in when they come', and at the contrasting states of mind which they represent, apprehension and joy, dejection and cheerfulness, spiritual sloth and renewed strength, confusion of mind and calmness of thought, we shall recognise these desert demons as indeed still familiar spirits and will see that the *Life* earned its great popularity because of the richness of its spiritual and psychological insight, a richness which was not matched by the many hagiographers who used it for a model. Some twenty years later, Jerome wrote his *Life of Paul the Hermit*. Paul, wealthy and highly educated, fled to the desert to escape persecution, and after living there into his nineties, he heard that there was a hermit even older than himself, Antony, then aged 113. After many adventures on the way, Paul eventually found Antony and the two talked happily together. As they talked a raven dropped them a loaf of bread and they argued till late in the evening about which of them should break it. Paul, as the younger, thought that Antony should, but Antony, as the host, thought that Paul should. The difficulty was resolved when each took one end of the loaf and both pulled at the same time. This scene from the desert of Egypt was later carved by a Northumbrian sculptor, probably during Bede's lifetime, and perhaps to symbolise the Mass, on the famous cross which now stands in the church at Ruthwell on the northern shore of the Solway Firth, and looking at this scene, as well as the others with which the cross is adorned, we can see at once how powerful was the appeal of popular hagiography to a largely unlettered population.

One of the most popular of the western hagiographies was the *Life of St Martin* written by Sulpicius Severus who was born in Aquitaine *c.* 360 and received his education at Bordeaux. Born into a pagan family in Pannonia, bordering the Danube, Martin became a soldier and after some years of military service found himself fighting in Gaul, then greatly harassed by barbarians' assaults. Remaining in the army for some time after his baptism he later entered the service of Christ and after receiving one of the minor orders, he returned to Pannonia to visit his parents. He travelled in Illyria and Italy before returning to Gaul where he finally established his famous monastery at Marmoutier, across the Loire from the old city of Tours. There he attracted many followers of whom some lived like himself in wooden cells and others in caves hewn from the rock. He travelled about northern Gaul, exposing a brigand who was being revered as a martyr, interrupting a pagan funeral which he had mistaken for a sacrificial procession, destroying old pagan temples and shrines, expelling demons and healing the sick. He is shown in association with Magnus Maximus, the same who had withdrawn troops from Britain in 383 in his bid for the western empire, and, though himself becoming a bishop, we find him portrayed as meeting much opposition, even to the extent of persecution, from the Gaulish episcopate, perhaps because his ascetic ideals had not proved easily acceptable to the wealthy land-owning magnates who were the Gaulish bishops of his age. It is not difficult to understand why a work such as this became so popular. It was a tale full of rich adventure and those who heard it read aloud in St Martin's church at Tours on his anniversaries would not have had their enjoyment spoilt by doubts about its historical veracity. Although it has moved a long way from the Athanasian attacks on the philosophical doctrines of Neo-Platonism, even here we find the opening chapter denouncing the folly of reading about the conflicts of Hector or the disputations of Socrates; eternal life was not to be sought by writing, fighting or philosophising, but through living a pious, holy and Godfearing life. The church at which Bertha, wife of King Æthelbert of Kent, worshipped in Canterbury before the arrival of the Augustinian mission, was dedicated to St Martin, as also was the church of St Ninian at Whithorn, but perhaps the most striking indication of the popularity of this work, and of Athanasius's *Life of St Antony*, in England is, that when a monk of Lindisfarne came to write the *Life* of his own Cuthbert, he prefaced the work with a chapter borrowed verbatim from the first chapter of the *Life of St Martin*, and later described Cuthbert's character in words which he took from Athanasius's *Life of St Antony* [2]

Following the pattern set by Athanasius, Jerome, Sulpicius Severus and others, many western churchmen, some known by name and others anonymous, rapidly turned hagiography into the most popular form of literary composition in the west, and not least in Brittany, Wales and Ireland. Since these areas were remote from the scenes of conflict with Aryanism and were but little affected by the struggle between Christianity and neo-pagan teaching descended ultimately from classical antiquity, there was no need for the western saints to be represented as the champions of orthodoxy against heresy. Instead they could devote their time to fighting against evil in more elementary,

and elemental forms. Inevitably the saint's *Life* tended to conform to a pattern, with his childhood, or even the very circumstances of his birth, foretelling his future sanctity, his maturity
marked by varying degrees of ascetical practices and by
triumphant struggles against devils in various guises, and his
death by edifying scenes followed at his tomb by a continuation
of the miracles of his lifetime. At their worst the hagiographers
produced no more than a tedious repetition of standard miracle
stories, such as were the common stock of any saint of good
standing, but at their best they could draw sympathetic and
lively portraits of men who had a profound effect upon their
contemporaries while they were alive, and an even more profound effect upon posterity after their death.

The historical, and perhaps also the literary, value of a saint's
Life depends largely on whether the subject was one remote
both in time and place, and therefore to be known only at many
removes, or whether he was a local saint whose *Life* was written
by one who had known him personally or at least at a time
when many of his contemporaries were still alive. Among the
former, from an English viewpoint, was St Felix of Nola, near
Naples, who lived in the third century. Late in the fourth
century Paulinus, a Gaulish churchman distinguished as a
poet, became bishop of Nola where he composed a series of
poems in honour of St Felix whom he adopted as his patron
saint. Some at least of these poems were known to Bede and
from them he wrote a *Life of St Felix*, perhaps prompted to do so
by the associations between Northumbria and the Naples area
of Italy. Similarly Bede wrote a *Life of Anastasius*, a Persian who
had been martyred as recently as 628 and had a church
dedicated to him outside Rome. In this instance Bede said that
he had corrected as best he could a *Life* 'which had been badly
translated from the Greek, and worse emended by some un-
skilled person'.[3] Bede's interest in the lives and deaths of saints
and martyrs – men whose good deeds would incite to imitation –
is witnessed by the pains which he took in assembling his
Martyrology, 'in which [he writes] I have endeavoured diligently
to note down all whom I could discover, and not only in what

day, but also by what sort of combat, and under what judge they overcame the world'.[4] The result was a work containing notices, derived from a great many different *passiones* and *vitae*, as well as other sources, of 114 martyrs or saints. Most of them were men and women who had lived in Mediterranean lands, but there was a small group from Burgundy, including the three in whose church Ceolfrith had been buried at Langres, as well as St Alban, Britain's protomartyr from Romano-British days, and three of English race, St Audrey of Ely and the two Hewalds, missionaries born in Northumbria and killed while preaching to the continental Saxons. Bede's *Martyrology*, compiled in the later years of his life, probably between 725 and 731, became the model from which all western martyrologies were descended, including the Roman Martyrology issued by Pope Gregory XIII in 1584.[5]

Bede's interest in the lives of saints and martyrs may well have owed something to his bishop, Acca, who succeeded Wilfrid at Hexham and who, as Bede himself later wrote, 'collected with the greatest industry the history of their passions'.[6] Bede was not an innovator in this field of composition and one suspects that he may have found the more extravagant claims of the hagiographers distasteful. For his *Martyrology* he assembled as much factual information as he could, and in his version of the *Lives* of Felix and Anastasius his main concern was to ensure that they should be presented in a simple and readily intelligible form. He was similarly concerned with form, rather than any originality of content, in the two versions of the *Life of Cuthbert* which he wrote, one in verse and one in prose, but both deriving from an earlier *Life* written by an unknown monk of Lindisfarne. This earliest *Life of Cuthbert* is one of a group of three surviving *Lives* all written in Northumbria during the earlier part of Bede's own lifetime, and all possessing characteristics which distinguish them from the common run of saints' *Lives* and give them great historical as well as literary interest. Two of them concern Northumbrian saints, Cuthbert and Wilfrid, but the third is a *Life of Gregory* written by a monk at Whitby and now the oldest surviving *Life* of the great pope who was regarded by the Whitby writer as the apostle of the English and the man who on the Day of Judgement would lead the English nation to the Lord. Although crude in its Latinity and in its presentation, the work is a valuable source of early traditions about the conversion of the English and an important witness to the veneration felt for Gregory himself. Uninfluenced by the writings of the early hagiographers – Athanasius, Jerome, Sulpicius Severus – it has the attractive simplicity of the primitive, though it was probably not known to Bede.

Wilfrid, intimately known to his biographer for many years, offered a life so rich in character and incident that it could not easily have been constrained within the accepted hagiographical conventions, and Eddius, the author, further enriched his material by a degree of enthusiasm for his subject which made him transparently partisan and tendentious. Bede was of course familiar with the work and he used it in his *Ecclesiastical History*, though he was carefully selective in his choice of material. It was, however, with the third, and undoubtedly the most attractive of the three Northumbrian saints' *Lives* that he was most particularly concerned, the *Life of St Cuthbert*. Using the anonymous Lindisfarne work, written between 699 and 705, as his main source, he compiled two versions of the saint's life, the first written in heroic metre and the second in prose. In the *Prologue* to the prose version, which he addressed to the bishop and whole congregation of Lindisfarne, he explained how, undertaking the work at their request, he first made scrupulous investigation into the details of Cuthbert's life and then began to make notes. When he had got what he calls his 'little work' arranged in proper order, though still in the form of notes, he showed it to a priest Herefrith who had formerly been abbot at Lindisfarne and came to visit him at Jarrow, and also to others who knew about Cuthbert's life. Bede composed this *Prologue* in about 721, some 34 years after Cuthbert's death, so that he would still have been able to get information about the saint from those who had known him personally. After revising his notes, he wrote down the *Life* on parchment and sent it to

Lindisfarne, where it was read for two days by the elders and teachers of the congregation who gave it their approval. Subsequently Bede learnt of further incidents in Cuthbert's life, but it did not seem to him fitting that fresh material should be added to a work which had been planned and completed. He does not say in this *Prologue*, though he does elsewhere,[7] that his chief source of information had been the earlier Lindisfarne *Life* of the saint. Though very seldom borrowing verbatim, he nonetheless followed his source closely. He added a little new material of interest, but these additions go only a small way towards accounting for the length of his own work which proved to be double that of his source. That he was a much better scholar than the Lindisfarne writer is certain, yet the direct simplicity of the Lindisfarne *Life*, containing many details of local interest which Bede omitted, seems nowadays to give a more faithful reflection of Cuthbert's age than the more elaborate prose of Bede.

The essence of hagiography was that it should be popular and easily understood by the unlettered, and perhaps it was because Bede found that his metric version of Cuthbert's life did not meet this need that he later superseded it by a prose version. The absence of any continuing tradition of classical scholarship in Britain prevented the development of affectations of style, deriving from rhetoric, of the kind disliked by some continental hagiographers, such as Verus, Constantius or Eugippius, who expressed their intention of writing in simple terms.[8] Such protestations might indeed become a mere literary convention, but little more than a glance at the Latin of Sidonius Apollinaris or Avitus of Vienne would show the need for reaction towards simplicity. Caesarius of Arles, formerly a monk of Lérins, pleaded in one of his sermons[9] that the ears of the learned should be content to bear with simple words, and that because ignorant and unlettered men could not rise to the heights of scholars, the latter should be ready to bow to the level of the former. There was, however, another form of affectation which had its roots in the delight taken by Irish scholars in bizarre words of obscure meaning and which has now become known as Hisperic Latin.

Bede, happily, was totally unaffected by this cult of the grotesque, though he may well have found some of its products in the Irish books of his library. Its English highpriest was Bede's contemporary Aldhelm who has left so little that can still be cherished by posterity because his learning became choked in the convolutions of its own ingenuity. One of those who came to be influenced by Aldhelm's style was Felix, the author of the *Life of Guthlac*, the fenland hermit, written shortly before or shortly after Bede's death. Hagiographies could range from the extreme of mere miracle-mongering to accounts of men's lives so plainly historical that they almost became biographies in the modern sense, and it was to such presentation that Bede himself was attracted. As we have seen, the history of his monastery can be told in considerable detail from its foundation until the abbacy of Hwætbert, almost half a century, from two works which were written there and which probably developed from commemorative sermons delivered on appropriate anniversaries, the *Life of Ceolfrith* whose author is unknown, and Bede's own *History of the Abbots* which was probably written between 725 and 731. Save for a final paragraph in the former, telling of signs and wonders at Ceolfrith's tomb at Langres, both are wholly free from the miraculous.

Many other stories about the lives and deaths of holy men and women were certainly current in England in Bede's day. Some, notably the *Life of Columba*, written by that same Adomnan who visited Jarrow *c.* 686, still survive, but others, like the little book in which Bede read about Ethelberga, abbess of Barking in Essex,[10] have perished, and yet others, about such saintly kings as Edwin and Oswald may only have circulated orally. Whatever their form, the *Lives* of the saints, both foreign and native, provided a considerable body of what would have been regarded as suitable reading within the monastic precinct, as well as a source of instructive discourse for the unlettered outside. We may suppose that it was through such material as this, and through the vernacular poetry associated with Cædmon and Whitby, that the monasteries carried out their task of spreading some knowledge of the elements of the Christian faith among the ordinary people of the countryside. It seems unlikely that there were many churches other than Wearmouth and Jarrow which possessed paintings of scenes from Scripture, but there may have been some. A passage in the *Life of Willibald*[11] records how in his infancy, i.e. *c.* 700, his parents dedicated him to Christ before a cross, since it was the custom of the times for crosses to be set up on many of the estates of the nobility where there were no churches. Whatever views may be held about the exact date of the most famous of the Northumbrian stone crosses, those of Bewcastle and Ruthwell, sculptured representations of Christ, of the Crucifixion and the Ascension, of John the Baptist, of John the Evangelist, of the Apostles, and also of scenes such as the flight of Mary into Egypt, of Paul and Antony in the desert, of the healing of the blind man and of the turning of water into wine, were probably to be seen on stone monuments standing in the countryside of Bede's age.

REFERENCES

1 W. Levison, *Bede: Life, Times and Writings*, 123.
2 *AVC* I, 2; II, 1; III, 7.
3 *HE* V, 24.
4 *Ibid.*
5 For Bede's Martyrology see Dom H. Quentin, *Les martyrologes historiques du moyen âge.* (2me ed. Paris 1908), 17–119.
6 *HE* V, 20.
7 *HE Praef.*
8 P. Riché, *Education et Culture*, p. 131.
9 No. LXXXVI, ed. Morin, *CCSL* CIII, 353.
10 *HE* IV, 7–11.
11 *C.* 1, ed. O. Holder-Egger, *MGH SS* XV, i, p. 88.

26

Secular and Christian Books

Bede himself never became so deeply immersed in works of scholarship as to be forgetful of the end to which it was devoted, or of the need for evangelists among the ordinary people. This was why he would give English translations of the *Credo* and the *Pater Noster* to priests and why, on his deathbed, he was translating St John's Gospel into English. But for him as for other churchmen of earlier ages, the task of establishing a new Christian literature in the place held by old pagan beliefs and philosophies can hardly have seemed an easy one. Two generations after Bede's death another Northumbrian scholar, Alcuin, wrote in the year 797 to the bishop of Lindisfarne whose monastery had suffered four years earlier from the first of the Viking attacks against the Northumbrian coast. 'When priests dine together', he wrote, 'let the words of God be read. At such a time it is fitting to listen to the reader, not to the harpist. What has Ingeld to do with Christ? Strait is the house and it will not be able to hold them both. The king of heaven will have no dealings with so-called kings who are heathen and damned, for this eternal king reigns in heaven while that pagan king who is damned groans in hell. The voices of readers should be heard in your houses, not the tumult of those who laugh in the streets.'[1] Alcuin here seems to be echoing words addressed by St Paul to the Corinthians – 'What communion hath light with darkness? What concord hath Christ with Belial?'[2] – words which were quoted by St Jerome who added, 'What has Horace to do with the Psalter, Virgil with the Gospel and Cicero with Paul? ... Although unto the pure all things are pure and nothing is to be refused if it be received with thanksgiving, still we ought not to drink the cup of Christ and the cup of devils at the same time.'[3]

It may seem incongrous to place the writings of Horace, Virgil and Cicero beside harpists' lays telling about the adventures of pagan Germanic heroes, but Jerome, writing in 384, when Britain was still part of the Roman empire, was facing the same problem voiced by Alcuin in 797 – the attitude to be adopted by Christians towards pagan literature. Within the context of Bede's England the problem, so far as it concerned Germanic paganism, admitted only one solution – total suppression – and how effective that solution was, is revealed by our present almost complete ignorance of the religious beliefs and the oral literature of the pagan Saxons. It cannot have been a church-man who chose to portray on a small whale-bone casket the three kings bringing gifts to the Virgin and Child in juxtaposition with one of the more gruesome legends from Germanic anti-quity, the story of Weland, the legend of Romulus and Remus, as well as the capture of Jerusalem by Titus.[4] Such mixed mythologies though doubtless common enough among lay people, could never have been endorsed by the Church. The pagan background could only be allowed to survive if, as in *Beowulf*, it had first been steeped in Christianity.

Germanic paganism was still immediately present to the world into which Bede was born, but since its literature and its mythology had never been put into writing, it presented no great problem to English churchmen of Bede's age. The dragons and spectres which might be supposed to haunt fens and water springs were harmless characters of rural superstition, not formidable intellectual opponents. But the poets, philosophers and historians of pagan classical antiquity could still be read by those who had access to manuscripts of their works, and herein lay a problem of quite a different order. At a time when there were no specifically Christian schools, the educated Christian, like any other educated man, had been taught in the grammar schools and the schools of the rhetors where the curriculum was based upon a study of classical authors. The problem became exceedingly acute for the great scholars like Jerome and Augustine who lived when the unity of the classical world had not yet disintegrated and when its literature was still widely read. For such, scarcely any other solution was possible save a compromise, not always itself stable, between the extremes which on the one hand encouraged the study of secular literature and on the other demanded its total rejection. Individual writers, attracted and repelled at one and the same time by very different philosophies of life, might well profess an attitude which they could not always put into practice in their writings, and perhaps for some the dilemma was insoluble.

Jerome, summoned before the seat of Judgement in his dream and professing himself a Christian was told: 'Thou liest; thou art a Ciceronian, not a Christian';[5] but though he may have abandoned the reading of secular literature for some years, he later returned to the classics and even wrote in defence of secular learning, attracted as much by classical humanism as he was by Christian asceticism.[6] Augustine, on the other hand, tended to move away from his earlier liberalism towards a more rigorously Christian position. In western Europe the problem gradually became less acute through the declining knowledge of the classics, and particularly of Greek, which accompanied the disturbed conditions of the fifth and sixth centuries. There were certainly bishops in Gaul, such as Sidonius of Clermont and Avitus of Vienne, whose writings were deeply influenced by their classical studies, but Caesarius of Arles, warned like Jerome in a dream, turned against secular literature and compared the third of the plagues of Egypt with the cunning of philosophy and the poisonous fabrications of heretics.[7]

Although ignorance of the Greek language, as well as the change of conditions wrought by the mere passage of time, might isolate both Isidore of Seville and Gregory the Great from much of classical antiquity, yet both had to face the problem of the Christian scholar confronted by pagan literature. If it was easy to denounce the immorality of poets who told of behaviour which ran counter to Christian teaching, it was less easy to deny all educative value to the work of some other writers, pagans though they might be. Isidore certainly recognised this value, accepting the coexistence of pagan and Christian writings, rather than searching the latter for means of confounding the former. Living himself in a world of transition, his attitude has been compared to that of Livy in offering several versions of the same historical episode without himself deciding to choose between them.[8] Discussing the portents of storm or fair weather in a chapter of his *De Natura Rerum*,[9] he could cite as successive authorities Virgil, Varro, Nigidius Figulus and Christ. We find the same weather lore expressed in almost identical terms in the corresponding chapter of Bede's *De Natura Rerum*,[10] but without any reference to either pagan or Christian authorities. It has been said of Isidore's *De Libris Gentilium*, a chapter of the third book of his *Sententiae*, that it is much less a condemnation of pagan literature than a long parallel between the formal attractions of the pagan books and the substance of truth contained in the Scriptures beneath an apparent poverty of form.[11]

The attitude adopted by Gregory the Great towards secular literature has often been unfairly judged from two seeming expressions of unqualified hostility. One of them is found in the dedicatory letter to Leander, brother of Isidore of Seville, with which he prefaced his *Commentary on Job*, and in which, after seeking to be excused for the inadequacies of his style, he expressed his firm conviction that the words of the Divine oracle ought not to be subject to the rules of Donatus. But this passage seems to be no more than an echo of a closely similar remark by Cassiodorus[12] and in any case is too short to carry much weight. Gregory is more outspoken in a letter which he wrote to Desiderius, bishop of Vienne, after word had reached him that the bishop had been teaching grammar to some people and had apparently been reciting poetry concerned with pagan topics. Gregory was forthright in his condemnation of the bishop's behaviour and remarked, much in the manner of Paul and Jerome, that it was not right for one and the same mouth to mix the praises of Christ with the praises of Jupiter. Desiderius must consider how offensive it was for a bishop to recite poetry which was not fit even for a lay Christian.[13] We do not know exactly what Desiderius had done, but if he had been giving public teaching in grammar and public readings of pagan texts, neither Gregory himself nor any other pope in this age could have failed to condemn a practice which was likely to give renewed life to pagan ideas. We find a more carefully considered statement of Gregory's attitude in his *Commentary* on the first Book of Kings (I Samuel) a work whose authenticity, formerly rejected by many, has now been established.[14] Commenting on the passage, 'Now there was no smith found throughout all the land of Israel',[15] Gregory remarks that we are to understand by this passage that 'it is by Divine and not by secular letters that we are taught to wage spiritual warfare. The faithful of the Lord do not wage war against evil spirits by knowledge of secular arts. But although knowledge of secular literature is of no avail in itself for spiritual warfare, if it is united with Holy Scripture it may lead to a more profound understanding of that Scripture. The liberal arts are to be learnt only in order that knowledge of them may lead to a more profound understanding of the Divine Word. Evil spirits take away the desire to learn from the hearts of some so that they are ignorant of secular letters and do not attain to spiritual heights. Evil spirits know that when we are taught secular letters we are helped in spiritual letters'.[16] In the light of this passage we cannot deny that Gregory set a considerable value upon the study of secular literature and the liberal arts, but always provided that they were recognised as being on a lower level from which it was the duty of the Christian to rise to greater heights. Commenting on the next verse – 'But all the Israelites went down to the Philistines to sharpen every man his share, and his coulter and his axe and his mattock' – Gregory remarks that we too are going down to the Philistines when we turn our minds to the study of secular books, but his thought surely was that the mind which did so turn was made sharper and more acute by the study of those books. Secular knowledge had been placed by God upon the plain, but it was for the Christian to climb up from the plain to the heights of spiritual knowledge. Gregory does not condemn: he merely differentiates between two different levels of understanding.

Bede knew the story of Jerome's dream,[17] but he evidently did not know Gregory's commentary on the first Book of Kings and it is instructive to compare the differing interpretations which the two writers give to the same passages. Gregory's comments on the function of secular literature, as preparing the reader to scale the greater heights of spiritual enlightenment, are entirely lacking from Bede's commentary which is confined to brief remarks about the land of promise falling into the hands of enemies, the virtues of the church becoming corrupted, for want of those who could manufacture spiritual arms. But where Gregory implied that those who went down to the lands of the Philistines, though leaving the heights for the plain, yet did so to sharpen their wits, Bede seems to be adopting an altogether more hostile attitude towards secular literatures. He writes: 'Today also there are those who go down, abandoning the height which they should have climbed in order to hear the word of God. They give ear to secular tales and the doctrines of devils. By reading the works of the logicians, the rhetors and the poets of the gentiles for the cultivation of their earthly talents, they go as it were unarmed and lacking spiritual knowledge to the blacksmiths of the Philistines to sharpen the iron tools of their woodland and rural husbandry.'[18]

Chapter 14 of the first Book of Kings tells of the victory won by Jonathan and his armour-bearer among the garrison of the Philistines and of how Jonathan, because he had not heard the command of his father that the people of Israel should not eat that day before evening, dipped his rod in a honeycomb and was told of the curse which his father had laid on any who should disobey his command. 'Then said Jonathan, My father hath troubled the land: see, I pray you, how mine eyes have been enlightened, because I tasted a little of this honey. How much more, if haply the people had eaten freely today of the spoil of their enemies which they found? for had there not been now a much greater slaughter among the Philistines?'[19] Gregory thus interprets the reference to the taste of honey: 'It is as if he is saying "I have grown in stature from the praise of my subjects, even as I have sought not to be backward in giving praises"', and Gregory then continues with a disquisition on the topic of praise. Bede, on the other hand, associates both verses symbolically with the attitude of the Christian towards the 'honey' of secular literature. He observes that Moses and Daniel had not forbidden the giving of instruction in the philosophy and writings of the Egyptians and the Chaldaeans, even though they feared their superstitions and their alluring delights, and moreover that even St Paul had put verses from the secular poets into his writings and sayings.[20] 'But we must use greater care in plucking the rose amid its sharp thorns than in gathering the lily in its soft foliage, and it is much safer to seek wholesome advice in the writings of the Apostles than in the pages of Plato. For even the bees themselves which make this kind of honey offer out of their mouths sweet sayings to soothe us, but keep in their hinder parts poisonous tales to kill.'[21]

The analogy of flowers and of roses with their thorns has of course a long literary history. Bede's use of it calls to mind two lines from the *Versus in Bibliotheca* which were inscribed on the book cases or on the walls of Isidore's library in Seville:

> *Prata vides plena spinis et copia floris;*
> *Si non vis spinas sumere, sume rosas.*[22]

Commenting further on Jonathan's claim that it would have been much better if all had been allowed to eat freely of the spoil of their enemies, Bede writes: 'These words of Jonathan's give support to anyone who does not think that the reading of secular works is harmful to those who are taught in church or even to those who teach. "You see," he says, "how much stronger, more intelligent and better prepared I have become in holding forth in a fitting manner because I have tasted a little of the flower of Tully's writings; if Christian people had learnt the doctrines and beliefs of the gentiles, would they not all the more boldly and surely laugh their errors to scorn and refute them; would they not the more devotedly rejoice in their own true faith and give thanks for it to the father of light?" It is not to be thought that Moses or Daniel wanted to acquaint themselves with secular philosophy for any other reason save that they might be the better able to destroy and overthrow the philosophy which they had learnt.'[23]

We can parallel Bede's hostility towards the reading of secular works by several passages in which he condemns the seductive allurements of rhetoric, dialectic, philosophy and astrology – the tapestries and fine linen from Egypt with which the prostitute decked her bed.[24] He was not far removed from the age of the great heresies and we can see why, as a theologian, he devoted so much space in his commentaries to refuting the views of Arius, Pelagius, Eutyches, Manichaeus, Plotinus, Sabellius and all the other preachers of heresy. But the problem which confronted Bede in his attitude towards the literature of classical antiquity was scarcely comparable with the problem which had faced Augustine and Jerome, men well-educated in a very wide range of classical works, both Latin and Greek. Unhappily we have no means of determining the extent to which classical literature was known in the England of Bede's age in general and to Bede himself in particular. It is of course possible to compile a list of the passages which Bede cites from classical works and such a list would include the names of Virgil, Ovid, Horace, Terence, Lucretius, Martial, Sallust and one or two others, but it would be folly to suppose that Bede drew his citations at firsthand from copies of the works of these writers in the libraries at Wearmouth and Jarrow. In most cases we can identify the same quotations in the works of the grammarians or of Isidore of Seville, but if even Isidore himself, so much nearer to possible sources of manuscripts, seems to have derived his knowledge of the writings of classical authors mainly at secondhand, we need strong evidence before we can admit that any of the works of classical antiquity were known to Bede at firsthand.

Educational manuals whose purpose was to serve as introductory textbooks for the study of the different branches of the liberal arts, *florilegia*, the compilations of the scholiasts and the works of the encyclopaedists were the principal means through which fragments of classical literature, perhaps several times removed from the originals, reached western Europe in the

times of Isidore and Bede. Much of this literature was ephem-
eral and surely only a small part of it has survived. If we can
show that Bede took about half of his quotations from Virgil
from such sources, we must suspect that the remainder were of
similar origin. When we find him misquoting a line from the
Second Eclogue we may suspect, not so much that his memory has
failed,[25] as that he had taken the line as he had found it, in a
corrupt form, from some grammarian's manual. We have seen
that the works of the Latin grammarians were copied in English
scriptoria and were taken to the continent by English missionaries, but, with one exception, there are no surviving manuscripts of any of the works of the pagan classical writers which
date from the age of Bede and which also show traces of having
been associated with or written in English scriptoria. The
exception is the Leyden manuscript which contains part of
Pliny's *Natural History* and which is thought to have been
written in northern England,[26] and it is significant that this is the
only work from classical antiquity which we can be certain that
Bede knew at firsthand, though even then he knew only parts of
it. A striking indication of the attitude of at least a part of the
western church towards classical texts is reflected in the
collection of palimpsests deriving from the Irish foundation at
Bobbio in northern Italy where we find that beautifully written
texts containing the works of Cicero, Seneca, Pliny, Lucan and
others were erased in order that the parchment might be used
again for repairing damaged Biblical manuscripts, for copying
patristic or grammatical treatises or for the works of Christian
poets such as Sedulius.[27] We would not nowadays suppose that
a casual reference to Scylla and Charybdis implied that its
author had read Homer's *Odyssey*, Virgil's *Eclogues* or Ovid's
Metamorphoses, nor should we make any such assumption when
the author of the reference was Ceolfrith, abbot of Wearmouth
and Jarrow.[28]

We are told that Bede was familiar with the native poetry of
his own people, but we do not know whether this was the new
religious poetry, such as had been composed at Whitby in
Cædmon's day, or older poetry deriving from the pagan past.

Some of the latter presumably survived beyond Bede's lifetime since there would otherwise have been no point in Alcuin's rebuke to the monks of Lindisfarne, but excepting only Cædmon's brief hymn to Creation, no vernacular poetry, whether pagan or Christian, now survives in manuscripts dating from Bede's age, and we are probably justified in thinking that such works as these, like the works of classical antiquity, were seldom, if ever, copied in English scriptoria in Bede's age. If we look at the content of surviving manuscripts which were either written in Anglo-Saxon monasteries, in England or on the continent, or which belonged to such monasteries during the age of Bede, extending the lower limit of date to cover the remainder of the eighth century after Bede's death, we find of course, as we have already seen, that by far the greater part consists of books from the Bible itself, especially the Gospels and the Psalter. But outside the Bible the works of some thirty other writers are represented. Among the Fathers, for example, the work of Ambrose is represented in a sixth-century uncial manuscript, now at Boulogne, which is believed to have been written in Italy, but which had come into English hands by the eighth century since it bears marginalia written in an Anglo-Saxon minuscule of that date.[29] It may have travelled from Italy to England and thence to France. Ambrose is also represented in an eighth-century manuscript which was probably written in Northumbria and which also contains Jerome's commentary on Ecclesiastes. This manuscript later went to the English foundation at Fulda and is now preserved at Cassel. Fragments of Jerome's commentary on St Matthew also survive, but in general eighth-century English copies of the writings of Ambrose, Jerome and Augustine are rare.[30] A notable manuscript, now at Durham and comparable in size with the Codex Amiatinus, contains Cassiodorus's commentary on the Psalms, with two full-page miniatures representing David.[31] Also at Cassel are fragments of a copy of the *Collationes* of Cassian written in an Anglo-Saxon minuscule hand of the eighth century.[32]

Among other theological works we find the writings of

Theodore of Mopsuestia on the Pauline Epistles, of Philippus on the Book of Job and Primasius on the Apocalypse.[33] A much rarer work, the commentary of Apponius on the Song of Songs, is preserved in an eighth-century manuscript which is now at Boulogne but which was written, probably in southern England, by a nun called Burginda who wrote her name at the end of a long subscription to an 'illustrious youth' for whose prayers she asked.[34] The writings of Christian poets are represented by Paulinus of Nola, by Sedulius, whose popular *Carmen Paschale* is found in three manuscripts, and by the English Aldhelm's *De Laudibus Virginitate*.[35] Historical works include the Latin translation which Rufinus made from the Greek History of Eusebius.[36] The Latin translation which Hegesippus made of Josephus's History of the Jews is found in a sixth-century Italian manuscript which had been damaged by damp and was restored in the eighth century by a scribe who wrote in Anglo-Saxon minuscule hand. This manuscript, now preserved at Cassel, found its way to Fulda, probably from England.[37] Another historical work is the abridgement which Justinus made of the history written by Pompeius Trogus. This manuscript, probably Northumbrian in origin, later passed to the continent where it became the ancestor of the whole transalpine transmission of the work of Justinus.[38]

Whereas the works of these and some other writers now survive in one, two or at most three manuscripts dating broadly from Bede's age and associated directly or indirectly with Anglo-Saxon scribes, there are four writers who, to judge from the strength of the Anglo-Saxon manuscript transmission were outstandingly popular among the English, whether at home or abroad. Applying the same criteria of date and of Anglo-Saxon associations, we find 13 manuscripts containing works of Jerome and 17 with those of Augustine of Hippo, but even these are outstripped by the works of two men living much nearer to the age of Bede, Isidore of Seville and Gregory the Great whose works are found in 21 and 28 manuscripts respectively, though in some cases no more than a fragment of a manuscript survives. The works of Isidore represented through the English transmission are the *Etymologiae* in four copies, the *Synonyma* also in four, the *De Natura Rerum* in three, the *Differentiae* in two, the *Prooemia* in two, the *De Ortu et Obitu Patrum* in two, the *De Ecclesiasticis Officiis* in two, the *Quaestiones in Testamentum Vetus* in one.[39] Although it does not now survive in an eighth-century manuscript with English associations, we know that Isidore's *Chronicon* reached England and was used by Bede. In the light of this evidence we cannot doubt that the works of Isidore of Seville were a major influence on the development of Anglo-Saxon intellectual life in the age of Bede, an influence whose power was rivalled, and perhaps exceeded, only by that of Gregory the Great.

The works of Gregory the Great are known to survive in some 95 manuscripts – some of them no more than fragments – which were written not later than the earliest years of the ninth century. Rather less than one third of this total, some 28 manuscripts in all, can be attributed either directly to monasteries in England or to continental monastic centres with strong English associations. The strength of the English contribution to the transmission of Gregory's works may have been even greater than these figures suggest. We know that an English scribe who called himself Peregrinus worked in the scriptorium at Freising in Bavaria and it is believed that two manuscript copies of Gregory's *Moralia* written at Freising derive from a common, but now lost, Anglo-Saxon exemplar.[40] It may well be that other manuscript copies of Gregory's writings from Freising likewise derive ultimately from lost English copies, even though they do not now reveal any distinctively English characteristics. English interest in Gregory's works is strikingly revealed by a manuscript of the *Homiliae in Evangelia* now preserved in Barcelona.[41] Its origin is uncertain but since it bears on f. 28 what appears to be a representation of a flamingo, southern origin, perhaps southern France or Spain, seems likely. Written in an uncial hand attributed to the seventh or eighth century, it bears upon it corrections and liturgical formulae which have been added by an English reader who wrote in an English uncial or minuscule hand of the eighth century. It may be that this manuscript had been lent to an English monastery and then returned, or it may be that an English scholar studied it in its original southern home. In addition to this manuscript which had certainly been used by an English reader, the *Homiliae in Evangelia* are represented in three or four other copies directly or indirectly of English origin. One of them, written in a rather clumsy majuscule, may be Kentish. A second, seemingly written in an Anglo-Saxon centre on the continent bears on f. 71v the female name *Abirhilt* which may be that of the scribe. A third, perhaps also written on the continent, bears the name *Erkanfrit* in runes on f. 71, and may have some Canterbury connections.[42] Gregory's *Homiliae in Ezechielem* are found in six manuscripts, of which one was written by the scribe Peregrinus who worked at Freising in the second half of the eighth century.[43] We find the same Peregrinus copying the works of Jerome and Isidore.[44] He wrote a characteristically English pointed minuscule and, from the name which he adopted, he was presumably an English monk who left his country as a pilgrim *pro amore Dei* and finally settled as a scribe at Freising in Bavaria, a monastery associated with English missionary activities. From Freising itself we have two copies of Gregory's *Moralia*, one of them written by Peregrinus himself and both deriving from a common English ancestor.[45] This work is also known from five other manuscripts with English associations, though in some instances mere fragments survive.[46] The *Dialogi* are also known from five manuscripts, but again sometimes only small fragments remain, in one case as the lower script of a palimpsest with the upper script dating from after 1500.[47] Finally the *Regular Pastoralis*, a book which certainly exercised a profound influence on Anglo-Saxon England in the age of Bede as well as that of Alfred, is known from six manuscripts. Three of them now survive only in a fragmentary state varying from a few scraps to six folios.[48] Two other copies likewise believed to have been written in England, and now preserved at Paris and Cassel respectively, have fared better, as also has the sixth which was written, probably at some English centre on the continent, by a scribe who called himself Willibald.[49] Bede was of course familiar with all five of these works of Gregory's – the two sets of homilies on Ezekiel and on the Gospels, the commentary on Job (*Moralia*) the four books on the Dialogues and the Pastoral Care (*Regula Pastoralis*) which last is thought to have been brought to England by Augustine when he came to Canterbury in 597. In addition to these major works, some minor Gregorian works were also known in England – some of the letters and also his *Libellus Responsionum* which were used by Bede in his own *History*, as well as the *Libellus Synodicus* relating to the Roman synod of 595. There would certainly be copies of all these works in the libraries at Wearmouth and Jarrow, and we are not likely to be mistaken in thinking that the major works of Gregory the Great were more frequently copied in Anglo-Saxon scriptoria in the age of Bede than those of any other writer. English scribes played a major part in spreading these works not only across England, but also across Germany as far as Bavaria.[50]

REFERENCES

1 *MGH Ep. Car.* II, 124.

2 II *Cor.* vi, 14–15.

3 *Ep.* 22, in *Select Letters*, ed. F. A. Wright (Loeb 1933), 124–5.

4 For an account of the Franks Casket see R. W. V. Elliott, *Runes, an Introduction* (Manchester 1959), 96–109.

5 *Ep.* 22.

6 H. Hagendahl, *Latin Fathers and the Classics* (Göteborg 1958), 269–309.

7 *Sermo* No. XCIX, ed. Morin *CCSL CIII*, 405–6. See also M. L. W. Laistner, 'The Christian Attitude to Pagan Literature', *History*, n.s. 20 (1936), 49–54.

8 J. Fontaine, *Isidore de Séville*, II, 801.

9 *C.* 38.

10 *C.* 36.

11 Cf. J. Fontaine, *op. cit.* 785–806.

12 *CI* I, xv, 7.

13 *GE* XI, 34.

14 P. Verbraken, 'Le Texte du Commentaire sur les Rois Attribué à Saint Grégoire', also 'Le Commentaire de Saint Grégoire sur le Premier Livre des Rois', *Rev. Bén.* 66 (1965), 39–62 and 159–217.

15 *I Sam.* 13, 19.

16 *Greg. In Librum Primum Regum*, ed. P. Verbraken, *CCSL* CXLIV (1963), 470–2.

17 *In I Sam.* p. 120, *lines* 2177–9.

18 *Ibid.* p. 112, lines 1853–9.

19 I *Sam.* 14, 29–30.

20 The ref. is to *Acts* 17, 28, and *Titus* 1, 12.

21 *In I Sam.* p. 121, *lines* 2216–21.

22 C. H. Beeson, *Isidorstudien, Quell. u. Untersuch. z. lateinischen Philol. des Mittelalters*, t. 4, 2 (München 1911), p. 157. Also Fontaine, *Isidore de Séville*, I, 760, n. 2.

23 *In I Sam.* p. 121, *lines* 225–36.

24 *Prov.* 8, 16, *PL.* XCI, 963.

25 As suggested by M. L. W. Laistner, *The Intellectual Heritage of the Early Middle Ages* (New York 1957), p. 97.

26 *CLA* X, 1578.

27 *CLA* III, 346, 363, 392 *et al.*, also *CLA* IV, *Intro.* pp. xx–xxvii.

28 See above, p. 188.

29 *CLA* VI, 735.

30 *CLA* VIII, 1134. See also N. R. Ker, 'Fragments of Jerome's Commentary on St. Matthew', *Medievalia et Humanistica*, XIV (1962), 7–14.

31 *CLA* II, 152.

32 *CLA* VIII, 1143.

33 *CLA* I, 4 and V**4; II, 234; VI, 740; II, 237.

34 *CLA* VI, 738.

35 *CLA* I, 87; II, 123; VII, 853; VIII, 1206; II, 135; VIII, 1207.

36 *CLA* X, 1515.

37 *CLA* VIII, 1139.

38 *CLA* IX, 1370.

39 The following are the *CLA* references:– *Etym.* VII, 983; VIII, 1189, 1225; IX, 1332; *Synon.* VII, 845; IX, 1426, 1435, 1437; *DNR*, VII, 842, 848; IX, 1369; *Diff.* VI, 827; VII, 849; *Prooem.* VI, 714; XI, 1618; *De Ort. et Ob.* VI, 714; VIII, 1184; *De Ecc. Off.* IX, 1432; XI, 1618; *Quaest. in Test. Vet.* IX, 1433.

40 *CLA* IX, 1263, 1278.

41 *CLA* XI, 1627.
42 *CLA* II, 121; IX, 1412, 1414.
43 *CLA* IX, 1253; and for the others I, 90; V, 634; VIII, 1095; IX, 1411; XI, 1591.
44 *CLA* IX, 1265, 1283.
45 *CLA* IX, 1263, 1278.
46 *CLA* II, 155; V, 596; VIII, 1144; IX, 1427; XI, 1664.
47 *CLA* VIII, 1070 (palimpsest,) 1186; IX, 1356, 1406; XI, 1595.
48 *CLA* II, 188, 229, 264.
49 *CLA* V, 651; VIII, 1138; IX, 1400.
50 For other evidence touching the esteem felt for Gregory the Great in England, see P. Meyvaert, *Bede and Gregory the Great* (Jarrow Lecture 1964).

27

Candela Ecclesiae

We have taken account of some of the books which Bede and his contemporaries read and copied – the Biblical commentaries both old and new, the lives of the saints, the works of the Christian poets, the historians of the Christian church – writings which would lead to a better knowledge and understanding of Scripture. We have also reviewed some of Bede's own writings – the schoolbooks on Orthography, on Metre and on Figures, the scientific treatises on Times and on the Nature of Things, the Lives of the Saints whether they had lived in the east or nearer at hand in Bede's own Northumbria, the history of his own monastery and of the abbots who ruled it. But these works, though a very considerable achievement for a scholar of this age, amount only to a small part of the totality of his writings. We may remind ourselves of his own remark that from the time of receiving priest's orders in his thirtieth year until he reached his fifty-ninth year he had been at pains, for his own needs and for those of his brethren 'to compile from the works of the venerable fathers brief notes on Holy Writ, and also to make additions according to the manner of their meaning and interpretation'.[1] It must be admitted that Bede's Biblical commentaries are not nowadays read save by those concerned with his theology or with tracing the different sources which he used and the particular methods which he employed. Passionate in his support of orthodoxy and in his condemnation of heresy, he was a traditionalist whose prime concern was with the diffusion of the accepted beliefs of the catholic church, as they had reached him through the works of the fathers, among people who, as we can all too easily forget, were still emerging from paganism. We may recall an occasion when some monks were caught by wind and tide and carried out to sea beyond the mouth of the Tyne, while rustics on the bank jeered at them. 'Let no man pray for them', they said, 'for they have robbed men of their old ways of worship, and how the new worship is to be conducted, nobody knows.'[2] It was towards the conduct of the new worship and to spreading a knowledge of its Scriptures that Bede devoted the greater part of his intellectual life. This was the achievement by which he himself, his contemporaries and the posterity of the European Middle Ages set the greatest store. The measure of that achievement is not easily gauged but we can appreciate something of its magnitude by merely learning that, apart from all his other writings, his Biblical commentaries on both the Old and the New Testament comprise about 45 books, some relatively short, others of considerable length. The influence of these books on the civilisation of western Europe is strikingly indicated by the fact that they can still be read in substantially more than 950 manuscripts scattered across every part of western Europe. Not all of his works achieved equal popularity. For example the four books of his commentary on Samuel are known in only eight manuscripts, perhaps because his extreme use of the allegorical method in this commentary proved distasteful. But his commentary on St Mark's Gospel is known in 95 manuscripts, on St Luke's Gospel in 90 and on the Catholic Epistles in more than 110. Bede's Biblical commentaries, already beginning to circulate in England during his lifetime, spread across Germany and France within a few years of his death.[3] Many of them were still being copied in the twelfth and thirteenth centuries.

Whatever importance different ages have attached to the different facets of Bede's intellectual achievement, whether as teacher, historian or theologian, he himself leaves us in no doubt that he would have supposed all his labours to have been in vain, if they had not born fruit in the daily lives of ordinary men and women. We must not suppose, because we know so little about the common incidents of his own daily life, that he was a recluse writing only for scholars more concerned with theological argument than with daily living. There is a passage in his commentary on the first book of Samuel in which he develops a homely analogy from the cook-house. We are being nourished, he writes, on food cooked on a griddle when we understand literally, openly and without covering those things which have been said or done to protect the health of the soul; upon food cooked in the frying-pan when, by frequently turning over the superficial meaning and looking at it afresh, we comprehend what it contains which corresponds allegorically with the mysteries of Christ, what with the state of the catholic church and what with setting right the ways of individuals; and afterwards we search in the oven when, by exerting our minds, we lay hold of those mystical things in the scriptures which as yet we cannot see, but which we hope to see in the future.[4] The analogy of the spiritual kitchen comes aptly from the pen of a man who had devoted his life to the preparation of healthy spiritual food for people hitherto nourished on a paganism, which, intellectually, had been untouched by the civilisation of classical antiquity, and aptly too from a scholar whose writings cannot fail to leave upon their readers an impression of intellectual humility. Bede could be stern and uncompromising in matters of sin and heresy – and such matters included the folly of those who did not celebrate Easter upon the proper date – but he was no less forthright in condemning arrogance. We do not know when he wrote his two books comprising fifty sermons on texts from the Gospels, but they seem to represent the maturity of his thoughts in later years, and they contain some passages which seem to reveal a little of the man himself. He writes in one of them: 'When we notice, while we are talking, that some of the less learned brethren cannot understand those mysteries of the Scriptures which we have not always known, but which we have gradually learnt to know with God's help, we are apt to be immediately puffed up. We despise them and boast about our learning as if it were uniquely profound and as if there were not a great many others much more learned than ourselves. We, who do not like to be despised by those who are more learned than us, delight in despising, or even ridiculing, those who are less learned than us. We do not

[300]

trouble to remember that the way to the kingdom is revealed not to those who only by meditation achieve understanding either of the mysteries of the faith or of the precepts of their founder, but rather to those who put into practice what they have been able to learn.'[5]

Bede was forthright in condemning the ways of those who delighted in taking part in lewd, boastful or blasphemous talk, in spreading slander and sowing discord among the brethren, as well as the hypocrisy of those who prolonged the services in the church with singing and prayer while their hearts were else-where.[6] Nonetheless he shows a compassionate understanding of the weaknesses of human nature and of the many ways in which a man's conduct of his life might be influenced by his failure to control his own thoughts. There were some thoughts which corrupted the mind by leading it directly into the committing of evil deeds. There were others which troubled the mind by causing it to indulge in the anticipation of evil, though falling short of the act itself. And there were yet other thoughts which, though they did not lead the mind astray, yet prevented it from the contemplation of good, 'as when we recall in memory the ghosts of things which we know that we have at some time done or said needlessly; memories which disturb rather than blind the spiritual sight, buzzing round the eyes of the heart like a cloud of midges'.[7] Man must learn to control his thoughts by constant perseverance in prayer. 'For whatsoever things we are more often in the habit of doing, saying or listening to, those same things inevitably return the more often to our minds, as if coming back to their own familiar homes. Even as pigs haunt their wallowing places in the mud, and doves the limpid streams, so do evil thoughts defile the impure mind while spiritual thoughts sanctify the chaste.'[8] Bede's thoughts on prayer are more fully expressed in the moving sermon which he composed *In Litaniis Majoribus*:

Citizens of the heavenly fatherland who are pilgrims upon earth are not forbidden to pray unto the Lord for times of peace, for bodily health, for abundance of crops, for fair weather and for the necessities of life – that is, if these things are not sought to excess, and if they are sought only that, with abundance of provision for the present, we may head the more freely towards the gifts that are to come. But there are some who demand temporal peace and prosperity from their Creator, not in order that they may obey that same Creator with greater dedication of spirit, but in order that they may have all the more opportunity for revellings and drunkenness, in order that they may the more easily and freely become slaves to the allurements of their own fleshly desires. Of such men it is rightly said that they pray in evil fashion. But truly all those who pray in this way, because they pray evilly, do not deserve to receive an answer. And so, my beloved brethren, let us strive both to pray well and to become worthy to receive those things for which we pray.[9]

No single work written by Bede was more frequently copied from the date of its completion until the age of the printed book than the work which he called *Historia Gentis Anglorum Ecclesiastica*. This great work, cast in the form of a continuous narrative of five Books, spans a period of almost eight centuries from Julius Caesar's invasion of Britain to within two or three years of Bede's own death in 735. A lifetime of labour in the fields of grammar, natural science, chronology, hagiography and Biblical exegesis had given to Bede a view of history not as a mere collection of unrelated episodes, but as an orderly chronological development extending over several millennia from the first creation of man. It was his profound sense for historical time which enabled him to depart from the type of dry annalistic record which was concerned with little else but battles and the deaths of kings. To find a work of comparable scale we must either look back to the historians of antiquity or forward to such as William of Malmesbury. Yet such comparisons do less than justice to Bede's achievement if they lead us to ignore the realities of that *alter orbis* in which he lived or to overlook his own views about the ends which were served by the writing of history. Bede wrote, as he expressly states in the *Preface, ad instructionem posteritatis*, believing that those who listened to, or themselves read, a work telling of the way in which their ancestors had been converted from paganism to Christianity would be inspired to imitate the good and shun the evil.

We must recognise that in Bede's sight, devotion to the catholic faith was the measure of good and that departure from catholic orthodoxy was a grave sin upon which there could be no compromise. This underlying belief, while allowing him to write generously of Aidan who came to Lindisfarne as a missionary of the Columban church in Iona, led him to write harshly of the British church whose clergy had failed to preach to the heathen Anglo-Saxons and still remained outside the fold of catholic orthodoxy in the observance of Easter. Modern readers, unfamiliar with the world in which Bede lived, may wonder at the place held by the miraculous in the *History*, but Bede would have answered that it was part of the true law of history (*vera lex historiae*) to commit to writing for the instruction of posterity all such things as could be gathered from common report. He knew that when, in his Gospel, St Luke called Joseph the father of Jesus, he did not do so because he was so in very truth, but because all men believed that he was. Bede could follow Jerome in thinking that it was part of the function of history to record what ordinary people believed. In his time, and for many centuries afterwards, popular opinion expected, and even demanded, the performance of miracles. If there is any occasion for surprise it is rather that the miraculous element in the *Ecclesiastical History* is so slight, and that it is totally absent from the *History of the Abbots*.

For the earlier part of the *History* Bede was naturally dependent on the writings of previous historians, and very few were available to him, but from the date of Augustine's arrival in Kent he was able to draw upon the letters of Gregory the Great of which copies were brought to him from Rome, upon tradition, upon information which he gathered from bishops and monasteries in the various English kingdoms and upon his own direct knowledge. Although we must not attribute to Bede himself the invention of the *annus domini*, his *History* was the first major historical work in which this Christian era was consistently used. Bede brought to the writing of the *History* a mastery of chronology, a consistently critical attitude towards his sources, a highly-developed sense for the dramatic which he could express in prose both lucid and vivid, a remarkable ability to coordinate details of widely diverse origin and a mind matured by a lifetime of scholarly study. These are the qualities giving greatness to the work which, by the common judgement of the medieval and the modern worlds, is Bede's masterpiece. Forgetful of all the resources that now lie at the service of any historian, it is easy, and currently fashionable, to be critical of the *History*, but the more deeply we delve into the world in which it was created, the more its greatness becomes apparent. Bede was not born, as were Jerome and Augustine, into a still-cohering Roman empire, nor even, like Isidore and Gregory, into a still literate society not yet severed from its classical roots. His most recent forebears belonged to the unlettered paganism of north-western Europe for whose enlightenment he bequeathed so much.

The *History* has never ceased to be read. More than 150 manuscript copies of it still survive and there are many other manuscripts which contain extracts from it. We have no autograph from Bede himself, nor anything else written in his own hand, but the work is known in several good eighth-century manuscripts and one or two of them are held to have been written at Wearmouth or Jarrow within a very few years of Bede's death. It was still being copied by hand in the fifteenth century when the first printed edition was produced by Heinrich Eggesteyn of Strasbourg in about 1475, and in the times of Reformation and counter-Reformation there were many who found it fresh grist for the Roman mill. It was translated into Old English in the time of Alfred the Great, or perhaps a little earlier,[10] and the first modern English translation was printed by John Laet at Antwerp in 1565. The author of this translation, Thomas Stapleton, prefaced his work with a long letter addressed to Queen Elizabeth I in which he wrote: 'In this history it shall appear in what faith your noble Realme was christened, and hath almost these thousand yeres continued: to the glory of God, the enriching of the Crowne, and great wealth & quiet of the realme. In this history your highness shall see in how many and weighty points the pretended refourmers of the church in your Grace's dominions have departed from the patern of that sounde and catholike faith planted first among Englishemen by holy S. Augustin our Apostle, & his vertuous company, described truly and sincerely by *Venerable Bede*, so called in all Christendom for his passing vertues and rare learning, the Author of this History.'

Bede continued the narrative of the *History* till midsummer of 731, but it probably did not reach its final form until 732, just three years before his death. As he surveyed the state of the nation in 731, he saw the English living peacefully with their neighbours, the Picts and the Scots, but many of the British were still hostile and persisting in their error about the observance of Easter. The times were secure and there were many among his own people, noblemen as well as others, who were laying aside the profession of arms and seeking to devote themselves as well as their children to the monastic life. Yet Bede was a man altogether too earnest in the pursuit of truth to close his eyes to signs of present and approaching ills, and we can sense something of his own anxiety in the closing paragraphs of the *History*. In 733, when he was already past his sixtieth birthday, he went to York to visit his former pupil, Egbert, who was then holding the bishopric. He had hoped to pay him a second visit in 734, but because he was too ill to travel, he wrote Egbert a letter instead, and this letter is the last work which we have from his pen. As Bede well knew, though he may not have known it more than three or four years, it had been the intention of Gregory the Great that Augustine's archbishopric in Canterbury should be balanced by an archbishopric in York, but this intention had been frustrated by the death of King Edwin and the subsequent flight of Paulinus to Kent. We may well be right in thinking that part of Bede's talk with Egbert had been about the archbishopric which was in fact established in 735, the year of Bede's death.

Perhaps more than any other of his works, the letter of 734 reveals the depths of Bede's concern with the immediate daily needs of his fellow-men. He wrote much about the conduct to be expected of one who held high office in the church, of the duty of teaching as well as of right behaviour. Among the Scriptures he commended particularly the letters of Paul to Timothy and Titus. He urged the bishop to pay close heed to the writings of Gregory, especially the *Regula Pastoralis*, to correct those bishops who were rumoured to be given up to laughter, jests, tales, feasting and drunkenness, and to read carefully in the Acts of the Apostles so that he might learn what kind of men worked with Paul and Barnabas. Within his own diocese he must ease the burden upon himself by ordaining more priests and appointing more teachers who would be able to visit the outlying villages and hamlets, some of which, as Bede had heard had never seen a bishop for years on end, even though they were all expected to pay their dues to the church. In preaching to the people, emphasis must be laid first and foremost upon the Apostles' Creed and the Lord's Prayer. It could be assumed that all those who had learnt Latin would be familiar with them, but those who knew no Latin must learn to repeat them in their own language. He must try to appoint more bishops, up to the number of twelve within the York metropolitan area as Gregory had urged, using monastic centres as episcopal seats, even though he might thereby meet opposition from abbots and monks. In particular he was to give his attention to eradicating certain grave abuses which had led to the growth of spurious forms of monasticism. Laymen had bought lands in many places under the pretext of founding monasteries, and had secured hereditary right in them by royal charters, even getting documents of privilege confirmed by the subscriptions of bishops and abbots. By such means men of rank had contrived to exempt themselves from military duties and their lands from secular taxation. So much land was coming under the control of these spurious monasteries, inhabited by laymen living with their wives and children, that the defences of the kingdom were endangered by the lack of fighting men and the sons of the nobility were moving overseas because there were no estates with which they could be endowed. There is indeed much in this letter to suggest that Bede was deeply concerned about the state of the church within his own kingdom of Northumbria, yet we must remember that he was writing not so much to praise the good which he found, as to guide his old pupil in the work which yet needed to be done. He could write in this same letter of the 'innumerable blameless people of chaste conduct, boys and girls, young men and maidens, old men and women' who were fully worthy to participate week by week in the observances of the celestial mysteries.

Bede died on the evening of 25 May 735, but because the Resurrection of Christ had so changed the order of time that the darkness of night had become joined to the light of the following day, the observances of the next day, itself Ascension Day, had already begun. Kalendars of later years show that the monks of Winchester and one or two other West Saxon monasteries, observed his festival on 26 May, a day which he shared with St Augustine of Canterbury but the two festivals were later separated with Bede's moved to 27 May. The manner of Bede's death is movingly described by Cuthbert who later became abbot of the monastery and who writes as one recalling what he himself had seen. Shortly before Easter of the year 735 Bede began to be troubled by increasing weakness and difficulty with his breathing, yet he continued not only with his teaching and chanting, but also with two other works which he was anxious to complete, a translation into English of part of the Gospel according to St John and a collection of extracts from the works of Isidore of Seville, seemingly from the *De Natura Rerum*: 'For', he said, 'I do not want my children to read what is false or to labour at this in vain after my death.' Bede's latest care seems to have been to ensure that his pupils in the school, not well versed in Latin, should not be led into error by faulty translations into English.

The rest is best told in the words of Cuthbert's letter:

But when we had got to the Tuesday before Ascension Day he began to find much greater difficulty in breathing, and a slight swelling appeared in his feet. Yet he went on teaching throughout the whole of that day, and dictating cheerfully. Now and again as he taught, he said:

'Learn quickly – for I do not know how long I shall live or if my Maker will soon take me away.'

[307]

But it seemed to us that perhaps he already well knew of his departure. And so he passed the night, wakeful in the giving of thanks. And when the day broke, that is the Wednesday, he bade us write diligently at what we had begun, and we did this until the third hour. From the third hour, as the custom of that day required, we walked in procession with the relics. And one of us who was with him said to him:

'There is still missing one chapter of the book you were dictating, but it seems hard for you that I should ask more of you.'

But he answered:

'It is easy – take up your pen and ink, and write quickly.'

And he did so. Then, at the ninth hour, he said to me:

'I have a few treasures in my wallet – some pepper, some napkins and some incense – so run quickly and bring the priests of our monastery to me so that I can distribute among them such small gifts as God has given me.'

And I did so greatly agitated. And when they had come he spoke to them, encouraging and beseeching each one individually to be diligent in offering prayers and masses for him. And they promised him that they would. And they all wept and were grieved, especially because he had said that they must not expect to see his face much longer in this world. Yet they rejoiced because he said:

'Now is the time, if it be my Maker's will, for me to be set free from this flesh and to come to Him who fashioned me from nothing when as yet I was not. I have lived a long time and my merciful judge has ordered my life well. The time of my delivery is at hand for my soul longs to see Christ my king in his glory'.

This and many other things he said for our enlightenment and so he passed his last day in gladness until the evening. Then the boy of whom I have spoken, Wilbert by name, said to him:

'Dear master, there is still one sentence not yet written down.'
And he answered:

'Very well, write it.'

And after a little while the boy said:

'Now it is done.'

[308]

And he said:

'Good – it is finished; truly have you spoken. Take my head in your hands, because I want to sit opposite the holy place where I used to pray, so that as I sit there I may call upon my Father.'

And so, upon the floor of his little cell, singing 'Glory be to the Father and to the Son and to the Holy Ghost', he breathed out the last breath from his body. And we may surely believe that, as he had always laboured with such great devotion in the praising of God, his soul was carried by the angels to the joys of Heaven for which he longed so much. All who heard and saw the death of our father Bede, used to say that they had never seen any other man end his life with such great devotion and peace of mind.'

REFERENCES

1 *HE* V, 24.
2 *BVC c.* III.
3 See D. Whitelock *After Bede* (Jarrow Lecture 1960). The figures for the MSS of Bede's works, not more than approximations, are counted from M. L. W. Laistner, *Hand-List*, to which many additions can now be made.
4 *In I Sam.* p. 87, *lines* 815–24.
5 *Hom.* I, 19, p. 138, *lines* 138–49.
6 *Ibid.* II, 6, p. 223, *lines* 115–21; I, 22, p. 160, *lines* 145–51.
7 *Ibid.* II, 12, p. 266, *lines* 201–12.
8 *Ibid.* I, 22, p. 160, *lines* 167–72.
9 *Ibid.* II, 14, p. 275, *lines* 112–25.
10 See D. Whitelock, 'The Old English Bede', *Proc. Brit. Acad.* XLVIII (1962), 57–90.

Select Bibliography

I BEDE'S WRITINGS

A COLLECTED WORKS

Giles, J. A., *Patres Ecclesiae Anglicanae*, 12 vols., London 1843–4.

Migne, J., *Patrologia Latina*, Vols. XC–XCIV, Paris 1862, Vol. XCV, 1861.

B INDIVIDUAL WORKS

1. *Biblical Commentaries*

Acts – *Expositio Actuum Apostolorum et retractatio*, ed. M. L. W. Laistner, *Medieval Academy of America Publication* No. 35, Cambridge, Mass. 1939.

Apocalypse – *Explanatio Apocalypsis*, PL XCIII, 129–206.

Catholic Epistles – *Super Epistulas Catholicas Expositio*, PL XCIII, 9–130.

Collectaneum on the Pauline Epistles – *Collectio Bedae presbiteri ex opusculis sancti Augustini in epistulis Pauli Apostoli*. Still unprinted, see *Select Bibliography s.n.* Charlier, Fransen.

Ezra and Nehemiah – *In Esdram et Nehemiam Prophetas Allegorica Expositio*, CCSL CXIX A, pp. 235–392.

Genesis – *Libri Quatuor in Principium Genesis usque ad Nativitatem Isaac et Eiectionem Ismahelis Adnotationum*, cura et studio C. W. Jones, CCSL CXVIII A, *Bedae Opera, Pars II, 1*, Turnholti MCMLXVII.

Habakkuk – *Super Canticum Habacuc Allegorica Expositio* PL XCI, 1235–1254.

Luke – *In Lucae Evangelium Expositio*, cura et studio D. Hurst, CCSL CXX, *Bedae Opera, Pars II, 3*, pp. 1–425, Turnholti MCMLX.

Mark – *In Marci Evangelium Expositio*, cura et studio D. Hurst, CCSL CXX, *Bedae Opera, Pars II, 3*, pp. 427–648, Turnholti MCMLX.

Proverbs – *In Proverbia Salomonis*, PL XCI, 937–1040.

– *In Proverbia Salomonis Allegoricae Interpretationis Fragmenta*, PL XCI, 1051–66.

Quaestiones XXX – *In Regum Librum XXX Quaestiones*, cura et studio

D. Hurst, *CCSL*, CXIX, *Bedae Opera, Pars II*, 2, pp. 289–322, Turnholti MCMLXII.

Samuel – *In Primam Partem Samuelis Libri IIII, cura et studio* D. Hurst, *CCSL*, CXIX, *Bedae Opera, Pars II*, 2, pp. 1–287, Turnholti MCMLXII.

Song of Songs – *In Cantica Canticorum Allegorica Expositio*, PL XCI, 1065–1236.

Tabernacle – *De Tabernaculo CCSL* CXIX A, pp. 1–139.

Temple – *De Templo Salomonis CCSL* CXIX A, pp. 141–234.

Tobit – *In Librum Patris Tobiae Allegorica Expositio PL* XCI, 923–38.

2. *Geography*
– *De Locis Sanctis*, ed. P. Geyer, *Corpus Script. Eccles. Latinorum* XXXIX, Vindobonae 1898, 301–24.

3. *Hagiography*
Vita Sancti Felicis PL XCIV, 789–98.

Vita Sancti Cuthberti, prose, ed. and tr. B. Colgrave, *Two Lives of Saint Cuthbert*, Cambridge 1940.

Vita Sancti Cuthberti, verse, ed. W. Jaager, *Metrische Vita Sancti Cuthberti*, *Palaestra* 198, Leipzig 1935 (and also separately with intro. Weimar 1935).

Martyrologium Bedae, H. Quentin, *Les martyrologes historiques du moyen Âge*, 2me ed. Paris 1908, pp. 17–119.

4. *History*
Historia Ecclesiastica Gentis Anglorum, ed. C. Plummer, Oxford 1896. See also J. E. King, *Baedae Opera Historica* (with translation), Loeb Classical Library, London 1930. For other translations see D. Whitelock *EHD*, No. 151 (with some chapters omitted), L. Sherley-Price, (revised ed. R. E. Latham) *A History of the English Church and People by Bede*, Penguin Classics 1968. A new edition of the *Historia Ecclesiastica* (edd. R. A. B. Mynors and B. Colgrave, with translation) is now in the press. Two of the eighth-century manuscripts, *The Leningrad Bede* (ed. O. Arngart, 1952) and *The Moore Bede* (ed. P. Hunter Blair, 1959) form vols. 2 and 9 respectively of the series *Early English Manuscripts in Facsimile*, Rosenkilde and Bagger, Copenhagen. *The Old English Version of Bede's Ecclesiastical History of the English People*, ed. and tr. T. Miller, *Early English Text Society*, O.S. 95–6, 1891, reprinted 1959.

Historia Abbatum Auctore Beda, ed. C. Plummer, *Venerabilis Bedae Opera Historica*, I, 364–387. See also J. E. King, *Baedae Opera Historica*, Loeb Classical Library, London 1930, II, 392–445.

5. *Homilies*
Bedae Venerabilis Homeliarum Evangelii Libri II, cura et studio D. Hurst, *CCSL* **CXXII**, *Bedae Opera, Pars III, Opera Homiletica*, Turnholti MCMLV.

6. *Letters*
Epistola ad Albinum, ed. C. Plummer, *Venerabilis Bedae Opera Historica*, Oxford 1896, I, 3.
Epistola ad Ecgbertum Episcopum, ed. C. Plummer, *op. cit.* I, 405–23. Tr. D. Whitelock, *EHD* No. 170.
Epistola ad Pleguinam, ed. C. W. Jones, *Bedae Opera de Temporibus*, Cambridge, Mass., 1943, 305–315.
Epistola ad Wicthedum, ed. C. W. Jones, *ibid.* 317–325.

7. *Hymns and Poems*
Liber Hymnorum Rhythmi Variae Preces, cura et studio J. Fraipont, *CCSL* **CXXII**, *Bedae Opera, Pars IV, Opera Rhythmica*, Turnholti MCMLV.

8. *School Treatises*
De Arte Metrica, ed. H. Keil, *Grammatici Latini*, Lipsiae 1880, VII, 227–60.
De Orthographia, ibid. 261–94.
De Schematibus et Tropis, ed. C. Halm, *Rhetores Latini Minores*, Leipzig 1863, 607–18. Tr. G. H. Tanenhaus, 'Bede's *De Schematibus et Tropis* – a translation', *Quarterly Journal of Speech* (Indiana), 48 (1962), 237–53.

9. *Scientific Works*
De Natura Rerum, PL *XC*, 187–278.
De Temporibus; De Temporum Ratione, ed. C. W. Jones, *Bedae Opera de Temporibus, Medieval Academy of America Publication No. 41.* Cambridge, Mass., 1943. For the *Chronica Minora* and the *Chronica Majora* which form integral parts respectively of the *De Temporibus* and the *De Temporum Ratione* see the edition by T. Mommsen, *MGH, Auct. Ant.* XIII. 247–327.

II BIBLIOGRAPHICAL

'Handschriften Antiker Autoren in Mittelalterlichen Bibliotheks-katalogen', M. Manitius, *Zentralblatt für Bibliothekswesen* Beiheft 67, Leipzig 1935, pp. 344–51.

Beda Venerabilis, Deutscher Gesamtkatalog, herausgegeben von der Preussischen Staatsbibliothek, 14, Berlin 1939, 697–707.

A Hand-List of Bede Manuscripts, M. L. W. Laistner and H. H. King, Cornell 1943.

An Anglo-Saxon and Celtic Bibliography (450–1087), W. Bonser, Oxford 1957, pp. 201–7, items 4154–4279, see also *Index* s.n. *Bede*.

Clavis Patrum Latinorum – ed. E. Dekkers, *Sacris Erudiri* 3, 2nd ed. Paris 1961, pp. 302–11.

'A Bede Bibliography: 1935–60', W. F. Bolton, *Traditio* XVIII (1962), 437–445.

Repertorium fontium historiae Medii Aevi (new Potthast), II, Romae 1967, 469–73.

III OTHER PRIMARY OR SECONDARY WORKS

Adamnan's De Locis Sanctis, ed. and tr. D. Meehan, *Scriptores Latini Hiberniae* III, Dublin 1958.

Addleshaw, G. W. O., *The Pastoral Organisation of the Modern Dioceses of Durham and Newcastle in the Time of Bede*, Jarrow Lecture 1963.

Æthelwulf, De Abbatibus, ed. A. Campbell, Oxford 1967.

Aldhelm – Aldhelmi Opera ed. R. Ehwald, *MGH Auct. Ant.* XV, 1919.

d'Alès, A., 'Tertullien chez Bède', *Recherches de science religieuse* XXVII (1937), 620.

Allison, T., *English Religious Life in the Eighth Century*, London 1929.

Anderson, O. S., *Old English Material in the Leningrad Manuscript of Bede's Ecclesiastical History*, Skrifter Utgivna av Kungl. Humanistiska Vetenskapssamfundet i Lund XXXI, Lund 1941.

The Anglo-Saxon Chronicle, A Revised Translation, ed. D. Whitelock with D. C. Douglas and S. I. Tucker, London 1961.

Antony – Life of St. Antony by St. Athanasius, tr. Sr. M. E. Keenan in *The Fathers of the Church*, ed. R. J. Deferrari, 15 (1952) 127–216.

Barley, M. W. and Hanson, R. P. C. (edd.), *Christianity in Britain, 300–700*, Leicester 1968.

Battiscombe, C. F., ed. *The Relics of Saint Cuthbert*, Oxford 1956.

The Beda Book, London 1957 – an anthology of articles reprinted from *The Beda Review*.

Beda der Ehrwurdige und seine Zeit, K. Werner, Wien 1881, recent undated reprint New York.

S. Beda Venerabilis, Ab. Capelle, B., Inguanez, M., Thum, B., *Studia Anselmiana* fasc. VI, Romae 1936.

Beeson, C. H., 'The *Ars Grammatica* of Julian of Toledo', *Studi e Testi*, 37 (1924), 50–70.

––––––– 'The Manuscripts of Bede', *Classical Philology* XLII (1947), 73–87.

Benedicti Regula, ed. R. Hanslik, *Corpus Scriptorum Ecclesiasticorum Latinorum* LXXV, Vindobonae 1960.

Beumer, J., 'Das Kirchenbild in den Schriftkommentaren Bedas des Ehrwürdigen', *Scholastik* XXVIII (1953), 40–56.

Bévenot, M., 'Towards Dating the Leningrad Bede', *Scriptorium*, XVI (1962), 365–9.

Bieler, L., '*Corpus Christianorum*', *Scriptorium* XVI (1962), 324–33 (esp. 330–1).

––––––– 'Some Recent Studies on English Palaeography', *Scriptorium* XVI (1962), 333–6.

––––––– '*Corpus Christianorum*', *Scriptorium* XIX (1965), 77–83 (esp. 82).

––––––– 'The Christianisation of the Insular Celts', *Celtica* VIII (1968), 112–25.

Bischoff, B., 'Das griechische Element in der abendländischen Bildung des Mittelalters', *Byzantinische Zeitschrift*, 44 (1951), 29–55.

––––––– 'Wendepunkte in der Geschichte der lateinischen Exegese im Frühmittelalter', *Sacris Erudiri*, VI (1954), 189–281.

Bolton, W. F., 'The Latin Revisions of Felix's *Vita Sancti Guthlaci*, *Mediaeval Studies* XXI (1959), 36–52.

Bonner, G., *Saint Bede in the Tradition of Western Apocalyptic Commentary*, Jarrow Lecture, 1966.

Boutflower, D. S., *The Life of Ceolfrid, Abbot of Wearmouth and Jarrow*, Sunderland 1912.

Boyer, B. B., 'Insular Contribution to Medieval Literary Tradition on the Continent', *Classical Philology* XLII (1947), 209–22, XLIII (1948), 31–9.

Brechter, S., *Die Quellen zur Angelsachsenmission Gregors des Grossen*, *Beitrage zur Geschichte des alten Mönchtums und des Benediktinerordens*, 22, Munster/Westf., 1941.

Brechter, S., 'Zur Bekehrungsgeschichte der Angelsachsen', *Settimane* XIV (Spoleto 1967), 191–215.

Bright, W., *Chapters of Early English Church History*, 3rd ed. Oxford 1897.

Brotanek, R., 'Nachlese zu den HSS der *Epistola Cuthberti* und des Sterbespruches Bedas', *Anglia* LXIV (1940), 159–90.

Browne, G. F., *The Venerable Bede, his life and writings*, London 1919.

Bruce-Mitford, R. L. S., *The Art of Codex Amiatinus*, Jarrow Lecture, 1967.

—— *The Sutton Hoo Ship-burial: a Handbook*, British Museum 1968.

Caesari Arelatensis Opera, Sermones, editio altera, ed. D. G. Morin, *CCSL* CIII, CIV Turnholti (1953).

The Calendar of St. Willibrord, facsimile ed. H. A. Wilson, Henry Bradshaw Society LV, London 1918.

Campbell, A., 'Some Linguistic Features of Early Anglo-Latin Verse and its Use of Classical Models.' *Trans. of the Philological Soc.* (1953), 1–20.

Canter, H. V., 'The Venerable Bede and the Colosseum', *Trans. and Proc. of the American Philological Assoc.* LXI (1930), 150–64.

Carroll, Sr. M. Th. A., 'The Venerable Bede: His Spiritual Teachings', *The Catholic University of America, Studies in Medieval History*, n.s. IX, Washington, 1946.

Cartularium Saxonicum, W. de G. Birch, 3 vols. and index, London 1885–99, reprinted 1964.

Chadwick, N. K., ed. *Studies in Early British History*, Cambridge 1954.

—— *Poetry and Letters in Early Christian Gaul*, London 1955.

—— ed. *Studies in the Early British Church*, Cambridge 1958.

—— ed. *Celt and Saxon*, Cambridge 1963.

—— *The Age of the Saints in the Early Celtic Church*, London 1963.

Chadwick, W. O., *John Cassian*, 2nd. ed. Cambridge 1968.

Chambers, R. W., 'Bede', Annual Lecture on a Master Mind, British Academy 1936, *Proc. British Acad.* XXII, 3–30.

Charlier, C., 'La compilation augustinienne de Florus sur l'Apôtre', *Rev. Bén.* 57 (1947), 132–67.

Clapham, A., 'Two Carved Stones at Monkwearmouth', *Archaeologia Aeliana*, 4th s. XXVIII (1950), 1–6.

Clausen, W., 'Bede and the British Pearl', *Classical Journal* 42 (1947), 277–80.

Colgrave, B., 'The History of the British Museum Additional MS. 39943', *EHR* LIV (1939), 673–7.

Colgrave, B., *The Venerable Bede and his Times*, Jarrow Lecture 1958.

Colgrave, B., and Masson, I., 'The *Editio Princeps* of Bede's Prose Life of St. Cuthbert, and its Printer's XIIth Century "Copy" ', *The Library* 4th s. XIX (1939), 289–303.

Colgrave, H., *Saint Cuthbert of Durham*, Durham 1947.

Collingwood, W. G., *Northumbrian Crosses of the Pre-Norman Age*, London 1927.

Columba – Adomnan's Life of Columba, ed. and tr. A. O. and M. O. Anderson, London/Edinburgh 1961.

Columbanus – Ionae vitae sanctorum Columbani, Vedastis, Iohannis, ed. B. Krusch, *Script. Rer. Germ. MGH* 1905.

Cordoliani, A., 'Études de comput – Note sur le manuscrit latin 7418 de la Bibliothèque nationale', *Bibliothèque de l'École des Chartes* CIII (1942), 61–5.

———— 'Á propos du chapitre premier du *De Temporum ratione*, de Bède', *Le Moyen Âge* LIV (1948), 209–223.

———— 'Un manuscrit de comput intéressant', *Scriptorium* XII (1958), 247–53.

Courtois, C., 'L'évolution du monachisme en Gaul de St. Martin à St. Colomban', *Settimane* IV (Spoleto 1957), 47–72.

Cowen, J. D., and Barty, E., 'A Lost Anglo-Saxon Inscription Recovered', *Archaeologia Aeliana*, 4th s. XLIV (1966), 61–70.

Cramp, R., *Early Northumbrian Sculpture*, Jarrow Lecture, 1965.

Craster, E., 'The Miracles of St. Cuthbert at Farne', *Analecta Bollandiana*, LXX (1952), 5–19.

Crawford, S. J., *Anglo-Saxon Influence on Western Christendom, 600–800*, Oxford 1933, reprinted for *Speculum Historiale*, Cambridge 1966.

Cremer, G., 'Das Fastenstreitgespräch (Mk. 2, 18–22 parr) bei Beda Venerabilis und Hrabanus Maurus', *Rev. Bén.* 77 (1967), 157–74.

Cuthbert – Two Lives of Saint Cuthbert, A Life by an Anonymous Monk of Lindisfarne and Bede's Prose Life, ed. and tr. B. Colgrave, Cambridge 1940.

———— *Life of Cuthbert*, tr. J. F. Webb, Penguin Classics 1965.

David, P., *Études historiques sur la Galice et le Portugal du VIe au XIIe siècle*, Lisbon, 1947.

Davis, R., 'Bede's Early Reading', *Speculum* VIII (1933), 179–95.

Deanesly, M., 'Roman Traditionalist Influence Among the Anglo-Saxons', *EHR* LVIII (1943), 129–46.

———— *The Pre-Conquest Church in England*, London 1961.

———— 'The Capitular Text of the *Responsiones of* pope Gregory I to

St. Augustine', *Journ. of Ecclesiastical History*, 12 (1961), 231–4.

——— *Sidelights on the Anglo-Saxon Church*, London 1962.

Deanesly, M., and Grosjean, P., 'The Canterbury Edition of the Answers of pope Gregory I to St. Augustine', *Journ. of Ecclesiastical History*, 10 (1959), 1–49.

Dillon, M., and Chadwick, N. K., *The Celtic Realms*, London 1967.

Dillon, M., 'The Vienna Glosses on Bede', *Celtica* 3 (1956), 340–4.

Dobiache-Rojdestvensky, O., 'Un manuscrit de Bède à Leningrad', *Speculum* III (1928), 314–21.

Dobbie, E. van K., *The manuscripts of Cædmon's Hymn and Bede's Death Song; with a critical text of the Epistola Cuthberti de obitu Bedae*, (Columbia University Studies in English and Comp. Lit., 128), New York 1937.

Druhan, D. R., *The Syntax of Bede's Historia Ecclesiastica*, Catholic University Studies in Medieval and Renaissance Latin 8, Washington D.C. 1938.

Duckett, E. S., *Anglo-Saxon Saints and Scholars*, New York 1947.

——— *Alcuin, Friend of Charlemagne*, New York 1951.

——— *The Wandering Saints*, London 1959.

Durrow, *The Book of*, – *Evangeliorum Quattuor Codex Durmachensis*, Olten-Lausanne-Fribourg 1960, Vol. I, facsimile, Vol. II contributions by A. A. Luce, G. O. Simms, P. Meyer, L. Bieler.

Elder, J. P., 'Did Remigius of Auxerre Comment on Bede's *De Schematibus et Tropis?*', *Mediaeval Studies* IX (1947), 141–50.

Eliason, N. E., 'The Age of Bede', *Lectures in the Humanities*, 14th and 15th series, University of North Carolina 1960, 23–37.

English Historical Documents, ed. D. C. Douglas, Vol. I, c. 500–1042, ed. D. Whitelock, London 1955.

Fischer, B., 'Codex Amiatinus und Cassiodor', *Biblische Zeitschrift*, n.f. 6 (1962), 57–79.

Fleming, J. V., 'The Dream of the Rood and Anglo-Saxon Monasticism', *Traditio* XXII (1966), 43–72.

Fontaine, J., 'Isidore de Séville et l'Astrologie', *Rev. des Études Latines*, 31 (1954), 271–300.

——— *Isidore de Séville et la culture classique dans l'Espagne wisigothique*, Études Augustiniennes, Paris, 1959.

——— *Isidore de Séville, Traité de la Nature*, Bibliothèque de l'École des Hautes Études Hispaniques, Fasc. XXVIII, Bordeaux, 1960.

Fransen, I., 'Les commentaires de Bède et de Florus sur l'Apôtre et saint Césaire d'Arles, *Rev. Bén.* 65 (1955), 262–6.

Fransen, I., 'Description de la Collection de Bède le Vénérable sur l'Apôtre', *Rev. Bén.* 71 (1961), 22–70.

Fructuosus – *The Vita Sancti Fructuosi*, ed. and tr. Sr. F. C. Nock, The Catholic University of America Press, Washington, D.C. 1946.

Furlong, P. J., 'On the Twelve Hundredth Anniversary of the Death of Bede', *Catholic Historical Review* XXII (1936), 297–303.

Gilbert, E., 'Some Problems of Early Northumbrian Architecture', *Archaeologia Aeliana*, 4th s. XLII (1964), 65–83.

Gillett, H. M., *Saint Bede, the Venerable*, London 1935.

Godfrey, J., *The Church in Anglo-Saxon England*, Cambridge 1962.

Green, C., *Sutton Hoo, The Excavation of a Royal Ship-Burial*, London 1963.

Gregory – *The Earliest Life of Gregory the Great*, ed. and tr. B. Colgrave, Lawrence 1968.

S. Gregorii Magni, Expositiones in Canticum Canticorum; Expositiones in Librum Primum Regum, ed. P. Verbraken, *CCSL*, CXLIV, Turnholti, 1963.

Gregorii Episcopi Turonensis Historiarum Libri Decem, ed. R. Buchner after B. Krusch, 2 vols., Berlin 1955–6.

Grierson, P., 'La fonction sociale de la monnaie en Angleterre aux VIIe–VIIIe siècles', *Settimane* VIII (Spoleto 1961), 341–62.

——— 'Les Foyers de Culture en Angleterre au Haut Môyen Age', *Settimane* XI, (Spoleto 1964), 279–95.

Grosjean, P., 'Le *De Excidio* chez Bède et chez Alcuin', *Analecta Bollandiana* LXXV (1957), 222–6.

——— 'Saints anglo-saxons des marches galloises', *Analecta Bollandiana* LXXIX (1961), 161–9.

Guthlac – *Felix's Life of Saint Guthlac*, ed. and tr. B. Colgrave, Cambridge 1956.

Haddan, A. W., and Stubbs, W., (ed.) *Councils and Ecclesiastical Documents relating to Great Britain and Ireland* (Oxford 1869–71).

Hagendahl, H., *Latin Fathers and the Classics, Studia Graeca et Latina Gothoburgensia* VI, Göteborg 1958.

Hamilton Thompson, A., ed., *Bede: His Life, Times and Writings*, Oxford 1935.

Hanning, R. W., *The Vision of History in Early Britain from Gildas to Geoffrey of Monmouth*, New York and London 1966.

Hennig, J., 'Studies in the Literary Tradition of the *Martyrologium Poeticum*', *Proc. Roy. Irish Acad.* 56 C (1953–4), 197–226.

——— 'A Critical Review of Hampson's Edition of the Hexametrical

Martyrologium Breviatum in BM Cotton Galba A XVIII', *Scriptorium* VIII (1954), 61–74.

Henry, F., 'The Lindisfarne Gospels', *Antiquity* 37 (1963), 100–10.

Hillgarth, J. N., *Irish Art in the Early Christian Period (to 800 A.D.)*, rev. ed. London 1965.

—— 'The East, Visigothic Spain and the Irish', *Studia Patristica* IV, Berlin 1961, 442–56.

—— 'Visigothic Spain and Early Christian Ireland', *Proc. Roy. Irish Acad.*, 62 (1962), 167–94.

—— Ed., *The Conversion of Western Europe 350–750*, New Jersey 1969.

Hilpisch, S., *Dier Doppelkloster; Entstehung und Organisation, Beiträge zür Geschichte des Alten Mönchtums und des Benediktinerordens*, 15, Münster, 1928.

Honoratus – St. Hilary, A Sermon on the Life of St. Honoratus, tr. R. J. Deferrari, in *The Fathers of the Church*, 15 (1952), 355–94.

Hopper, V. F., *Medieval Number Symbolism*, New York 1938.

Hornung, H., 'Ein Fragment der Metrischen St. Cuthbert-Vita des Beda im Nachlass der Brüder Grimm', *Scriptorium* XIV (1960), 344—6.

Hughes, K., 'The Changing Theory and Practice of Irish Pilgrimage', *Journ. Eccles. Hist.* XI (1960), 143–51.

—— *The Church in Early Irish Society*, London 1966.

—— 'Irish Monks and Learning', *Los Monjes y los Estudios*, Poblet 1963, 61–86.

Hunter Blair, P., 'The *Moore Memoranda* on Northumbrian History', in *The Early Cultures of North-West Europe*, ed. C. Fox and B. Dickins, Cambridge 1950.

—— *An Introduction to Anglo-Saxon England*, Cambridge 1956.

—— *Bede's Ecclesiastical History of the English Nation and its Importance Today*, Jarrow Lecture, 1959.

—— 'The Historical Writings of Bede', *Settimane* XVII (Spoleto 1970), 197–221.

Jenkins, C., 'A Newly Discovered Reference to the Heavenly Witnesses' (I John v. 7, 8) in a Manuscript of Bede', *Journal of Theological Studies* XLIII (1942), 42–5.

Jones, C. W., 'Bede and Vegetius', *Classical Review* XLVI (1932), 248–9.

—— 'The "Lost" Sirmond Manuscript of Bede's "Computus" ', *EHR* LII (1937), 204–19.

Jones, C. W., 'Manuscripts of Bede's *De Natura Rerum*', *Isis* **XXVII** (1937), 430–40.

——— 'Two Easter Tables', *Speculum* XIII (1938), 204–5.

——— *Bedae pseudepigrapha: scientific writings falsely attributed to Bede*, Ithaca, N.Y., 1939.

——— 'Bede as early Medieval Historian', *Medievalia et Humanistica* IV (1946), 26–36.

——— *Saints' Lives and Chronicles in Early England*, New York 1947.

Jones, P. F., 'The Gregorian Mission and English Education', *Speculum* III (1928), 335–48.

——— *A Concordance to the Historia ecclesiastica of Bede*, Medieval Academy of America Publication No. 2, Cambridge, Mass., 1929.

Kellett, F. W., *Pope Gregory the Great and his Relations with Gaul*, Cambridge 1889.

Kendrick, T. D., *Anglo-Saxon Art to A.D. 900*, London, 1938.

Ker, N. R., 'The Hague Manuscript of the *Epistola Cuthberti de obitu Bedae*', *Medium Ævum* VIII (1939), 40–44.

——— 'The Provenance of the Oldest Manuscript of the Rule of St. Benedict,' *The Bodleian Library Record*, II (1941), 28–9.

——— *Medium Ævum* XIII (1944), 36–40 – review of Laistner, *Hand-List*, with many additional MSS.

——— *Catalogue of Manuscripts Containing Anglo-Saxon*, Oxford 1957.

——— 'Fragments of Jerome's Commentary on St. Matthew', *Medievalia et Humanistica*, XIV (1962), 7–14.

Kirby, D. P., 'Bede and Northumbrian Chronology', *EHR* LXXVIII (1963), 514–27.

——— 'Bede's Native Sources for the *Historia Ecclesiastica*', *Bulletin of the John Rylands Library*, 48 (1966), 341–71.

Laistner, M. L. W., 'Source-marks in Bede Manuscripts', *Journ. of Theological Studies* XXXIV (1933), 350–54.

——— 'The Spanish Archetype of MS Harley 4980 (Bede's Exposition of Acts)', *Journal of Theological Studies* XXXVII (1936), 132–7.

——— 'The Western Church and Astrology during the Early Middle Ages', *Harvard Theological Review*, XXXIV (1941), 251–75.

——— 'An Addition to Bede in MS. Balliol 177', *Journal of Theological Studies* XLIII (1942), 184–7.

——— 'A Fragment from an Insular Manuscript of Isidore', *Medievalia et Humanistica*, II (1944), 28–31.

Laistner, M. L. W., *Thought and Letters in Western Europe, A.D. 500–900*, revised ed. London 1957.

—— *The Intellectual Heritage of the Early Middle Ages*, selected Essays by Laistner ed. C. G. Starr, New York 1957.

—— 'The Christian Attitude to Pagan Literature', *History*, n.s. XX (1936), 49–54.

Laistner, M. L. W., and King, H. H., *A Hand-List of Bede Manuscripts*, New York 1943.

Lambot, C., 'La tradition manuscrite Anglo-saxonne des sermons de S. Augustin', *Rev. Bén.* 64 (1954), 3–8.

Leclerq, J., 'Le IIIe livre des Homélies de Bède le Vénérable', *Recherches de Théologie Ancienne et Médiévale* XIV (1947), 211–18.

Lehmann, P., 'Das Verhältnis der abendländischen Kirche (bis 800) zu Literatur und Gelehrsamkeit', *Settimane* VII (Spoleto 1960), 613–32.

Leoba (Leofgyth) – *Vita Leobae*, ed. G. Waitz, *MGH Script.* XV, pt. I (1887), 118–131.

Levison, W., 'Modern Editions of Bede', *Durham University Journal*, n.s. 6 (1945), 78–85.

—— 'The Inscription on the Jarrow Cross', *Archaeologia Aeliana*, 4th s., XXI (1943), 121–6.

—— *England and the Continent in the Eighth Century*, Oxford 1946.

Lindisfarne Gospels – *Evangeliorum Quattuor Codex Lindisfarnensis*, Olten-Lausanne-Fribourg, Vol I (1956) facsimile, Vol. II (1960) contributions by T. D. Kendrick, T. J. Brown, R. L. S. Bruce-Mitford, H. Rosen-Runge, A. S. C. Ross, E. G. Stanley, A. E. A. Werner.

Loomis, C. G., 'The Miracle Traditions of the Venerable Bede', *Speculum* XXI (1946), 404–18.

Lowe, E. A., 'An Eighth-Century List of Books in a Bodleian MS. from Würzburg and its Probable Relation to the Laudian *Acts*', *Speculum*, III (1928), 3–15.

—— 'An Autograph of the Venerable Bede?', *Rev. Bén.* 68 (1958), 200–2.

—— 'A Key to Bede's Scriptorium', *Scriptorium* XII (1958), 182–90.

—— 'The Script of the Farewell and Date Formulae in Early Papal Documents as Reflected in the Oldest Manuscripts of Bede's *Historia Ecclesiastica*', *Rev. Bén.* 69 (1959) 22–31.

—— *English Uncial*, Oxford 1960.

Lowe, E. A., 'A Sixth-Century Italian Uncial Fragment of Maccabees and its Eighth-Century Northumbrian Copy', *Scriptorium* XVI (1962), 84–5.

—— *Codices Latini Antiquiores, A Palaeographical Guide to Latin Manuscripts prior to the ninth century*, Oxford 1934–66.

Luff, S. G., 'A Survey of Primitive Monasticism in Central Gaul (c. 350–700)', *Downside Review*, LXX (1952), 180–203.

Macdonald, Sir G., 'Bede and Vegetius', *Classical Review*, XLVII (1933), 124.

Machielsen, L., 'L'origine anglo-saxonne du supplément canonique à l'Histoire ecclésiastique de Bède', *Rev. Bén.* 73 (1963), 33–47.

—— 'Le supplement à l'Histoire ecclésiastique de Bède dans la littérature canonique jusqu'au Décret de Gratien', *Rev. Bén.* 73 (1963), 314–16.

McGalliard, J. C., 'Beowulf and Bede' in *Life and Thought in the Early Middle Ages*, ed. R. S. Hoyt, Minneapolis 1967, 101–21.

McGurk, P., 'Two Notes on the Book of Kells and its relation to other insular Gospel Books', *Scriptorium*, IX (1955), 105–7.

—— *Latin Gospel Books from A.D. 400 to A.D. 800*, Paris-Bruxelles 1961.

McKee, L., 'A Fragment of Bede's *De Temporum Ratione* in Vat. Reg. Lat. 838,' *Manuscripta* X (1966), 43–4.

Malone, K., 'The meaning of Bede's *Iutae*', *Beiblatt zur Anglia* 51 (1940), 262–4.

Markus, R. A., 'The Chronology of the Gregorian Mission to England: Bede's Narrative and Gregory's Correspondence', *Journ. of Ecclesiastical History*, XIV (1963), 16–30.

Martin – for the *Life of St. Martin* see *Sulpicius Severus*.

Mason, A. J. (ed.), *The Mission of St. Augustine to England according to the Original Documents*, Cambridge 1897.

Maycock, A. L., 'Bede and Alcuin (735–1935)', *Hibbert Journal* XXXIII (1935), 402–12.

Mercer, E., 'The Ruthwell and Bewcastle Crosses', *Antiquity*, 38 (1964), 268–76.

Meyvaert, P., '*Colophons dans des Manuscrits de Bède*, *Rev. Bén.*, 69 (1959), 100–101.

—— 'Les *Responsiones* de S. Grégoire le Grand à S. Augustin de Cantorbéry', *Rev. d'histoire ecclésiastique*, LIV (1959), 879–894.

—— 'Bede and the *Libellus Synodicus* of Gregory the Great', *Journ. of Theological Studies*, n.s. XII (1961), 298–302.

Meyvaert, P., 'The Bede "Signature" in the Leningrad Colophon', *Rev. Bén.*, 71 (1961), 274–286.

——— 'Towards a History of the Textual Transmission of the *Regula S. Benedicti*', *Scriptorium*, XVII (1963), 83–110.

——— *Bede and Gregory the Great*, Jarrow Lecture, 1964.

——— 'A New Edition of Gregory the Great's Commentaries on the Canticle and I Kings', *Journal of Theological Studies* n.s. XIX (1968), 215–25.

Misonne, D., ' "Famulus Christi". A propos d'un autographe de Bède le Vénérable', *Rev. Bén.*, 69 (1959), 97–9.

Montmollin, V. de, *Revue du Moyen Age Latin*, IV (1948), 395–6 – review of Laistner, *Hand-List*, with additional MSS.

Moore, W. J., *The Saxon Pilgrims to Rome and the Schola Saxonum*, Fribourg Dissertation, printed 1937.

Morris, J., 'The Dates of the Celtic Saints', *Journal of Theological Studies*, n.s. XVII (1966), 342–91.

Mozley, J. H., '*Bede, Hist. Evang.* bk. V, ch. 2' – (*sic* for *Hist. Eccles.*) – *Latomus* XIX (1960), 578. (A comment on *clymeterium*.)

Murray, G., *Gregorian Chant According to the Manuscripts*, London 1963.

Musca, G., 'Un secolo di studi su Beda storico' in *Studi storici in onore di Gabriele Pepe*, Dedalo Libri 1969.

Mynors, R. A. B., *Durham Cathedral Manuscripts to the End of the Twelfth Century* Oxford, 1939.

Ogilvy, J. D. A., *Books Known to the English, 597–1066*, Medieval Academy of America Publication No. 76, Cambridge, Mass. 1967.

Orchard, P., 'Bede the Venerable', *Downside Reivew*, LIII (1935), 344–68.

Page, R. I., 'The Bewcastle Cross', *Nottingham Medieval Studies*, IV (1960), 36–57.

Palmer, R. B., 'Bede as Textbook Writer: A Study of his *De Arte Metrica*', *Speculum* XXXIV (1959), 573–84.

Paul the Hermit – St. Jerome, The Life of Paul the Hermit, tr. Sr. M. L. Ewald in *The Fathers of the Church*, ed. R. J. Deferrari, 15 (1952), 218–238.

Peers, C. R., 'The Inscribed and Sculptured Stones of Lindisfarne', *Archaeologia* LXXIV (1925) 255–70.

Peers, C., and Ralegh Radford, C. A., 'The Saxon Monastery of Whitby', *Archaeologia* LXXXIX (1943), 27–88.

Pepperdene, M. W., 'Bede's *Historia Ecclesiastica* – a new perspective', *Celtica* IV (1958), 253–62.

Petersohn, J., 'Neue Bedafragmente in Northumbrischer Unziale Saec. VIII', *Scriptorium* XX (1966), 215–47.

Poole, R. L., 'The Chronology of Bede's *Historia Ecclesiastica* and the Councils of 679–80', *Journ. of Theological Studies* XX (1918), 24–40.

Porter, W. S., 'Early Spanish Monasticism', *Laudate*, X (1932), 2–15, 66–78, 156–67; XI (1933), 199–207; XII (1934), 31–52.

Prestwich, J. O., 'King Æthelhere and the battle of the Winwaed', *EHR* LXXXIII (1968), 89–95.

Quentin, H., *Les Martyrologes historiques du moyen Âge*, 2me ed. Paris, 1908.

Raby, F. J. E., 'Bede, 735–1935', *Laudate*, 13 (1935), 140–55.

Riché, P., *Éducation et culture dans l'Occident barbare, VIe–VIIIe Siècles*, *Patristica Sorbonensia* 4, Paris 1962, 2me ed. 1967.

—————— 'Les Foyers de Culture en Gaule Franque du VIe au IXe Siècle,' *Settimane* II (Spoleto, 1964), 297–321.

Roger, M., *L'enseignement des lettres classiques d'Ausone à Alcuin*, Paris 1905.

Ryan, J., 'The Early Irish Church and the See of Peter', *Settimane* VII (Spoleto, 1960), 549–74.

Sawyer, P. H., *Anglo-Saxon Charters, An Annotated List and Bibliography*, *Royal Historical Society Guides and Handbooks* No. 8, London 1968.

Saxl, F., 'The Ruthwell Cross', *Journal of the Warburg and Courtauld Institute* 6 (1943), 1–19.

Schapiro, M., 'The Religious Meaning of the Ruthwell Cross', *Art Bulletin* 26 (1944), 232–45.

—————— 'The Decoration of the Leningrad Manuscript of Bede', *Scriptorium*, XII (1958), 191–207.

Schreiber, H., 'Beda in Buchgeschichtlicher Betrachtung', *Zentralblatt für Bibliothekswesen* 53 (1936), 625–52.

—————— 'Beda Venerabilis und die mittelalterliche Bildung', *Studien und Mitteilungen zur Geschichte des Benediktiner-Ordens und seine Zweige – herausgegaben von der Bayerischen Benediktineakademie*, 55 (1937), 1–14.

Schütt, M., 'Ein Beda-Problem', *Anglia* 72 (1954), 1–20.

Scott, F. S., 'The Hildithryth Stone and the other Hartlepool Name-Stones', *Archaeologia Aeliana*, 4th s. XXXIV (1956), 196–212.

Silvestre, H., 'Le Hand-List de Laistner-King et les MSS Bruxellois de Bède', *Scriptorium*, VI (1952), 287–93.

—————— *Les manuscrits de Bède à la Bibliothèque Royale à Bruxelles*, Léopoldville 1959.

Silvestre, H., 'À propos de quelques manuscrits de Bède', *Scriptorium* XVII (1963), 110–13.

Sparks, H. F. D., 'A Celtic Text of the Latin Apocalypse Preserved in Two Durham Manuscripts of Bede's Commentary on the Apocalypse', *Journal of Theological Studies*, n.s. V (1954), 227–31.

Stengel, E. E., 'Imperator und Imperium bei den Angelsachsen', *Deutsches Archiv für Erforschung des Mittelalters* 16 (1960), 15–72.

Stenton, F. M., *Anglo-Saxon England, The Oxford History of England*, Vol. II, 2nd ed. Oxford 1947.

Ström, H., *Old English Personal Names in Bede's History, Lund Studies in English* VIII, Lund 1939.

Sullivan, R. E., 'The Papacy and Missionary Activity in the Early Middle Ages', *Medieval Studies*, XVII (1955), 46–106.

Sulpicius Severus – The Writings of Sulpicius Severus, tr. B. Peebles in *The Fathers of the Church*, ed. R. J. Deferrari, 7 (1949), 79–254.

—— *Sulpice Sévère Vie de Saint Martin*, ed. and tr. J. Fontaine, *Sources Chrétiennes*, Nos. 133–5, Paris 1967–9.

Sutcliffe, E. F., 'The Venerable Bede's Knowledge of Hebrew', *Biblica*, 16 (1935), 300–6.

Tanenhaus, G. H., 'Bede's *De Schematibus et Tropis* – a translation', *Quarterly Journal of Speech* (Indiana), XLVIII (1962), 237–53.

Taylor, H. M., *English Architecture in the Time of Bede*, Jarrow Lecture, 1961.

—— 'Rediscovery of Important Anglo-Saxon Sculpture at Hexham', *Archaeologia Aeliana*, 4th s. XLIV (1966), 49–60.

Taylor, H. M., and J., *Anglo-Saxon Architecture*, 2 vols., Cambridge 1965.

Thompson, E. A., 'Christianity and the Northern Barbarians', *Nottingham Medieval Studies*, I (1957), 3–21.

Torreta, L., 'Coscienza nazionale e ideale d'universalità nella *Historia Ecclesiastica* del venerabile Beda', *Atti del 5° Congresso di Studi Romani* 3 (1942), 9–20.

Verbraken, P., 'Le Texte du Commentaire sur les Rois Attribué à Saint Grégoire', *Rev. Bén.*, 66 (1956), 39–62.

—— 'Le Commentaire de Saint Grégoire sur le Premier Livre des Rois', *Rev. Bén.*, 66 (1956), 159–217.

Vespasian Psalter, Facsimile ed. D. H. Wright, *Early English Manuscripts in Facsimile*, Vol. 14, Copenhagen 1967.

Vincent of Lérins, The Commonitories, tr. R. E. Morris in *The Fathers of the Church*, ed. R. J. Deferrari, 7 (1949), 257–332.

Visentin, P., 'La posizione di S. Beda e del suo ambiente riguardo alla traslazione del corpo di S. Benedetto in Francia', *Rev. Bén.*, 67 (1957), 34–48.

Wallace-Hadrill, J. M., 'Rome and the English Church; some questions of transmission', *Settimane* VII (Spoleto 1960), 519–48.

—— *The Long-Haired Kings*, London 1962.

—— *Bede's Europe*, Jarrow Lecture, 1962.

Watkin, A., 'Farne Island and St. Cuthbert', *Downside Review*, n.s. LXX (1952), 292–307.

Weber, R., *Le Psautier Romain et les autres anciens Psautiers latins*, Rome 1953.

Werckmeister, O-K., *Irisch-northumbrische Buchmalerei des 8. Jahrhunderts und monastische Spiritualität*, Berlin 1967.

Whitbread, L., 'A Study of Bede's *Versus de Die Iudicii*', *Philological Quarterly* XXIII (1944), 193–221.

—— 'Note on a Bede Fragment', *Scriptorium* XII (1958), 280–1.

—— 'The Old English Poem *Judgement Day II* and its Latin Source', *Philological Quarterly* XLV (1966), 635–56.

Whitelock, D., *The Beginnings of English Society*, Pelican History of England, 2, London 1952.

—— *After Bede*, Jarrow Lecture, 1960.

—— 'The Old English Bede', Gollancz Memorial Lecture British Academy 1962, *Proc. British Acad.* XLVIII, 57–90.

Wilcock, P., *Lives of the Abbots of Wearmouth and Jarrow*, Sunderland 1910.

Wilfrid – The Life of Bishop Wilfrid by Eddius Stephanus, ed. and tr. B. Colgrave, Cambridge, 1927.

– Frithegodi monachi Breuiloquium vitae beati Wilfredi, ed. A. Campbell, Turici 1950.

Wilmart, A., 'La Collection de Bède le Vénérable sur l'Apôtre', *Rev. Bén.*, 38 (1926), 16–52 and 216.

—— 'Sommaire de l'exposition de Florus sur les Epitres', ibid. 205–16.

—— 'Un Témoin Anglo-Saxon du Calendrier Métrique d'York', *Rev. Bén.*, 46 (1934), 41–69.

Wormald, F., *The Miniatures in the Gospels of St Augustine, Corpus Christi College MS. 286*, Cambridge 1954.

Wrenn, C. L., 'The Poetry of Caedmon,' *Proc. Brit. Acad.* XXXIII (1947), 1–19.

Wright, D. H., 'The Date of the Leningrad Bede', *Rev. Bén.*, LXXI (1961), 265–73.

——— 'Some Notes on English Uncial', *Traditio* XVII (1961), 441–56.

Wynn, J. B., 'The beginning of the year in Bede and the Anglo-Saxon Chronicle', *Medium Ævum* XXV (1956), 71–8.

Bibliographical Addenda

Campbell, J., 'Bede' in *Latin Historians*, ed. T. A. Dorey, London 1966.

Bolton, W. F., *A History of Anglo-Latin Literature*, Princeton 1967.

Grosjean, P., 'La date du Colloque de Whitby', *Analecta Bollandiana*, 78 (1960), 233–74.

Meyvaert, P., 'Diversity within Unity, a Gregorian Theme', *The Heythrop Journal* 4 (1963), 141–62.

——— 'The *Registrum* of Gregory the Great and Bede', *Rev. Bén.*, 80 (1970), 162–6.

Ross, A. S. C., 'A Connection between Bede and the Anglo-Saxon Gloss to the Lindisfarne Gospels?', *Journ. of Theological Studies*, 20 (1969), 482–94.

Bede's Ecclesiastical History of the English People, ed. and tr. B. Colgrave and R. A. B. Mynors, Oxford Medieval Texts, Oxford 1969, supersedes earlier editions and translations of the *History*. Unfortunately its publication came too late for me to be able to use it in this book.

P.H.B.

Bibliographical Addenda (1990)

Primary sources: Nearly all of Bede's exegetical and pedagogical writings are now available in *CCSL* editions; of those discussed above note especially the *opera didascalica* (3 vols., *CCSL* 123A–C), ed. C. W. Jones *et al.*, including *De orthographia*, *De arte metrica* and *De natura rerum* as well as the computistical treatises. The edition of Bede's *Historia ecclesiastica* by B. Colgrave and R. A. B. Mynors (Oxford,

1969), appeared too late for Hunter Blair to use; it is now to be used in combination with J. M. Wallace-Hadrill, *Bede's Ecclesiastical History of the English People* (Oxford, 1988).

Collaborative volumes: A collection of 22 essays in commemoration of the 1300th anniversary of Bede's birth (1973) appeared as *Famulus Christi*, ed. G. Bonner (London, 1976). The following also contain much of relevance to Bede: *Bede and Anglo-Saxon England*, ed. R. T. Farrell, British Archaeological Reports 46 (Oxford, 1978); *Saints, Scholars and Heroes: Studies in Medieval Culture in Honour of Charles W. Jones*, ed. M. H. King and W. Stevens, 2 vols. (Collegeville, MN, 1979); *Ideal and Reality in Frankish Society: Studies presented to J. M. Wallace-Hadrill*, ed. P. Wormald, D. Bullough and R. Collins (Oxford, 1983); and *St Cuthbert: His Cult and Community to AD 1200*, ed. G. Bonner, D. Rollason and C. Stancliffe (Woodbridge, 1989).

Collected papers: P. Meyvaert, *Benedict, Gregory, Bede and Others* (London, 1977) [5 essays on Bede]; P. Hunter Blair, *Anglo-Saxon Northumbria* (London, 1984); and J. Campbell, *Essays in Anglo-Saxon History* (London–Ronceverte, 1986) [4 essays on Bede; much more of direct relevance].

Studies on Bede: There is a brief but excellent introduction to Bede, with helpful bibliography, by G. H. Brown, *Bede the Venerable* (Boston, 1987); see also T. Eckenrode, 'The Venerable Bede: A Bibliographical Essay 1970–81', *American Benedictine Review* 36 (1985), 172–91. Note also: G. Bonner, 'Bede and Medieval Civilization', *Anglo-Saxon England* 2 (1973), 71–90; P. Meyvaert, 'Bede and the Church Paintings at Wearmouth-Jarrow', *Anglo-Saxon England* 8 (1979), 63–77; A. C. Dionisotti, 'On Bede, Grammars and Greek', *Revue Bénédictine* 92 (1982), 11–41; R. Ray, 'Bede's *Vera Lex Historiae*', *Speculum* 55 (1980), 1–21; *idem*, 'What do we know about Bede's Commentaries', *Recherches de théologie ancienne et médiévale* 49 (1982), 5–20; *idem*, 'Bede and Cicero', *Anglo-Saxon England* 16 (1987), 1–15.

Background studies: For general guidance see S. D. Keynes, *Anglo-Saxon History: A Select Bibliography* (Binghamton, NY, 1987). On the Gregorian mission (above, chs. 5–8), see H. Mayr-Harting, *The Coming of Christianity to Anglo-Saxon England* (London, 1972); on Canterbury (ch. 9), see N. Brooks, *The Early History of the Church of Canterbury* (Leicester, 1984); on Northumbria, see P. Hunter Blair, *Northumbria in the Days of Bede* (London, 1976); on Whitby, see P.

Hunter Blair, 'Whitby as a Centre of Learning in the Seventh Century', in *Learning and Literature in Anglo-Saxon England*, ed. M. Lapidge and H. Gneuss (Cambridge, 1985), pp. 3–32; on western England, see P. Sims-Williams, *Religion and Literature in Western England, 600–800* (Cambridge, 1990); and on grammatical studies, see V. Law, *The Insular Latin Grammarians* (Woodbridge, 1982). The excavations at Jarrow have not yet been published; see, for now, R. J. Cramp, 'Monastic Sites', in *The Archaeology of Anglo-Saxon England*, ed. D. M. Wilson (London, 1976), pp. 201–52. For Yeavering, see B. Hope-Taylor, *Yeavering: An Anglo-British Centre of Early Northumbria* (London, 1977).

Index